Existentialism

A Reconstruction

Second Edition

David E. Cooper

The right of David E. Cooper to be identified as the author of this work has been asserted in accordance with the Copyright, Designs and Patents Act 1988.

First published 1990

Second edition published 1999

2 4 6 8 10 9 7 5 3 1

Blackwell Publishers Ltd
108 Cowley Road
Oxford OX4 1JF
UK

Blackwell Publishers Inc.
350 Main Street
Malden, Massachusetts 02148
USA

Library of Congress Cataloging-in-Publication Data

Cooper, David Edward.
    Existentialism : a reconstruction / David E. Cooper. — 2nd ed.
      p.   cm. (Introducing philosophy ; 8)
      Includes bibliographical references (p.   ) and index.
      ISBN 0–631–21322–8 (hbk : alk. paper). — ISBN 0–631–21323–6 (pbk : alk. paper)
      1. Existentialism.   I. Title.   II. Series.
  B819.C62   1999
  142'. 78—dc21   98–52529
                                                    CIP

British Library Cataloguing in Publication Data

A CIP catalogue record for this book is available from the British Library.

Typeset in 10 on 12 pt Bembo
by Pure Tech India Ltd, Pondicharry.
http://www.puretech.com
Printed in Great Britain by MPG Books,
Victoria Square, Bodmin, Cornwall.

This book is printed on acid-free paper.

Existentialism

Introducing Philosophy

Introducing Philosophy is a series of textbooks designed to introduce the basic topics of philosophy for any student approaching the subject for the first time. Each volume presents a central subject of philosophy by considering the key issues and outlooks associated with the area. With the emphasis firmly on the arguments for and against a philosophical position, the reader is encouraged to think philosophically about the subject.

Contents

Preface to the Second Edition

In the preface to the first edition of this book, a decade ago, I listed a number of reasons which had moved me to write the book. I mentioned, for example, that hardly any general works on existentialism had appeared since around 1970, so that the few books still available were showing their wrinkles. In part this was because their authors did not have the benefit of reading works by Heidegger, Sartre and other leading figures which only appeared, for the most part posthumously, in the 1970s and 1980s. But in part it was because the authors, children of their time, focused on the philosophical preoccupations of a previous generation. My book, equally a child of its time, attempted to bring existentialist discussions to bear on such 'hot' issues as 'anti-realism' and 'communitarianism'. Do human thought and talk contribute to the very constitution of the world? Is an individual's self-identity dependent on the community to which he or she belongs?

A further problem, as I described it, with previous general books on existentialism is that nearly all of them were done, in an Australian student's words, 'by blokes' – in the form, that is, of chapters, often barely connected, on individual existentialist thinkers. This, I suggested, was hardly the way to make salient the cohesiveness and thematic progression to be found in existentialist thinking.

I did not, I hastened to add, write the book simply to fill a gap in the market. Nor was my main reason a certain nostalgia for a youthful enthusiasm born of visits to Sartre's plays and haunts in the Paris of the late 1950s. The book was also written in response to the silly attitudes towards existentialist philosophy which, though on the wane, were still familiar in many British philosophy departments in the 1980s – departments in which Heidegger was still the 'joke' which, according to Michael Dummett, he had always been in Oxford, and Kierkegaard, Sartre and Nietzsche were condescendingly recognized only as 'psychologists'. (The situation across the Atlantic, thanks to the work of such philosophers indebted to existentialist writing as Charles Taylor, Richard Rorty, Hubert L. Dreyfus and Frederick A. Olafson, had for quite a while been a more cheerful and sensible one.)

In order to counter those silly attitudes, I aimed, first, to get rid of certain persistent misunderstandings (existentialism is *not*, for instance, a 'subjectivist' philosophy counselling depair and solitude), and second, to locate existentialism within a movement of thought which, as our century closes, is increasingly perceived as the distinctive direction of that century's philosophizing. This has been the repudiation of the Cartesian premises which set the agenda for three centuries. As I put it in my original preface, 'Along with American pragmatists, the later Wittgenstein and contemporary deconstructivists, existentialists reject not only any representational theory of knowledge and the search for certain foundations, but the whole idea of the isolated subject caught in an "egocentric predicament" of trying to acquire knowledge about a public world on the basis of private experience.' Where existentialists differ from many other critics of 'Cartesianism', I added, was in relating the overcoming of that tradition to the conduct of an 'authentic' life and in preserving one important ingredient in Descartes' thinking – his insistence on an individual's responsibility for his or her stance towards the world.

I repeat a further point from the original preface. My book does not attempt to be encyclopedic and 'scholarly'. It is not done 'by blokes', with the result that some existentialist thinkers hardly get a mention. Indeed, the main figure in the book is not Sartre, Heidegger or any actual thinker, but the Existentialist – the embodiment of the best wisdom to be gleaned from existentialist writings. Nor does it attempt to discuss all the issues which some existentialist author or another has addressed. My primary concern was, through the mouth of the Existentialist, to reconstruct a coherent and challenging structure of thought. To that extent, the book was intended as a contribution to, and not mere reportage of, existentialist thinking.

I have been gratified by the reception of the book over the last ten years. Reviewers, teachers and students have generally been kind in their comments. More gratifying still, perhaps, has been the interest it has aroused in several readers who are not professionally engaged in philosophy, but who find their thoughts and sympathies drawn towards existentialist themes.

Time has also been kind to the book. The 'hot' issues I wanted to focus on have not yet gone cold and other issues, notably in that most striking 'growth area' of the 1990s, the philosophy of mind, are also ones to which I devote a fair amount of attention. The time of which the book was a child has not yet passed. Existentialism itself, I am pleased to observe, attracts more attention than it did ten years ago, benefiting from the accelerating demolition of an 'iron curtain' between 'analytic' and 'continental' philosophy. Heidegger, of course, continues to be the focus of a whole critical industry and Sartre, whose reputation was in the doldrums when I wrote the book, is enjoying a deserved renaissance. Those two philosophers, as well as Kierkegaard and Nietzsche, have each been honoured by a *Cambridge Companion*, and it is encouraging to count the number of pages devoted to existentialist authors and topics in the massive Routledge *Encyclopedia of Philosophy*. New anthologies of existentialist writings have been published, and although relatively few books *about* existentialism have been published since 1990, something better has appeared: books which *use* existentialist insights in addressing live philosophical issues in, say, philosophical psychology. (A stimulating book by Gregory McCulloch is significantly titled *Using Sartre*.)

For such reasons, my publisher and I have been encouraged to bring out a new, revised edition. Preparing revised editions is not an unalloyed pleasure. There are bound to be things said which, ten years on, an author no longer subscribes to, so that an awkward choice is forced, whether to let those things stand or to embark on what might amount to a new book. I have, in the main, taken the first option in a spirit of leaving well alone. There isn't, anyway, *much* I would want to take issue with, and certainly I am generally content with the direction and thrust of the book – especially the centring of the discussion on the theme of 'alienation'. Indeed, I have become more convinced than I was in 1990 that the great philosophical debates gather around that theme – something of which I try to persuade readers in my *World Philosophies: An Historical Introduction*.

A new edition does, however, afford the opportunity for some repair jobs. While I have more or less left the existing text alone, I have made various additions. First, in response to the disappointment expressed by some students and readers at the lack of discussion of religious topics, I have written a section, 'Religious intimations', which comes at the end of chapter 8. Second, I have added a longish appendix on the relation between the philosophies of the two men who figure most frequently in the book, Heidegger and Sartre. I do so partly in response to the criticism that my approach in the book rests on an over-assimilation of their philosophies. Thirdly, I have expanded a number of notes, by way of both making occasional qualifications to claims made in the text and referring to relevant material published during the last decade (including 'primary' texts such as Sartre's *Truth and Existence*). Finally, the bibliography has been expanded by the inclusion of recent publications.

I would like to reiterate my thanks to those who read and commented on various chapters when they were first written – to Professors Timothy Sprigge, E.J. Lowe and Joy Palmer. And thanks again to Ann Walker, erstwhile secretary of the Department of Philosophy at Durham, for translating my handwriting onto a word-processor. I am also grateful now to the many reviewers, colleagues, students and other readers who, over the last ten years, have commented on the book. If I have not altered much in response to those comments, that is only because an adequate response would have meant writing a whole new book.

1
Preliminaries

The Sources of a Name

None of the great existentialist tomes contains the word 'existentialism'. Reports on its origin differ, but it seems to have been coined towards the end of World War II by the French philosopher Gabriel Marcel as a label for the currently emerging ideas of Jean-Paul Sartre and his close friend Simone de Beauvoir. According to the latter, neither of them initially appreciated this baptism.

> During a discussion organized during the summer [of 1945], Sartre had refused to allow Gabriel Marcel to apply this [word] to him: '...I don't even know what existentialism is'. I shared his irritation...But our protests were in vain. In the end, we took the epithet...and used it for our own purposes.[1]

Sartre, in fact, 'took' it rather quickly, for in the autumn of that year he delivered the lecture which became the most widely read of existentialist writings, *Existentialism and Humanism*.

The label was soon to be stuck on many other writers. To begin with, it was attached to the two German philosophers of *Existenz*, Martin Heidegger and Karl Jaspers, whose influence upon Sartre had been considerable. Heidegger bridled at this, quickly disowning the title in a piece published in 1947.[2] Jaspers, while unwilling to be identified too closely with Sartre, was sufficiently enamoured of the term to claim that a book of his own, written back in 1919, was 'the earliest writing in the later so-called existentialism'.[3] Then the label was fixed, unsurprisingly, on a number of Sartre's French contemporaries and friends, notably Albert Camus and Maurice Merleau-Ponty, eventually returning like a boomerang upon the neologizing Marcel. None of these readily welcomed the title either – not so much, as is sometimes suggested, because they were against systems and '-isms' as because no one other than Sartre, in his lecture, had tried to define the word, and this was not a definition under which they could immediately see their own ideas falling. One could hardly expect the Catholic Marcel, for example, to embrace a term which, as defined by Sartre, made the notion of a religious existentialist a virtual self-contradiction.

The next stage was to rake through the remoter philosophical past in search of thinkers deserving of the label, the prime candidates being the two *enfants terribles* of the nineteenth century, Søren Kierkegaard and Friedrich Nietzsche, both of whom were known to have influenced Heidegger, Jaspers and Sartre. This intellectual archaeology was soon to know no bounds, with Pascal, Montaigne, even St Thomas Aquinas and St Augustine, newly excavated as heralds of existentialism. And this labelling game was not confined to the field of philosophy. Novelists reckoned to have concerned themselves with such typically Sartrean themes as anxiety and conflict with others were soon included – Franz Kafka, for example. Nor, as Simone de Beauvoir relates, did the label attach only to people and their thoughts.

> The existentialist label had been attached to all our books . . . and to those of our friends . . . and also to a certain style of painting and a certain sort of music. Anne-Marie Cazalis had the idea of profiting from the vogue . . . she baptized the clique of which she was the centre, and the young people who prowled between the *Tabou* and the *Pergola*, as existentialists . . . [They] wore the new 'existentialist' uniform . . . imported from Capri . . . of black sweaters, black shirts, and black pants.[4]

In short, existentialism was not only a philosophy, but as any potted history of our century will point out, it had also become a 'movement' and a 'fashion'.

Although the name 'existentialism' is only of wartime vintage, the special use of the word 'existence' which inspired the name is older. Both Heidegger and Jaspers put it to this use, the latter in fact referring to his writings of the 1920s and 1930s as *Existenzphilosophie*. The two Germans had, in turn, taken up this special use of 'existence' from Kierkegaard who, in Jaspers' words, had provided its 'historically binding meaning'.[5] The story does not end there, since Kierkegaard was apparently only giving a new twist to the word as used by German idealists like Schelling, whom he heard lecturing in the Berlin of 1840 – but I shall not pursue the story that far.

What is this special sense of 'existence' from which existentialism derives its name? A full answer would amount to little less than a complete account of existentialism, so for the moment I only indicate an answer. First, 'existence' refers only to the kind of existence enjoyed by human beings. Second, it refers only to those aspects of human being which distinguish it from the being of everything else – 'mere' physical objects, for instance. Human beings have digestive systems, but since these are 'merely' physical in nature, they are not a constituent of human *existence*. A cardinal sin, from the existentialist viewpoint, is to conceive of human existence as being akin to the kind of being enjoyed by 'mere' things. The word 'sin' is to be taken with some seriousness here, for it is not just an error to think in this way, but self-deception or 'bad faith'.

Humans differ from non-humans in countless ways, of course. They can laugh, for example. So what are the distinctive traits which the word 'existence' is seeking to highlight? First of all, human existence is said to have a concern for itself. As Kierkegaard puts it, the individual not only exists but is 'infinitely interested in existing'.[6] He is able to reflect on his existence, take a stance towards it, and mould it in accordance with the fruits of his reflection. Or, as Heidegger would say, humans are such that their being is in question for them, an issue for them.[7] Second, to quote Kierkegaard again, 'an existing individual is constantly in the process of becoming.'[8] The same, you might say, is true of objects like acorns or clouds. But the difference is supposed to be this: at any given point in an acorn's career, it is possible to give an exhaustive description of it in terms of the properties – colour, molecular structure, etc. – which belong to it at that moment. But no complete account can be given of a human being without reference to what he is in the process of becoming – without reference, that is, to the projects and intentions which he is on the way to realizing, and in terms of which sense is made of his present condition. As Heidegger puts it, the human being is always 'ahead of himself', always *unterwegs* ('on the way').

The two features of human existence just mentioned lend one sense to that most famous of existentialist dicta, 'existence precedes essence.' What a person is at any given time, his 'essence', is always a function of what he is on the way to becoming in pursuit of the projects issuing from a reflective concern for his life. Unlike the stone, whose essence or nature is 'given', a person's existence, writes Ortega y Gasset, 'consists not in what it is already, but in what it is not yet . . . Existence . . . is the process of realizing . . . the aspiration we are.'[9]

Such characterizations obviously call for elucidation, and existentialism might be thought of as the sustained attempt to provide this, and to explore the implications for people's relationship to the world, each other and themselves. As they stand, these characterizations are little more than promissory notes. Nor do we progress much further, at this stage, by trawling in some of the further characterizations which many people associate with the existentialist picture of human being. Existence, they will have heard, is a constant *striving*, a perpetual *choice*; it is marked by a radical *freedom* and *responsibility*; and it is always prey to a sense of *Angst* which reveals that, for the most part, it is lived *inauthentically* and in *bad faith*. And because the character of a human life is never *given*, existence is *without foundation*; hence it is *abandoned*, or *absurd* even. The reason why recitation of this existentialist lexicon does not, of itself, advance our understanding is that, without exception, these are terms of art. None of them should be taken at face value, and the thinking of Sartre and others is badly misconstrued if they are.

Why do existentialists employ the word 'existence' to express their conception of human being? Partly because of precedent. Kierkegaard so employed the word, and those who more or less shared his insights followed suit. But there is more to it than that. For one thing, Kierkegaard's adoption of the term was not arbitrary. According to a venerable tradition, to hold that a certain thing exists is to hold that certain essences or 'universals' are instantiated, or that certain concepts or definitions are satisfied, by it. The number 2 exists, while the greatest number does not, because in the one case, but not the other, the appropriate essences – such as being between 1 and 3 – are instantiated. It was Kierkegaard's contention that, however matters may stand with numbers, this doctrine was mistaken when applied to individual *persons*. A person has a 'concreteness', 'particularity' and 'uniqueness' which make it impossible to equate him with an aggregate of instantiated universals. Søren cannot be 'reduced' to the entity instantiating the following universals . . . since there is no way of completing the list. Moreover, even if Søren's friends need to have an essence or concept of Søren in mind in order to recognize him, Søren himself does not. He is aware of his existence directly, 'unmediated' by concepts. To know who he is, he does not have to check through a list of definitions to make sure he fits them all. Kierkegaard's constant references to 'the existing individual', 'the existing thinker' and the like are intended to remind his readers – versed, presumably, in the traditional doctrine or its more recent Hegelian variation – that, with human beings, their existence is peculiarly 'particular', and known to themselves 'immediately'.[10]

A more decisive reason, having to do with the etymology of the word 'exist', helps to explain Heidegger's use of it. In some of his writings he spells the word with a hyphen, 'ex-ist', thereby drawing attention to its derivation from the Greek and Latin words meaning 'to stand out from'. This etymology is fairly apparent in related words like 'ecstasy', for the ecstatic mystic is someone whose soul is liberated from, and so stands outside of, his body. When this origin of 'exist' is borne in mind, it is an apt word for expressing the existentialist thought mentioned above, that in some sense a person is always already 'beyond' or 'ahead' of whatever properties characterize him at a given time. If, as it is sometimes put, the person is 'in' the future towards which he moves, he stands out from his present. He ex-ists.

An annoying complication is that some existentialists use the word in a more restricted way, applying it only to what others would call *authentic* existence.

Although human being is radically unlike that of anything else, people may think and behave as if this were not so, like Sartre's man of bad faith who takes his cowardice or homosexuality to be a fixed and inevitable property, and behaves accordingly. Some of our writers prefer to withhold the term 'existence' in the case of lives marked by chronic bad faith. Kierkegaard distinguishes 'existing essentially' from 'loosely called existing', reserving the former for the life of a person who has 'willed . . . ventured . . . with full consciousness of one's eternal responsibility'.[11] Jaspers is equally demanding: 'I *am* only in the earnestness of choice' and '*Existenz* . . . is present when I am authentic.'[12] I shall not follow this practice of loading the term with an evaluation. 'Existence' will refer to the distinctive being of humans which can then be qualified by words like 'authentic' and 'inauthentic'.

The word 'existentialism' has an additional and very important source. For many philosophers, the word 'existential' is most at home in the expression *existential phenomenology*. There is general agreement that the most significant versions of twentieth-century existentialism are developments, welcome or perverse, from phenomenology, the philosophy elaborated by Edmund Husserl in the early years of the century. Heidegger describes *Being and Time* as a work of phenomenology, while Merleau-Ponty and Sartre use the word in the title or subtitle of their main works. For our immediate purposes, the exact character of phenomenology does not matter. (I discuss it, in some detail, in chapter 3.) But its central feature, crudely expressed, is a focus upon the *meanings* (in a rather special sense) and acts of meaning in virtue of which we refer, and otherwise relate, to the world. What does matter here is that, according to Husserl, this examination could only be properly conducted by first suspending our usual assumptions about the actual existence of things in the world. In a procedure akin to Descartes' methodological doubt, the phenomenologist must suspend belief, or 'put in brackets', any reality beyond consciousness and the 'meanings' in which consciousness trades. The scientist studies colour by examining its physical properties, but the philosopher concerned with the 'meaning' of colour must put aside the assumption of real, physical existence made by the scientist. Otherwise, the phenomenological investigation will be contaminated by irrelevant, contingent data having nothing to do with 'meanings'.

Heidegger, Merleau-Ponty and Sartre are unanimous that this programme of 'pure' phenomenology is impossible. One can neither doubt nor seriously pretend to doubt the reality of the world. Even 'to ask oneself whether the world is real,' writes Merleau- Ponty, 'is to fail to understand what one is asking.' Consciousness cannot imagine itself divested of a world, for 'it always finds itself at work *in* the world.'[13] There is no prospect for examining 'meaning' and the 'meaning'-making activities of conscious beings unless these latter are taken to be practically and bodily engaged in the real world. Human being is, in Heidegger's phrase, Being-in-the-world, so that phenomenological understanding must be 'existential', not 'pure'.

Is the word 'existential' ambiguous, then: expressing, on the one hand, a special conception of human being and, on the other, the insistence that the world cannot be 'bracketed'? This would be to overlook an intimate connection between the themes of human existence and existential phenomenology. For Heidegger and those who follow him, it is precisely because the being of humans takes the form of existence that any account of it must presuppose their engagement in the real world. Only if we were creatures of a quite different sort – immaterial souls, say – could we perform even the thought-experiment of divorcing ourselves from the surrounding world. Conversely, the possibility of an existential phenomenology requires that conscious being takes the form of existence. For the 'meaning'-making activities upon which it focuses could only be those of creatures who ex-ist. Instead of treating 'existential' as ambiguous, then, we should approach existentialist philosophy – at least in its paradigmatic forms – along two different, but converging routes.

Existentialists and 'the Existentialist'

I described the rapid spread of the 'existentialist' label after 1945, but how do we determine when the label is appropriate? Who are to count as existentialists? I shall say a little by way of an answer before suggesting that we should not overtax ourselves in search of a precise one.

It is sometimes said that the reason it is hard to draw up an exact list is that existentialism is a mere 'tendency', rather than a coherent philosophy. Now while I do not want to minimize the differences between individual writers, I do hope to demonstrate that there is a coherent, definable philosophy of existentialism – no less, though perhaps no more, homogeneous than logical positivism, say, or pragmatism. The reason it is hard to place certain thinkers is not that the characterization of existentialism must be vague, but because they fit the characterization in some respects and not others. The taxonomist, then, has a weighting problem on his hands.

Existentialism is what existentialists embrace, and existentialists are people who embrace existentialism. How do we break into this circle? It is generally agreed that if Heidegger and Sartre are not existentialists, then no one is. A natural policy, therefore, is to apply the name to these two, and then to others according to their kinship with them. This policy is not, however, without problems. For one thing, the thinking of both men underwent large changes. Heidegger's 'turn' (*Kehre*) in the 1930s was in a direction away from the existentialist position of *Being and Time*; and some people find precious little of Sartre's earlier views in his Marxist writings of the 1960s and thereafter. But this is not a serious problem: we can stipulate that by 'Heidegger' and 'Sartre' we mean the authors of certain works only.

A more serious criticism is that the policy exaggerates the affinity between Heidegger and Sartre. It is ludicrous to hold that 'no kinship ever bound the two philosophers... that they are radically opposed in every respect',[14] but the days are gone when Heidegger was treated merely as an impenetrable precursor of Sartre. There is now a tendency to read Sartre as a wayward pupil who produced a bowdlerized version of the master's thoughts. Hubert Dreyfus, for instance, thinks that Sartre's revamping of Heidegger was a 'disaster', and that the latter had some justification for calling *Being and Nothingness* *'Dreck'* ('rubbish').[15]

This tendency is as unfortunate, I believe, as the one it succeeded. I discuss the relation between Heidegger and Sartre in the appendix, but even before that the book will, I hope, have indicated their affinities. But here are a couple of remarks in advance. First, one should not take Heidegger's own hostile judgement on Sartre too seriously. Only the first few pages of his copy of *Being and Nothingness* were cut open, a little *Dreck* being enough, it seems. By 1946, moreover, when Heidegger wrote his criticism of *Existentialism and Humanism* – not the most dependable expression of Sartre's views, incidentally – he had moved a long way from the ideas which had inspired Sartre. When, a few years after the war, Sartre visited Heidegger in his mountain retreat, his disillusioned verdict was that Heidegger had gone mystical.[16]

More important, the new tendency rests on misunderstandings of Sartre. It treats him as a Cartesian, wedded to Descartes' notion of the *cogito* as the substantial subject of consciousness, and to a dualistic division of reality into the Being-for-itself of consciousness and the Being-in-itself of things. Despite some of Sartre's misleading remarks in these connections, it will emerge, I hope, that:

1 He is as opposed as Heidegger to any Cartesian notion of the *cogito*. ('"Cartesianism" is simply used [by Sartre] as the name of the view that consciousness is always aware of itself,' writes Mary Warnock.)[17]
2 'Subjectivity', as Sartre explains, is simply a name for something Heidegger himself insists upon: that 'man is... something which propels itself towards a future and is aware that it is doing so.'[18]
3 The For-itself/In-itself distinction is a clumsy reiteration of Heidegger's between the being enjoyed by humans (*Dasein*) and that possessed by things. For neither of them is the distinction, in one crucial sense, dualistic: since they insist that it is impossible to conceive of conscious activity and the world in isolation from one another.

These remarks are contentious and, at this early stage, will not be intelligible to some readers. Their point is to herald the affinity between the two men which warrants the policy of understanding existentialism, initially, by reference to them. But which other philosophers are sufficiently close to these two to belong on the list? There are some whose very style and vocabulary make them prime candidates – Jaspers, Merleau-Ponty, Ortega y Gasset and Simone de Beauvoir. The much neglected Ortega, for example, wrote a couple of essays in 1940, three years before the publication of *Being and Nothingness*, in which several pages could be mistaken for elegant summaries of Sartre's book.[19] There are others who would never pass the stylistic and lexical tests, but whose concerns and conclusions are close to those of the people already mentioned: Marcel, for instance, and the author of existentialism's most lyrical work, Martin Buber. *I and Thou*, which appeared in German in 1923, might compete with Jaspers' *Psychology of World-Views* for the description, 'the earliest writing in the later so-called existentialism'.

Each of these writers subscribes to the two main themes (described above, 'The Sources of a Name') of the distinctive character of human existence and existential phenomenology. (This is so even when they do not indulge in the terms of art of phenomenology and *Existenzphilosophie*.) Each of them emphasizes how, in its being an 'issue' for itself and 'ahead' of itself, human existence is to be contrasted with the being of whatever is 'thing-like'. And each of them insists upon our engagement with a real world as a precondition for understanding those most fundamental of our activities, the making and grasping of 'meanings'. For each of them, the world and human existence are only intelligible in terms of one another. Merleau-Ponty's dictum, 'The world is wholly inside me, and I am wholly outside myself,'[20] might have been spoken by any of them.

There is something else these writers share – something, I shall be arguing, which serves to motivate and guide the whole existentialist enterprise. This is the sense that the most serious question with which philosophy has to deal is that of *alienation* in its various forms – alienation from the world, from one's fellows, from oneself. It is to the alienation threatened by a dualism of mind and body and by the scientific image of an objective reality untainted by human concerns, and not to the spectre of scepticism, which philosophy must, before all else, respond. Existentialism itself is just such a response.

Given all this, there is at least one writer who, although he is often included, does not really belong on the list – Albert Camus. *The Myth of Sisyphus* is, to be sure, peppered with some favourite existentialist terms, like 'absurdity', but I have already remarked that, as used by Sartre and others, these are terms of art. What Camus means by 'absurdity' is quite different from Sartre (see p. 141

below). One reason for excluding Camus is that, unlike the rest of our writers, it is not at all his aim to reduce or overcome a sense of alienation or separateness from the world. In the attitude of Meursault, *The Outsider*, for example, we find a defiant pleasure taken in our alienated condition. Sisyphus, the 'absurd hero', feels a 'silent joy' in living in a world where 'man feels an alien, a stranger...his exile...without remedy.'[21] Camus wants to invert Merleau-Ponty's dictum into 'The world is wholly outside me, and I am wholly inside myself.' Moreover Camus was, by his own admission or boast, not interested in the weighty philosophical topics which occupied his Parisian friends, Sartre and Merleau-Ponty – the nature of consciousness and perception, the mind–body relation, the problem of 'other minds' and so on. Existentialism, as treated in this book, is not a mood or a vocabulary, but a relatively systematic philosophy in which topics like these are duly addressed. I shall have rather little to say about those, like Camus, who make a virtue out of being neither a philosopher nor systematic.

A question which has vexed a number of commentators is where to place Kierkegaard and Nietzsche. It was Kierkegaard's use of 'existence' which inspired the very name of existentialism, and his notions of 'dread' and the 'Public' are echoed in Heidegger's discussions of *Angst* and the 'they' (*Das Man*) (see chapters 7 and 8). But some of the things said about Camus also apply to Kierkegaard. Despite the endless repetition, he does little to develop his intuitions about existence as 'striving' and 'becoming', and some of those large philosophical topics which failed to disturb Camus scarcely bothered Kierkegaard either. Like Camus, as well, he seems to enjoy the thought that men are aliens in their world. It is only if people do view themselves as 'homeless' that they will then seek that personal relationship with God, which is the pivot of Kierkegaard's concerns.

Nietzsche presents the taxonomist with different problems. Unlike the Dane, he tackles most of the philosophical questions which occupy later existentialists; and in his doctrines of the will to power and perspectivism he is arguing against a dualism of mind and reality. 'We laugh as soon as we encounter the juxtaposition of "man *and* world"'; we are 'sick' of 'the whole pose of "man *against* the world"'.[22] But Nietzsche also makes claims which at least seem to contradict those of later existentialists. For example, he denies that we can act freely. More generally, his *naturalism*, his urge to treat man as *just* one species of 'domestic animal', runs counter, on the surface anyway, to claims about the distinctive character of human existence. But if Nietzsche's name appears less often in this book than it may deserve to, the main reason is that he is too large a figure to be contained within it. If proper attention were given to his views, he would, I fear, take things over. (I speak with some experience, having written a book on Nietzsche that was not originally intended to be that.)[23]

Once reasons for and against including Kierkegaard and Nietzsche on the list are given, it matters little whether they are classified as wayward existentialists or, less anachronistically perhaps, as precursors of existentialism. This might matter more if the book were being done 'by blokes', but as indicated in the preface the aim is, rather, to reconstruct a certain structure of thought. The important thing is not the card-carrying credentials of this or that writer, but his contribution to the development of that structure. It is because I am uncertain or plain ignorant about the contribution of some people often described as existentialists – Berdyaev and Bultmann, for example – that they scarcely appear. Some of these exclusions may be unjust, but exclusions anyway have to be imposed if the book is not to degenerate into a mere encyclopaedia of existentialist writings.

The main figure in this book, however, is not Heidegger, Sartre nor any of those mentioned above, but the Existentialist. He is not to be identified with any particular author, but nor is he the 'average' existentialist, stripped of whatever opinions distinguish one author from another. A figure who did not take sides on issues which divide these authors would be a pale one indeed. He is, rather, the 'ideal' existentialist, who embodies the best wisdom, in his creator's view, to be gleaned from actual existentialist writers. Put differently, he represents a 'rational reconstruction' of existentialist thought.

This book could be regarded as a journey of thought undertaken by the Existentialist. Its starting-point is the issue which, in his opinion, is the largest one to which philosophy should respond – that of *alienation*. As for Hegel and Marx, the issue for him is how alienation is to be 'overcome' (chapter 2). It is in Husserl's phenomenology that he finds the clue to this, though Husserl's 'pure' phenomenology must first be converted into an 'existential' one (chapter 3). The Existentialist is then equipped to provide a systematic account of our Being-in-the-world, which emphasizes both the logical interdependence of mind and world, and the unique character of human existence (chapter 4). This account enables him to 'dissolve' a number of traditional dualisms, like that of mind versus body, which have contributed to people's sense of alienation (chapter 5).

His account, however, throws into relief the depressing possibility of other dimensions of alienation: estrangement from oneself and estrangement from others. He needs, then, to discuss the notion of self, and the relation between this and experience of others (chapter 6). The Existentialist is now able to describe the forms of self-estrangement, such as 'bad faith', which have their basis in relations to others (chapter 7). But to justify his description of our everyday condition as self-estranged, he needs to find evidence that we are capable of a different, 'authentic' existence. He finds this in the experience of *Angst*, the 'anticipation' of death, and the sense of absurdity (chapter 8).

Whatever else an 'authentic' existence is, it is one of a certain kind of freedom – 'existential freedom' (chapter 9). Finally, the Existentialist considers what this authentic life of freedom might imply by way of an ethic to guide our relations with one another (chapter 10).

The Existentialist's journey is one of the most serious a philosopher could make. Not only does it encounter some of the largest and toughest philosophical questions, but it passes through some of the more sombre areas of human enquiry. It is serious, finally, because it is undertaken to 'overcome' threats to human integrity and dignity which all but the self-narcoticized must on occasion experience.

I once heard a distinguished analytic philosopher express the wish that his epitaph should read, 'This man discovered a new sense of the word "If".' (He has since died, but I do not know if his wish was fulfilled.) The Existentialist's ambitions are of a different order, surely more faithful to the original spirit of philosophy.

Some Misconceptions

Existentialism is something everyone has heard of. It belongs among those '-isms', like cubism and surrealism, whose *succès de scandale* makes them part of the consciousness of our century. The popular image is, however, full of misconceptions which need to be scotched if understanding of the philosophy examined in this book is not to be prejudiced.

These misconceptions are prevalent among those who have picked up their existentialism from dictionaries, encyclopaedias and popular histories of ideas. Typical is the description of existentialism as 'the metaphysical expression of the spiritual dishevelment of a post-war age'.[24] So, too, is one historian's description of it as 'the assertion that life is more than logic ... that the subjective and personal must be more highly valued and the objective and intellectualized must be depreciated'.[25] The *Concise Oxford Dictionary* entry of 1964 is particularly wayward: 'An anti-intellectual philosophy of life, holding that man is free and responsible, based on the assumption that reality as existence can only be lived, but can never become the object of thought'.[26]

The inaccuracy of these descriptions will become plain in the following chapters, but it will be useful here to indicate some reasons for their currency and to preview some of their deficiencies. Such descriptions encourage a popular view which might be expressed in something like the following words: 'Existentialism was a philosophy born out of the *Angst* of post-war Europe, out of a loss of faith in the ideals of progress, reason and science which had led to Dresden and Auschwitz. If not only God, but reason and objective value are dead, then man is abandoned in an absurd and alien world.

The philosophy for man in this "age of distress" must be a subjective, personal one. A person's remaining hope is to return to his "inner self", and to live in whatever ways he feels are true to that self. The hero for this age, the existentialist hero, lives totally free from the constraints of discredited traditions, and commits himself unreservedly to the demands of his inner, authentic being.'

One thing which encourages this kind of view is a failure sufficiently to distinguish existentialist philosophy from the existentialist vogue among black-clad youths prowling between the *Tabou* and the *Pergola*, which Simone de Beauvoir described. Film of the young Juliette Greco singing in the late 1940s gives an idea of the chic appeal which feigned *ennui* and despair apparently had for young Parisians of the time. Few of them, presumably, waded through the six hundred pages of *Being and Nothingness*, and their interpretation of existentialist freedom as a licence to act as unconventionally as possible, *pour épater les bourgeois*, was a complete distortion of Sartre's and de Beauvoir's notion. In fact, they had less affinity with these writers than with the 'hippies' of the 1960s or the 'punks' of the 1970s.

A second factor has been over-reliance on existentialist fiction. This is compounded when Camus' novel, *The Outsider*, is taken as paradigmatic of the genre. Many people, I find, discover the quintessential 'existentialist hero' in Meursault: casually smoking on his mother's coffin, indifferent to God and to marriage, unrepentant at killing an Arab, and unable to find value in anything. In fact, Meursault is no more 'authentic' in Sartre's sense than the bourgeois with his 'respectability' and fake 'sincerity'. Not that the 'message' of Sartre's own novels is always grasped correctly. In *The Age of Reason* the central character, Mathieu, proclaims, 'I recognise no allegiance except to myself... All I want is to retain my freedom.' This is his defence of his refusal to marry his pregnant girlfriend. But it is not, as sometimes imagined, Mathieu who is Sartre's mouthpiece, but his 'respectable' brother, Jacques, who says: 'I should myself have thought that freedom consisted in frankly confronting situations into which one has deliberately entered and accepting one's responsibilities. You have reached the age of reason, my poor Mathieu... But you try to pretend you are younger than you are.'[27] I shall be discussing various works of existentialist fiction, but this is no substitute for examination of the 'straight' philosophical works.

The most popular of those works is Sartre's lecture *Existentialism and Humanism*, and over-reliance on it is a third source of misconceptions. The lecture was written hurriedly and Sartre soon regretted its publication. For there are passages here which do encourage the view that commitment and moral decision can only be irrational *actes gratuits*, or based upon nothing but inner conviction. It is here, too, that there is much talk of abandonment and despair, but not set in the wider context of Sartre's philosophy which lends proper sense to such notions. Sartre's posthumously published notes, *Cahiers pour une morale*, give a much more accurate, if far less punchy, expression to his views at the time than the lecture does.

Let us now take some of the misconceptions one by one. It is quite wrong, first, to regard existentialism as the expression of post-war 'dishevelment', despair or malaise. To do so rather obviously confuses existentialism as a philosophy and existentialism as a vogue. All the best-known existentialist works, it should be noted, were written either before the war began or before it ended. To describe existentialism as an expression of an age, moreover, is to suggest that its claims could be only temporarily and locally valid. But if the accounts of the distinctiveness of human existence, of the interdependence of mind and world, of our existential freedom and so on are true at all, they are true of human beings at all times and in all places. These accounts, furthermore, stem from reflections on the perennial condition of human beings, and not the particular situation obtaining in post-war Europe. Existentialism, in other words, belongs to philosophy, not to the social sciences.

None of this is to deny that existentialism is historically located. In its mature form, it could not have developed much earlier than it did. The same, though, is true of quantum physics, but it would be absurd to describe that as an 'expression' of a particular age. Existentialism grew, in part, out of Husserl's phenomenology, which in turn was a critical response to nineteenth-century materialism and positivism. So existentialism can certainly be placed in intellectual history: it was not a bolt from the blue. Nor do I want to deny that existentialists have things to say which both help to explain and are especially pertinent to modern times. Heidegger, Buber and Marcel all believed that the most salient tendencies of the times, technology and consumerism, are the fall-out from that Cartesian schism between mind and world which turns the latter into a foreign territory, to be conquered and exploited. Existentialism is, in part, directed to the 'overcoming' of that schism.

One reason existentialism gets described as a 'metaphysical expression' of its age is because it is alleged to give voice to an *Angst* and despair which, it is said, are peculiarly symptomatic of the twentieth-century condition. It is true that several existentialist writers speak much of these notions, but it is crucial here to recall my warning about their use of words as terms of art. As used by Kierkegaard, 'despair' refers not to a mood of hopeless gloom, but to the position of someone whose life, a contented one perhaps, 'hinges upon a condition outside of itself'.[28] Sartre uses it to refer to the recognition that 'there is no God and no prevenient design, which can adapt the world ... to my will.'[29] As for *Angst*, existentialists do not have in mind that fear before a dangerous, uncertain world recorded here by Virginia Woolf:

> The war...has taken away the outer wall of security. No echo comes back. I have no surroundings... Those familiar circumvolutions...which have for so many years given back an echo...are all wide and wild as the desert now.[30]

Existential *Angst* is, rather, a sense of freedom, of a capacity to strike out on one's own in the formation of a scheme of beliefs and values. If *Angst* has special significance in modern times, this is not because life has become too 'dishevelled' or 'wide and wild', but because it has become too *comfortable*. Beliefs and values are too easily and readily received from what Kierkegaard called the 'Public', Nietzsche the 'herd', and Heidegger the 'they'. This *Angst* is not something to be 'treated'; on the contrary, we need to be called to it, and away from a state of 'tranquillization' induced through bad faith (see chapters 7 and 8).

The wayward definitions of existentialism quoted on p. 11 echo the widespread impression that it is an 'anti-intellectualist' philosophy, which sets itself against reason to the point of preaching irrationalism − or worse: 'Existentialism...is nothing other than radical nihilism...the absolute negation of everything, which leaves only a chaotic and meaningless activity.'[31] This is nonsense, but more sober versions of the 'anti-intellectualist' interpretation require some comment.

The first thing to say is that the Existentialist is not an irrationalist in the sense of supporting his claims by appeal to mystical insight, 'gut' feeling, or other non-rational founts of knowledge. He argues, typically, by close description of everyday life, by drawing out people's own implicit understanding of themselves and by exposing the incoherence of rival claims. He proceeds, that is, as a philosopher, not a seer. Even the gnomic-sounding Buber argues for the presence of the divine 'Thou' in human life by interpreting familiar experiences, and not by appeal to esoteric knowledge.[32]

Second, existentialism does not, in the manner of a Rimbaud or a D. H. Lawrence, exhort us to cultivate wild or 'vital' lives in conscious rejection of the exercise of reason. We are not to think with our hearts or our blood. The only possible exception here might be Kierkegaard. The virtue, it seems, of the 'knight of faith', like Abraham in *Fear and Trembling*, is to obey God's will despite its logical absurdity. The absurdity of faith makes it all the greater. But it is not clear that the pseudonymous 'author' of the book represents Kierkegaard's own settled view, and even the 'author' is equivocal: 'While Abraham arouses my admiration, he also appals me.'[33] Moreover, Kierkegaard is contemptuous of those who would make a virtue of 'absurd belief' in everyday life: it is warranted, if at all, only in very special situations where God issues certain calls to us.

There are, it is true, passages in *Existentialism and Humanism* where Sartre may seem to suggest that rational deliberation is impossible in the area of moral choice, so that the choice is a mere 'invention', an *acte gratuit*. I shall show later how this is a misinterpretation of Sartre (chapters 5, 9 and 10).

While the Existentialist is not, in any serious sense, an irrationalist, he is certainly not a 'rationalist' in the philosophical sense that contrasts with 'empiricist'. He does not hold, that is, that the mind is innately equipped with, or predisposed towards, knowledge of certain truths about the world. This is not because he is an 'empiricist', holding that all knowledge is the product of experience. The issue between the two camps is one of several which, for the Existentialist, rest on the false premise that mind and world are logically independent of one another, like a spectator and the show before him. The 'rationalist' differs from the 'empiricist' only in holding that the spectator arrives with a rich intellectual apparatus through which the passing scene gets filtered.

When cultural historians refer to Western rationalism, they intend something broader than 'rationalism' as against 'empiricism'. They mean a tradition which culminates in the Enlightenment and in the positivist conviction that the true repositories of knowledge are the sciences. Existentialism shares no such conviction, and in that respect might be labelled 'romantic'. Its hostility to the pretensions of science, however, is not that of the romantic primitivist, for whom Western science has got things wrong, while African magic or Yin – Yang cosmology has got them right. Rather, the claim of science to provide fundamental understanding of the world rests on misconceptions about understanding, the world, and the relation between the two. The vehicles of the fundamental understanding presupposed by all further knowledge are not the theories and products of science or 'cognition', but practical activities and 'moods'. (Heidegger speaks of 'cognition' reaching 'far too short a way compared with the primordial disclosure belonging to moods'.)[34] Before we can 'cognize' the world, we must first encounter it, both understandingly and affectively, as a world of things to be embraced, avoided, used, discarded and the like. The world described by the scientist has no claim, therefore, to be the one real world. On the contrary, it is parasitic upon the *Lebenswelt*, the 'life-world' in which we move and acquire our primary understanding. Physics may, in its own sphere, possess an 'absolute truth', but that 'makes no difference to that other absolute, which is the world of perception and *praxis*'.[35]

Moreover, the scientific pretension requires that it is possible and necessary for the conquest of real knowledge that the world be stripped of everything which human beings have 'projected' upon it – from colours to meanings, from smells to values. But this is to suppose that mind and world, subject and object, can be treated in logical isolation from one another and separately examined. This dualism, however, is one of those inherited from Descartes which most stand in need of dissolution. For not only is it incoherent, but it is also partly responsible for the sense of the world as alien, as a place of 'unimaginable otherness', accessible if at all only to the man in the laboratory, *au fait* with event-horizons, closed space-times and other postulates of contemporary physics.[36]

One might, I suppose, characterize the Existentialist's insistence on the 'humanness' of the world as a denial of its 'objectivity'. But it would be quite wrong to conclude that existentialism is therefore a 'subjectivist' philosophy, though the term is often applied. For the Existentialist, the question of whether descriptions of the world are objective or subjective is a bad one. They are not objective, if this means being of a kind which a scrupulously detached spectator would provide, for a spectator completely disengaged from the world could have no conception of it at all. But nor are they subjective, if this means that they are glosses smeared over, and therefore occluding, the world as it is in itself. This idea presupposes, no less than the 'objectivist' one does, that there could, at least for God, be a direct, unhindered view of reality 'with its skin off' (as Heidegger puts it).

Nor, of course, is existentialism a form of 'subjective idealism', according to which so-called external things are really contents of the mind or constructs of the imagination. This view contradicts the main tenet of existential phenomenology, that no sense can be made of mind except as engaged, through embodied activity, in a world which cannot, therefore, be contained 'inside' it.

This same point about mind having to be 'out there' in the world as praxis should scotch the strangely entrenched idea that existentialism is 'subjectivist' in being a philosophy primarily concerned with the 'subject', in roughly the Cartesian sense of a mental substance or self underlying consciousness. Robert Solomon, for example, describes existentialism, in France at least, as 'undeniably Cartesian', and the 'culmination' of what he calls 'the transcendental pretence', which includes belief in 'the remarkable inner richness and expanse of the self'.[37] This is the reverse of the truth, for one of the most salient aspects of existentialism, Gallic versions included, is the onslaught on Cartesian notions of self or subject, and on the dualisms which they inspire. For Nietzsche, the self is a 'fiction', invented by people who required something inside others to blame, and inside themselves to go on to an afterlife.[38] Heidegger writes that a person is 'never anything like a substantive inner sphere',[39] while Marcel regards the 'pure subjectivism' of Descartes' *cogito* as among 'the most serious errors of which any metaphysics has been guilty'.[40] Sartre, we saw, refers to the 'subjectivity' which is a 'principle' of existentialism, but makes clear that this is not what belongs to the Cartesian subject: it merely indicates that 'man is a project which possesses a subjective [that is, self-aware] life, instead of being a kind of moss... or a cauliflower.'[41] His animosity towards the Cartesian self is plain enough: it is a 'bloodthirsty idol which devours all one's projects', and the 'subjectivity' it possesses is 'magical'. For, just as magical thought invests objects with spirits, like fetishes and jujus, so philosophers like Descartes have 'reified' our mental acts by locating them in a fictitious 'subjectivity-object' that they call 'self' or 'ego'.[42]

I could continue considering further senses in which existentialism is not a subjectivist philosophy, but let me mention only one more. The Existentialist certainly does not embrace a subjectivist theory of truth, if by that is meant the view propounded by Protagoras in Plato's *Theaetetus*, to the effect that each man is the measure of truth, that truth can only be *for me, for you*, or whoever. While he cannot accept a definition of truth as correspondence with a reality independent of all human conceptions of it, the Existentialist is perfectly able to accept that beliefs can be objectively true in the sense of being warranted by criteria on which there is tried and tested public agreement.

People may have been misled here by Kierkegaard's notorious statement that 'truth is subjectivity [and] to seek objectivity is to be in error.' Kierkegaard's meaning, though, cannot be Protagoras', since he immediately adds that 'subjective truth' is 'an objective uncertainty held fast in... the most passionate inwardness'[43] – which implies, of course, that there *can* be an objective truth of the matter. He is, in fact, trying to make two points, neither of them Protagorean, in connection with a comparison he makes between a Christian who lends merely intellectual assent to his religion, and a heathen with his passionate, lived faith. The former's belief has greater objective truth, but the latter is more 'in the truth'. This is, first, because the heathen, although his God is not the true one, better appreciates God's essential nature: for God is not a Being to whom, if that nature is grasped, a person can remain emotionally indifferent. Second, the heathen's faith is a truer, more authentic expression of human existence than the cool theology of the Christian. This is because 'essential existing', as against 'loosely-called existing', demands passion and commitment. Whatever one thinks of these points, and Kierkegaard's paradoxical way of making them, they are not subjectivist ones in the sense under discussion.

Finally, it is worth recording one aspect of existentialist thinking which might, at a pinch, be described as subjective. An important existentialist thesis is that 'moods' and emotions can be vehicles of understanding. Now there is a tendency among our writers to focus on the more personal and solitary 'moods', those farthest away from the grief or delight which people display in unison at funerals or football matches. I have in mind, for example, the sense of guilt which, for Jaspers, is indicative of the 'unpeaceful', 'antinomial' nature of *Existenz*; or the 'fidelity' a person may feel towards a dead friend which, for

Marcel, indicates the presence of a God who is the source of fidelity. These sombre moods might be described as 'subjective' by way of contrast to the 'social' ones we display alongside others. Existentialists concentrate upon these because they are, arguably, the most distinctively human; the ones, therefore, which are liable to be most disclosive of the character of human existence. Those television nature programmes which specialize, in the 'naked ape' tradition, in telling us how we imitate the beasts and they imitate us, would find it hard to discover analogues in the feline or marsupial worlds to Jaspers' guilt or Marcel's fidelity. It is important to note, though, that if we do describe these 'moods' as 'subjective', there are other senses in which they are certainly *not* subjective. They are not, for example, irretrievably 'private' and incommunicable. Nor are they 'merely' subjective, in the sense of having no significant connection with how reality is. On the contrary, they are supposed to be feelings to which, as William James puts it, things are *known*. (I return to the topic of 'subjectivity' in chapter 5 and the appendix.)

This completes my preliminary survey of some misconceptions about existentialism and of some reasons behind them. The book as a whole will, I hope, confirm that these are indeed misconceptions. We are now ready for the Existentialist to begin the journey whose route I outlined earlier.

Notes

1　Simone de Beauvoir, *Force of Circumstance*, 1987, pp. 45–6.
2　'Letter on humanism', in *Martin Heidegger: Basic Writings*, ed. D. F. Krell, 1978.
3　'Philosophical autobiography', in *The Philosophy of Karl Jaspers*, ed. P. A. Schilpp, 1957, p. 28. He is referring to his *Psychology of World-Views*.
4　*Force of Circumstance*, pp. 151–2.
5　Quoted in K. Hoffman, 'The basic concepts of Jaspers' philosophy', in *The Philosophy of Karl Jaspers*, ed. Schilpp, p. 100.
6　*Concluding Unscientific Postscript*, 1974, p. 268.
7　*Being and Time*, 1962, p. 42H. (The 'H' refers to the pagination of the German original, *Sein und Zeit*, which is given in the margins of the English translation.)
8　*Concluding Unscientific Postscript*, p. 79.
9　'Man the technician', in his *History as a System and Other Essays towards a Philosophy of History*, 1962, pp. 112–13.
10　*Concluding Unscientific Postscript*, pp. 107ff., 268ff.
11　Ibid., p. 270.
12　Quoted in Charles F. Wallraff, *Karl Jaspers: An Introduction to his Philosophy*, 1970, pp. 101–2.
13　Maurice Merleau-Ponty, *Phenomenology of Perception*, 1962, pp. 344, 432.

14 Michel Haar, 'Sartre and Heidegger', in *Jean-Paul Sartre: Contemporary Approaches to his Philosophy*, ed. H. Silverman and F. Elliston, 1980, p. 168. For a more responsible account, see Joseph J. Fell, *Heidegger and Sartre: An Essay on Being and Place*, 1979.

15 In conversation with Bryan Magee on the BBC Television series, The Great Philosophers, also available as a book with the same title (1987).

16 De Beauvoir, *Force of Circumstance*, p. 301.

17 *The Philosophy of Sartre*, 1965, p. 35.

18 *Existentialism and Humanism*, 1966, p. 28.

19 'Man the technician' and 'History as a system', in his *History as a System and Other Essays*.

20 *Phenomenology of Perception*, p. 407.

21 Albert Camus, *The Myth of Sisyphus*, 1986, pp. 13, 110.

22 Nietzsche, *The Gay Science*, 1974, p. 286.

23 *Authenticity and Learning: Nietzsche's Educational Philosophy*, 1983.

24 *The Oxford Companion to French Literature*, 1959, p. 261.

25 J. M. Roberts, *Europe 1880–1945*, 1977, p. 467.

26 Fifth edn 1964 p. 424. By the eighth edition (1990) the definition had improved.

27 *The Age of Reason*, 1961, p. 107.

28 *Either/Or*, 1974, vol. 2, p. 240.

29 *Existentialism and Humanism*, p. 39.

30 *Diaries*, entry for June 1940.

31 M. A. Gillespie, *Hegel, Heidegger and the Ground of History*, 1984, p. 20. The author's subsequent explanation of the possible senses of 'nihilism' does not confirm the cover-blurb's reference to his book as a 'marvel of clarity'.

32 *I and Thou*, 1937, p. 77.

33 *Fear and Trembling*, 1985, p. 89.

34 *Being and Time*, p. 134H.

35 Jean-Paul Sartre, *Cahiers pour une morale*, 1983, p. 529.

36 Bas van Fraasen, quoted by Anthony O'Hear, *The Element of Fire: Science, Art, and the Human World*, 1988, p. 12. The first chapter of this book gives a good description of the alienating effect of an exclusively scientific conception of understanding.

37 *Continental Philosophy since 1970*, 1988, pp. 173, 2. I have no idea how Solomon reconciles these remarks with his correct appreciation that Sartre 'insists that there is no self at the core of consciousness...[and that] the self...is created only through living' (p. 174). Generally, I should add, this is an illuminating book.

38 See *The Will to Power*, 1968, section 485, and *The Genealogy of Morals*, 1968, Part 2.

39 *The Basic Problems of Phenomenology*, 1982, p. 170.

40 *Being and Having*, 1949, p. 27.

41 *Existentialism and Humanism*, p. 28.

42 Sartre, *Cahiers pour une morale*, pp. 497, 431.

43 *Concluding Unscientific Postscript*, pp. 181–2.

2
Philosophy and Alienation

Battling against Bewitchment

In this chapter I shall be suggesting that there is a truth, though not perhaps the one intended, in the popular idea that existentialism is a practical philosophy, one to be 'lived'. The conception of a philosophy as something to live, and a philosopher as somebody who lives one, is venerable. For many Socrates is *the* philosopher, not because of theories he taught, but because of his enquiring, honest, courageous life. The Daoist sage is not a man who simply knows things, but a *hsien* (man of the mountains) who manifests his knowledge through renunciation of social and worldly ambitions.

Underlying such conceptions is the thought that there are kinds of understanding which transform a person's stance towards reality, and hence his life. How he lives, or *is*, thereby becomes a test of what he knows. (The person who escapes from the cave and 'sees' the 'Form of the Good' is metamorphosed, which is why, Plato says, it will be almost impossible to get him to return to the cave and lead others out of it.) I shall argue that the Existentialist aims at an understanding of this kind, and for the sake of the transformation it effects. Whether existentialism is a 'practical' philosophy in the stronger sense of offering concrete guidance on how people ought to behave; whether, if you like, it issues in an ethic – these are questions I postpone until chapter 10.

I shall approach the matter from what might seem an unlikely direction. Followers of the later Wittgenstein sometimes like to describe philosophy as a therapy, even as a relative of psychoanalysis. They are inspired in this by such well-known remarks of Wittgenstein's as 'philosophy is a battle against the bewitchment of our intelligence by means of language' and 'a philosophical problem has the form "I don't know my way about."' Philosophy, to cite his famous analogy, must endeavour to show the fly out of the bottle in which it is trapped.[1] The idea, it seems, is this: language, when it functions in normal communication, is perfectly 'in order' as it is. But when it is allowed to 'go on holiday', and is unmoored from its usual functions, language can seduce us into a whole array of misconceptions, for example, the illusion that all nouns, even ones like 'thought' and 'meaning', must stand for thing-like entities of however mysterious a kind.

Wittgenstein was not, in one sense, offering any prescription for living, for he thought that most people would sensibly avoid the questions that render them liable to the seductions and bewitchments of language. Better to work as a shop-assistant, was his advice to one aspiring philosopher. Still, for those who fail to heed such advice, philosophy should not be the task of providing new knowledge, of constructing large theories, nor even of solving substantial questions. These are the tasks of science. Philosophy, rather, should be an activity through which the victim of bewitchment helps himself escape from the fly-bottle, or appease the disquiet into which he has fallen. The right-minded philosopher is distinguished by a certain stance towards language, and his success is measured by the mental peace he attains as a result of this 'therapy'.

Now by far the most important bewitchments against which Wittgenstein thinks we must battle are those which lead us to postulate two fictitious, complementary realms: first, that of the 'inner', 'private' mental life in which invisible processes of meaning, desiring, thinking, etc. are conducted; second, an 'objective', 'transcendent' realm of things and events possessed of 'essences' which are quite independent of our particular conceptual schemes, 'language-games' and 'forms of life'. Such bewitchments produce dualisms like those of inner versus outer, mind versus body, language versus reality, private versus public, or word versus essence.

It is of great interest that it is against bewitchments of just this kind that the sages of several very ancient traditions are also portrayed as struggling. The Daoist, for example, recognizes both the relativity to human thought of all the properties we purport to discover in the world, and that the 'I', since it requires the presence of the 'He', cannot be a discrete psychic entity like a soul.[2] Comparisons like this prompt the thought that the battle is not simply to relieve intellectual cramps, but to remedy a whole distorted stance towards the relation between man and world – one which inclines our ambitions, our treatment of other people, our relationship to God, our very lives in fact, in certain directions.

The further thought is then suggested that the deepest urge to philosophy may be the need to overcome, dissolve, or come to terms with the dualistic thinking which informs that stance. Neither puzzlement nor awe, neither a thirst for knowledge nor a craving for clarity, has been the abiding inspiration for philosophy. Rather, this has been the perpetual threat posed by the sense that men are hopelessly alienated from their world.

This thought must sound odd to the contemporary student of philosophy. The subject is usually introduced to him through discussion of Descartes' doubts about the material world, the validity of mathematics and so on. Other writers are then brought in by locating them in the debate about scepticism. Do Plato's Forms serve as objects of absolutely certain knowledge? Does Berkeley's 'esse est percipi' guarantee the existence of tables and trees by equating them with our 'sense-data'? Did Kant establish that the very possibility of experience requires physical objects and causal laws? In short, the contemporary student must gain the impression that philosophy revolves primarily around 'the problem of knowledge'. The topic of alienation will then sound a fairly marginal one, the province of oriental exoticism or Teutonic brooding.

I can hardly intend, in a few paragraphs, to rewrite the history of philosophy, but I think that the student just described has matters the wrong way round. The problem of knowledge perhaps owes its endurance to being just one aspect of the larger issue of alienation. What is really disturbing in Descartes' 'methodological doubt' is not that it gets people to wonder seriously if the world exists. Indeed, one must ask with Wittgenstein and Heidegger what it would be like to entertain such worries. Can one even pretend to entertain them? How could such doubts, 'idle' at best, be the well-spring of philosophy?

Descartes tries to show that my experiences could be just as they are even though there exists no world for them to be experiences of. And what is disturbing in this is not the worry that perhaps there really is no world, but the sense that I am a self-enclosed realm, 'cut off' in logical isolation from the world.[3] If I could exist despite the absence of things and other people, then it cannot be essential to my being that I have a body and am in the company of others. Descartes' subsequent reintroduction of the material world, via a God who would not fool us about its reality, can do nothing to restore the intimacy between myself and my body and world which his initial arguments have dissolved. This is especially so, given the kind of world he reintroduces: for this is the world of science, and our ordinary image of the world as replete with colours, sounds, meanings and beauty is relegated to a mere subjective effect of the scientists' 'real' world. Not only is the world inessential to my being, but it turns out to be one that I cannot comprehend. The scientist may comprehend this 'real' world, but is in the schizoid position of experiencing a completely different one.

If the above account of the significance of Cartesian 'doubt' is plausible, then we need to look again at philosophers usually construed as attempting to solve the problem of knowledge. Perhaps even Descartes is misconstrued if read as a genuine 'doubter'. An alternative reading would be this: Descartes was at once convinced by the mechanistic, Galilean account of the world and perturbed by it – for what space does that account leave for God and for the Christian idea that the world is there, in some sense, for *our* sake? Descartes' main aim, perhaps, was to re-establish that space and that idea. As he explained in a letter of 1638 to Vatier, the only sure way to prove God's existence was to show that what is left after the world has been 'bracketed', the *cogito*, could only operate as it does if there is a God providing it with some of its thoughts (notably, that of perfection).[4] In that event, the Galilean world which Descartes then reintroduces must be something which is not only created by this God, but ordered by Him to behave in harmony with ourselves, His creatures. This, perhaps, is the most we can hope for by way of intimacy with the world in the age of science.

The usual way of reading the other thinkers mentioned earlier may also be guilty of mistaken emphasis. For Plato, the Forms surely have a more significant role than to serve as items of indubitable knowledge. Being eternal and immaterial, they are *akin to* the minds which come to the acquainted with them, unlike physical objects which are alien to the nature of the soul. As Plato puts it, the philosopher attains knowledge of the Forms 'with the faculty which is akin to reality, and which approaches and unites with it'.[5] Berkeley, too, rejects matter, not only because it would be unknowable, but because it would be an unnecessary *intrusion*. If the only reality outside of our own minds and their ideas is God, then nothing exists which is incommensurate to, or unfitting for, the mental. Berkeley's attitude towards matter is one of *indignation* at something so 'stupid' and alien to ourselves. It is 'repugnant' to suppose that the world might exist without mind.[6] Only if it is so many 'signs' provided by God for 'informing, admonishing and directing' us is the world suited to human intelligence.[7]

To judge from the reception among his immediate philosophical successors in Germany, Kant's dramatic contribution was not to have laid Hume's scepticism to rest, but his postulation of a 'noumenal' reality of unknowable 'things-in-themselves' standing behind the empirical world. Kant himself thought that the primary importance of this was moral rather than epistemological, for it secured room for free will and responsibility. (In the empirical order, the will is, like everything else, causally determined.) For many of his successors, though, the 'noumenal' world was not something to welcome, but an emotional as well as an intellectual disaster. As the poet Kleist put it in a letter to his fiancée, the effect of putting the 'real' world outside of experience was to render 'every effort to earn a possession which follows us into the grave ... in vain ... my single, highest goal is sunk, and I have no other.'[8] Kleist was not exaggerating, for he committed suicide shortly after.

These selective remarks will not convince anyone to read the history of the subject in a new way, but they support the thought that a perennial concern of philosophy has been to confront an alienation of man from the world which science, language or metaphysical speculation may threaten. For example, the opposing charms of materialism and idealism may reside less in their solutions to the problem of knowledge, than in suggesting how men may be 'at one' with the world. Either man is just one more kind of thing in nature, or nature is itself a constituent of his consciousness.

It can hardly be denied, at any rate, that for some philosophers of the first importance alienation has been the explicit focus, and I shall shortly be turning to two of these. Before that, it is worth remarking, following Hegel, that philosophy so considered is at once brought into immediate proximity with those other great endeavours of the human spirit, religion and art. It is, of course, a cliché that a main inspiration for religion is a need for unity with 'something larger than oneself'. This need is most obviously manifested in religions of a pantheistic hue, or in ones, like that of the *Upanishads*, where the soul is identified with the principle of the cosmos. But even where there is worship of a more personal God, the endeavour is to envisage a *humanized* world, one created and governed by a Being recognizably like ourselves (even if, as Marx argued, the net effect is to make the actual world *more* alien).

It is a cliché, too, that some of the greatest art has endeavoured to forge, or to record, a unity between the human spirit and the world. The artist 'humanizes' a shapeless world by lending it form, or he attunes himself to the world's rhythms. From the anonymous poets of the *Vedas* to Tagore, from Theocritus to Wordsworth and Goethe, this unity has been a salient motif of poetry. 'The skies were mine, and so were the sun and moon and stars, and all the world was mine,' wrote the seventeenth-century poet Thomas Traherne, on behalf of countless members of his calling. And countless painters would no doubt hope that the following description of Van Gogh's *Crows over the Wheatfield* might also apply to their own works. It presents an 'all-absorbing essence in which at last subject and object, part and whole, past and present, near and far, can no longer be distinguished'.[9]

This will all sound much too romantic to some ears, and it will have escaped nobody's notice that the terminology in which I have so far discussed alienation – 'at home with', 'separated from', etc. – is both vague and figurative. It may be that the sense of alienation is resistant to literal, analytical definition. Perhaps it is a sense which can, finally, be registered only through the practices and metaphors of religion and art. But this would be a pessimistic attitude. At the very least, alienation is a many-sided notion whose sides need to be individually exposed. This task is of a piece with trying to indicate the various respects in which alienation is held to be so important to 'overcome' or, at any rate, come to terms with. The best way to approach these tasks is by considering the views of two writers, Hegel and Marx, who explicitly undertook them.

This will also put us in a position of being able to compare and contrast the Existentialist's treatment of the matter.

Hegel and Marx

For Hegel, alienation is not so much the central issue of philosophy as the *only* one, with the sole test of a philosophy being its ability to 'overcome' alienation. Philosophy aims to ensure that 'everything foreign has vanished and *Geist* [mind, spirit] is . . . at home with itself.'[10] But Hegel has still more startling claims to make.

The first is that alienation is *the* fundamental feature of consciousness throughout its history – one which begins with *Geist*'s 'separation from itself', its opposing itself to the world of Nature. Its subsequent history is that of further 'withdrawal out of its happy natural life, into the night of self-consciousness'; followed by the long attempt to 'reconstruct . . . the reality . . . from which it has been separated'.[11] More than this, though, history itself is 'the development of *Geist* in time', and that development is the 'endless labour' of *Geist* to overcome its self-alienation.[12] History's parade of civilizations, 'world-historical' individuals, religions and so on, is that of the 'vehicles' commandeered by *Geist* in its struggle to recapture a lost unity with Nature.

Philosophy, finally, does not merely discuss alienation; it is a peculiarly significant manifestation of it. It is 'the spirit of the age . . . as present to itself in thought' and, as such, must reflect *Geist*'s struggles against alienation, as do religion and art. Philosophy thus ends when alienation does; when, having once 'elevated' itself above 'immediate unity with Nature', it manages 'by the activity of thinking to restore the unity again'.[13] In short, from the dawn of self-consciousness the condition of *Geist* has been one of alienation. This condition, in its various twists and turns, has dictated the history of civilization, including that of philosophy, whose task is to restore a lost unity. The unity regained, however, will not be the original 'dull', 'naïve' sort, but one which is thought and understood, not just felt.

Hegel grounds these remarkable claims on two central propositions. First, there is the idealist insistence that 'the Absolute is *Geist*.' Gods, numbers, men, mice, stones – all these are aspects of a single reality whose nature is spiritual or mind-like. To suppose that reality is not like this, Hegel thinks, yields contradictions. The second proposition is that *Geist* is an activity or process whose goal is that of self-knowledge. Nothing, Hegel argues, can count as mind-like unless it is rational; and no activity is rational that is not distinguished by reflection on, and understanding of, its own character.

From these propositions it follows that *Geist* only realizes its aim, self-knowledge, when it appreciates that it is the whole of reality. It must 'recognize itself in everything in heaven and on earth', and see that there is no 'out and out other' besides itself.[14] During the whole period prior to that recognition, consequently, *Geist* has laboured under a misunderstanding, for it has supposed that heaven and earth are 'out and out other' than itself. It has, in fine, been alienated from itself, regarding as 'foreign' what are really aspects of itself. At this point, it is worth bearing in mind the etymology of the German word, '*Entfremdung*', which gets translated as 'alienation'. It comes from '*fremd*' ('strange', 'foreign'), so that the translation which better captures Hegel's notion would be 'estrangement'. Like the lover estranged from the woman who is, if he would only realize it, 'a part of him', so *Geist* is estranged from the world or Nature that, more literally for Hegel, is a part of it.

We can now see how Hegel is able to make his startling claims about history, philosophy and alienation. First, if the very essence of *Geist* is to achieve self-knowledge, then its fundamental feature during its 'endless labours' is that so far it has failed in this task. Just as the crucial thing about a seed is that it has not yet 'actualized' its potential as a fruit, so, Hegel says, the crucial thing about *Geist* has been to have remained only potentially what it is essentially. Second, the history of the world – its great civilizations and men, its religions and art-forms – will indeed be that of alienation if it is merely the manifestation of a *Geist* whose nature, we now know, is to have 'externalized' or 'estranged' itself. This historical struggle is conducted, in part, at the self-conscious level which we call 'philosophy'. So, finally, 'the spectacle afforded by the history of philosophy' will be precisely the struggle of *Geist* against alienation. And philosophy only concludes its task when, in the shape of Hegel's system, it achieves its 'aim to grasp the Absolute as *Geist*'.[15]

Most people find these claims hard to digest, choking most of all on the notion of *Geist*. It would be cheering, certainly, if that notion could be 'brought down to earth', and the simplest way would be to construe the word as an over-dramatic, collective label for individual human minds or consciousnesses. Unfortunately this would be unfaithful to Hegel, who frequently *contrasts Geist* with the totality of human beings. On the other hand, he does insist that *Geist* is no 'soul-thing' which exists independently of ourselves. It is only 'truly actual through . . . its necessary self-manifestation' in the concrete, embodied or intellectual activities of people.[16] So while *Geist* cannot be equated with human being, we can expect assertions about it to imply corollaries about ourselves. *Geist* can then be 'brought down to earth' by setting aside worries about its final metaphysical status and concentrating upon these corollaries about human beings. This is just what Hegel himself does in *The Phenomenology of Spirit* and *The Philosophy of History* where, at the levels of psychology and political history, he concerns himself with *Geist*'s 'self-manifestations' in human affairs.

It would be good, in particular, to grasp the concrete corollaries of the claim that the history of *Geist* is one of alienation and the struggle to overcome it. We want to know, too, just why alienation is so undesirable; why not only philosophy, but religion, art and statecraft struggle to overcome it. Hegel makes it clear that not only is the state of alienation one of misunderstanding, but it is also 'wretched', 'unhappy' or 'uncanny'. History, he laconically remarks, is not 'the theatre of happiness'.[17]

There is, of course, a puzzle as to why *Geist* ever alienated itself in the first place. 'Brought down to earth', the point seems to be that humans will only recognize their true place in the order of things – as privileged aspects of an essentially spiritual reality – if they first treat that order as 'objective', outside of themselves. Only if they do this will they develop the articulated understanding of Nature which will eventually transmute into the recognition that it is not, after all, intelligible as independent of themselves. The analogy might be with the artist Rembrandt, say, who must first 'externalize' himself in self-portraits in order that, by looking at them, he can understand his own character. Hegel's view in fact extends an ancient theological tradition according to which God creates the world so that, through this image of Himself, he may come to know His own nature.

Whatever the reason, humans have come to view reality as external to themselves, and their history is one of trying to correct that view. Hegel indicates at least five 'grim' aspects of alienation which, surfacing at various points in history, induce men to overcome it.

To begin with, once men contrast themselves *qua* spiritual beings with Nature, they thereby contrast-themselves with their own *bodies*. This is an especially acute aspect of what Hegel calls 'the unhappy consciousness', which characterizes medieval, ascetic Christianity. Alienated from the natural world, people think of themselves as immaterial souls. Their 'animal functions' then become an 'embarrassment' in which 'the enemy reveals himself'. Sensual desires pose a threat to one's 'real' self, to be warded off by the devices of asceticism, from self-flagellation to celibacy. What should be matters of enjoyment turn into 'a feeling...of wretchedness'.[18] Men feel 'split' and, like St Augustine, they plead for chastity and continence – only 'not yet'.

If I set myself off against the world and my body then I also do so against my fellow men. This sense of separation from others looms large at a number of the stages of consciousness described by Hegel. His famous discussion of 'lordship and bondage' describes the manner in which people assert themselves, though to no avail, by trying to enslave the freedom of others. And he criticizes the societies of his own day for having become mere 'heaps' of human 'atoms', held together only by mutual self- interest. In such societies there is lacking any identification, in heart and soul, with one's community.

There is another aspect of alienation which, Hegel thought, was particularly visible in the century into which he was born. Indeed, he refers to the eighteenth-century Age of Enlightenment as 'the world of self-alienated spirit'.[19] Although no defender of the myths and superstitions which the Enlightenment challenged, he did think that, in their crude way, these captured the important truth that the world is replete with *meaning*. (One thinks here of the medieval and Renaissance image of the world as the Book of God.) By treating the world as a mere mechanism, and meaning or value as a purely 'subjective' contribution, Voltaire and his friends made Nature a more rational, but also a more foreign, place − one which only the scientist, in his cool moments, can properly measure. Where the Gods of old had shown themselves in symbols for man to read, the God of the Enlightenment was the distant 'Supreme Being', a clock-maker with whom no one could feel an affinity. From this picture of the world as a meaningless mechanism, it was a short step, Hegel believed, to the nihilism of the French Revolution where society too became a mere mechanism to be taken apart and reassembled at will.

Fourth, the alienating bifurcation between Mind and Nature can induce in men a sense of being completely *inessential* to the way things are. This is part of Hegel's point in the early chapters of the *Phenomenology* where he discusses 'perception' and 'understanding'. To conceive of ourselves as mere perceivers of an objective reality is to deny that we have any responsibility for the articulation of reality. While it is an advance if we also come to understand the world in terms of causal laws, it remains that the world is not, in an important sense, *our* world.

Finally, alienated man cannot be *free*. The two crucial features of Hegel's complex theory of freedom are that a person is only free if he is not dependent on anything outside of himself, and that 'a man is only free when he knows himself [to be free].'[20] To be free, people must not only be independent of anything standing over against them, but they must feel that they are thus independent. The alienated person, however, feels that objects 'dominate' him, and that he is a 'victim' of his sensual, 'animal' desires. Hence, the attempt to overcome alienation is one with the urge towards freedom: 'the nature of *Geist* [is] to alienate itself in order to find itself again. This movement is just what freedom is . . . By reverting to itself, *Geist* achieves its freedom . . . where everything foreign has vanished . . . *Geist* is absolutely free, at home with itself.'[21]

Alienated men, in sum, are doomed at some point to feel divorced from their own bodies and from their fellows; and to regard the world, devoid of meaning and value, as an order to which they are quite inessential, and in which they cannot realize their freedom. It is these 'grim' aspects of the alienated stance which, as well as its intellectual incoherence, drive men on to overcome it.

Two points about Hegel remain outstanding, but these are best made during a brief outline of Karl Marx's account of alienation.

In line with his famous dictum that philosophers must change the world, Marx wrote that 'philosophy can only be realized by the abolition of the proletariat' and vice versa.[22] This is because the aim of philosophy, as for Hegel, is to overcome alienation, and because this requires society to be rid of economic class division. It is difficult to exaggerate the role played by alienation in Marx's early writings. Neither the injustices of class society nor the inevitability of its disappearance constitutes his case for communism, but solely the belief that overcoming alienation requires the abolition of classes. Originally, indeed, alienation is the cause, not the effect, of class division, though the connection later becomes reciprocal. Against Hegel, however, Marx believed that alienation, in turn, had an economic origin. 'How can it be that [men's] relationships become independent of them... [and] gain control over them? The answer in a word is – the division of labour.'[23]

The young Marx was led to these conclusions not only by reading Hegel, but by reflecting on the contemporary state of religion, especially the issue of Jewish emancipation in Germany. His crucial claim was that religion *per se* was a symptom of alienation, in which case it was hopeless for Jews or anyone else to seek emancipation through religious tolerance. *All* religion is an 'opium' to which alienated people turn for tranquillization. This is a radical extension of a point of Hegel's, for while he was not, of course, an enemy of religion in general, he was critical of those beliefs which conceive God as transcendent or 'outside' of the world. Such beliefs not only contribute to our sense of alienation, as we saw in the case of the ascetic's 'unhappy consciousness', but are also a product of that sense. An extra 'grim' aspect of alienation, therefore, is that it induces people, incapable of reconciling themselves to the real world, to manufacture illusory ones. Marx goes beyond Hegel in regarding *all* religions as so many illusions.

Marx further departs from Hegel in rejecting the whole metaphysics of *Geist*. Alienation is not primarily a matter of misunderstanding the proper relation between Mind and Nature: hence it cannot be overcome by a mere correction of thought, by philosophy. Marx concedes that for Hegel alienation cannot be ended purely cerebrally, and recognizes his insistence that men must also live in the kind of political state described in *The Philosophy of Right* if they are to feel 'at home' in the world. But this, Marx thinks, is still not enough, for 'political emancipation by itself cannot be human emancipation.'[24] Political life belongs to society's 'superstructure', and not the economic 'substructure' where the determinants of the human condition operate. The end of alienation therefore demands transformation of 'existing social conditions' – private property, the division of labour – and not simply of the political forms which reflect these conditions.

Marx exaggerates his distance from Hegel here, for he underplays the latter's *holism* – the way in which *everything* in human affairs, being a manifestation of *Geist*'s latest development, hangs together. People will only philosophize truly, and only constitute themselves into the Hegelian state, as part and parcel of a total transformation of consciousness that affects, *inter alia*, their religion and art, their family relations and their attitude towards work. (This great emphasis upon holism is the second of the two points I left outstanding.) It remains, however, that Hegel does not, in the manner of Marx, envisage an economic revolution in 'existing social conditions' as required for ending human alienation.

It would take us too far from the concerns of this book to recount Marx's analysis of alienation into its various modes – alienation from others, from one's work and its products, and so on. It does need to be stressed, however, that the 'subjective' aspect of these modes – how things appear to people, how they are felt – is just as important to Marx as the 'objective' economic circumstances. People are alienated from their work because it is done under compulsion; but also because they 'feel beside [themselves] in work', and 'at home' only away from work, when performing their least human, 'animal functions'.[25] Marx, then, is adding to the list of 'grim' experiences which motivate people to overcome their alienation.

One of Marx's modes of alienation deserves special mention – what he calls alienation from 'species-being' (or 'species-essence': German '*Gattungswesen*'). This is a rich concept which underlies all the modes of alienation he cites, and which provides a materialist twist to the Hegelian idea of *Geist* coming to grasp the world as an extension of itself. 'Species-being' is man's *essence* as a free, creative producer who co-operates with his fellows in lending form and meaning to their world by transforming it through work. We 'humanize' the world, not by thinking about it in the right way, but by making it into one whose contents bear our stamp and reflect back to us our scale of values and significance. (Faithful Marxists, with their picture of Nature as wax in man's hands, are at the opposite pole from today's 'deep ecologists'.)[26] It is from this 'species-being' that we have, above all, become alienated. Instead of producing freely and 'according to the laws of beauty', people produce out of need, and 'alienated labour . . . makes [a man's] life-activity, his essence, a mere *means* for his existence.'[27]

Existentialism and Alienation

I am hardly the first to have suggested that issues of alienation are pivotal in existentialist thought. William Barrett, for example, writes that 'alienation and estrangement' constitute the 'whole problematic' of existentialism: one which 'unfolds from the historical situation [of] bourgeois society in a state of dissolution', notably 'the *human* debacle' of 1914–18.[28] My understanding, however, is fundamentally at odds with Barrett's on two counts. First, the Existentialist does not regard alienation as the product of recent historical circumstance, like the 'dissolution' of bourgeois society. With Hegel, he holds that millennia of Western thought have reinforced a tendency, implicit in the very nature of consciousness, to posit an independent, 'objective' world. Second, Barrett treats existentialism as a *celebration*, heroic or masochistic, of alienated man's 'nakedness' and 'solitariness' before the world. Here, I suspect, Camus' Sisyphus is exerting too much influence. The Existentialist in fact follows Hegel and Marx in assigning to philosophy the task of curing people of the misunderstandings which promote a sense of alienation.

This sense of alienation is to be overcome, not simply because it rests on misunderstanding, but because it makes for an unhappy consciousness. Existentialists endorse the lists of 'grim' aspects of alienation drawn up by Hegel and Marx. Marcel, for example, draws attention to the impossibility, once 'the opposition between subject and object is treat[ed] as fundamental', of my 'getting back to the original consciousness' of 'incarnation', of being indissolubly '*bound* to a body'.[29] Sartre takes up the point that, in alienation, the sense is lost that man is 'essential' to the constitution of the world, that he has a 'mission' to ensure that there is a structured reality at all.[30] Heidegger repeats Hegel's observation that people have come to view the world as devoid of significance, with values and meanings being stuck, as an afterthought, upon the neutral world of which science speaks. Nietzsche, like Marx, attributes the temptation to invent illusory realms, such as heaven, to the desire for refuge from a world which is perceived as alien instead of something which people bear the responsibility for 'creating'.[31]

Despite the continuity with Hegel and Marx, the Existentialist follows neither of them all the way in his diagnosis of alienation and his proposed remedies. He does not, for instance, share Marx's almost exclusive emphasis on economic conditions and exploitation. These may reinforce people's sense of living and working in a hostile world, but as Sartre succinctly puts it, 'alienation precedes oppression.'[32] The Existentialist is closer to Hegel in diagnosing alienation as a 'spiritual' condition, but he does not embrace, nor perhaps understand, Hegel's metaphysics of reality as self-bifurcating *Geist*. There is no mind except that of individuals. Nor does he share Hegel's optimistic belief that history is a long process, destined to be successful, of attempting to overcome alienation. Indeed, the Existentialist is more impressed by what he sees as the disingenuous ploys whereby people stave off the sense of alienation which is implicit in their view of the world: their treatment of themselves as *merely* natural objects, for example.

This last remark introduces something crucial. The Existentialist's departures from Hegel and Marx confront him with some serious questions which did not arise for them. First, if Nature is not 'contained' in Mind, nor vice versa, how is it possible to avoid the dualist picture of conscious subjects confronting a world of independent objects? The question is particularly acute given that, by definition, existentialism emphasizes the unique, 'unthing-like' character of human existence.

The second, more complicated question concerns the relation between the various modes of alienation identified by Hegel and Marx – alienation from the world, from others and from oneself. Although Hegel and Marx distinguish between them, each holds that these modes hang together. In Hegel's account, alienation from the world is a form of self-alienation of *Geist* from itself. For Marx, a person who is alienated from the world in which he works is *ipso facto* estranged from his fellow workers and from his own 'species-essence'. For both of them, alienation in each of its modes is overcome when people live together in a certain kind of community – the Hegelian state, or the classless society.

The Existentialist, on the other hand, does not see the modes of alienation, and their remedies, hanging together in these ways. On the contrary, he thinks that, for the most part, people suppress a sense of alienation from the world by becoming 'absorbed' in or 'tranquillized' by the comforting, ready-made schemes of beliefs and values which prevail in their societies. This has two implications. First, since this 'tranquillized' life is at odds with the exercise of existential freedom, it is the life of people estranged from what is most essentially their own, hence from themselves. Second, since an authentic existence in which this freedom is exercised requires a person to disengage himself from the ways of the 'Public', the 'herd' or the 'they', the remedy for self-estrangement is inherently liable to bring him into conflict with his fellows. There is a striking contrast between Hegel's belief that a person realizes his freedom and human essence by becoming an 'accident' of a communal 'substance', the state, and Kierkegaard's conviction that the only way to 'become an individual' is by withdrawal from, or opposition to, the 'Public'.[33]

The Existentialist therefore faces a difficulty which Hegel and Marx did not: that of delineating forms of thought and existence in which people are 'at home' with their world and each other, but not at the cost of 'losing themselves'. He will succeed in his self-appointed philosophical task only if he brings off this delicate manoeuvre.

Over the last few pages I have helped myself to some terminology from Heidegger and others, but my description of the Existentialist's position on issues of alienation does not match the way any particular existentialist writer has put matters. It has been an example of what I called 'rational reconstruction': one which, I hope, many existentialists would accept as a way of articulating an important motif in their work. Whether it is acceptable and illuminating must be judged on the basis of the book as a whole, but it would be encouraging to have some reason in advance for thinking that the reconstruction is not fantasy. So I shall consider, very briefly, how it fares in the cases of two of our writers – an easy and a hard case.

The 'easy' case is that of Martin Buber, whose *I and Thou* is saturated in the vocabulary of alienation. The person who regards the world as an 'It' lives in 'severance and alienation', and is without a 'home, a dwelling in the universe'.[34] The philosopher's task is to return men to that relationship to the world, God and others which, 'split asunder', has polarized into 'I' versus 'It'. This proper relationship is that of 'I–Thou', Buber's metaphor for the condition in which men are not estranged. It is a common mistake to suppose that Buber's 'Thou' refers only to persons and to God. In fact, anything – a tree, for example, or the eyes of a cat – can belong in the 'Thou', just as any*one* can be an 'It' for us. Something figures as 'It' when, for example, it is considered solely as an object of perception, possessed of properties deemed to exist independently of ourselves. It is 'Thou' when it 'has to do with me', in the dual sense that I am essential to its being and it is to mine. 'A subject deprived of its object is deprived of its reality.'[35]

The features which characterize the 'I – It' relation, moreover, map the 'grim' aspects of alienation adumbrated by the Existentialist. For instance, the world as 'It' has 'become adverse to meaning', and one in which we cannot view ourselves as free. Within it, social life becomes a 'collection of human units that do not know relation'.[36] Despite the Hegelian tone of some of his remarks, Buber is not a philosophical idealist. To suppose that 'there really is no world at all' is an 'illusory' way to 'put [oneself] at ease'.[37] Nor is he sympathetic to Hegel's political remedies. It would be to 'see man only as a part' to imagine that he could be saved from 'cosmic and social homelessness' by becoming so integrated in a community as to be a mere 'accident' of it.[38]

Finally, Buber shares the Existentialist's view that a tendency to regard the world as alien, as 'It', is implicit in the very nature of consciousness: a tendency aided and abetted by dualistic metaphysics. It belongs, he says, in the nature of experience to minimize the contribution made by the one who is experiencing to the constitution of the object experienced. This encourages people to 'split' experience, wrongly, into two independent factors: a 'ghostly I' and a 'ready-made world'.[39]

The 'hard' case is Heidegger, whose writings during the *Being and Time* period contain hardly any explicit discussion of alienation. He does occasionally use the term, but always in the sense of self-estrangement, not estrangement from the world. Nor, it seems, does he think of philosophy as having a practical task, but only the very 'pure' task of investigating Being. This is not to be contaminated by either the study of particular beings, which is the job of the sciences, or the advocacy of 'world-views'.[40] Let me explain why I do not find any of this disturbing for my reconstruction.

There is no doubt, first of all, that the main targets of the early chapters of *Being and Time* are precisely those dualisms of thought in which the Existentialist locates the source of a sense of alienation from the world. They include those of subject versus object, mind versus body, and fact versus value. Nor is there any doubt that, like the Existentialist and like Buber, Heidegger recognizes a proneness to dualistic thinking in the intrinsic nature of human experience, in its so-called 'intentionality'.

Second, we should attend to Heidegger's later writings, where a constant theme is our 'estrangement from Being'. Especially in the writings on technology, the vocabulary of alienation becomes pervasive. Man is described, time and again, as 'homeless' and in search of a true 'dwelling'. Endorsing the words of Rilke, Heidegger writes that 'man stands over against the world. He does not live immediately in the drift and wind of the whole draught.'[41] Now it is made clear in these writings that his concern for 'homelessness' is not new. It is simply that in the earlier writings this 'homelessness' was taken for granted and the emphasis placed instead on the generally inauthentic responses people make to its incipient threat: notably their willingness to become 'absorbed' and 'tranquillized' in the ways of the 'they'. This was why, when the word 'alienation' did occur, it was in the sense of self-estrangement.

In the later writings, finally, the task of philosphy is very much to 'rescue' us from our estrangement from Being. (To be precise, this is the task of 'thinking', Heidegger having discarded the word 'philosophy' as hopelessly contaminated with dualist metaphysics.) This sounds at odds with the earlier, 'pure' conception of philosophy as the study of Being as such. In fact, however, *Being and Time* never gets beyond what, for Heidegger, is supposed to be a preparatory stage: examination of how human beings understand and misunderstand the Being which is an 'issue' for them. Two points about this examination should be noted. First, an exposé of people's misunderstandings about Being – notably their tendency to equate it with the spatio-temporal universe investigated by scientists – is *ipso facto* a therapeutic critique of their attitudes and practices. This is because people's 'understanding of Being and [their] comportment to beings do not come together only afterward and by chance'.[42] Second, most of *Being and Time* has only the remotest connection with the stated goal of a study of Being as such. Much of it consists of earthy discussions of the practices and ploys, the desires and deceptions of those particular beings, ourselves, who for the most part are at odds with either the world, each other, or themselves.

I suggest, then, that it may be illuminating to read the works of the *Being and Time* period in the light of the Existentialist's concern with issues of alienation; and that Heidegger himself, to judge from later remarks, came to read them in this light as well.

Most readers would be disappointed to be told that existentialism is in no manner a 'practical' philosophy, one to be 'lived'. Fortunately this is not what I am saying, even though existentialism's relevance to life has often been distorted. For example, its message is certainly not that we should prowl about committing *actes gratuits* as we wallow in a defiant mood of despair. It may well be that the Existentialist can offer us something by way of concrete guidance to attitudes and actions. That is something to consider later. In this chapter I have indicated a prior, if more modest, sense in which existentialism bears upon life. In the first instance, it addresses a number of dualistic illusions to which we are prone. As for the Daoist and the Wittgensteinian, for Hegel, Goethe and Marx, so for the Existentialist these are not merely intellectual errors which love of truth alone obliges one to dispel. They are illusions which 'bewitch' us and pervade our lives; illusions which generate a sense of being 'homelessly' abandoned in a world devoid of meaning and value, a world whose 'unimaginable otherness' is, at best, partly accessible only to the man in the laboratory. Dissolution of these dualisms is not a victory, therefore, for right thinking alone. It can transform the view we take on our position in the order of things, and free us for a new comportment towards our world.

There are, however, many ways and many philosophies through which it is possible for people to view themselves as 'at home' in the world. Several of these can be accepted and followed only at the expense of a proper understanding of, and fidelity to, the distinctive character of individual human existence. (The Existentialist would include here the philosophies of Hegel and Marx, and various other brands of idealism and materialism.) Existentialism is not to work for people like a drug, to provide a means of 'coping' with one's situation which only people in bad faith could swallow. If existentialism is a philosophy to live, it is to be lived by men and women who have not become estranged from themselves.

The issue of alienation will not return in any detail until chapter 5. Before that we need to appreciate the Existentialist's understanding of the world, human existence and the relation between the two, as articulated in his existential phenomenology.

Notes

1   Ludwig Wittgenstein, *Philosophical Investigations*, 1969, pp. 47, 49, 103.
2   Chuang-Tzu, in *Wisdom of the Daoist Masters*, 1984, ch. 2.
3   A similar point is made by John McDowell in his excellent paper, 'Singular thought and the extent of inner space', 1986.
4   René Descartes, *Philosophical Letters*, 1970, p. 46.
5   *The Republic*, 1986, p. 284.

6 George Berkeley, *Philosophical Writings*, 1952, p. 167.
7 Quoted from Berkeley's *Alciphron* by John Passmore, *Man's Responsibility for Nature*, 1980, p. 15.
8 Quoted by Karl Popper, *The Open Society and its Enemies*, 1963, vol. 2, p. 382.
9 Meyer Schapiro, *Van Gogh*, n.d. p. 34.
10 G. W. F. Hegel, *Introduction to the Lectures on the History of Philosophy*, 1985, p. 80. None of the usual translations of '*Geist*' is adequate, so I leave it in German.
11 Ibid., p. 42.
12 Hegel, *The Philosophy of History*, 1956, p. 72; *The History of Philosophy*, p. 42.
13 Hegel, *The History of Philosophy*, pp. 25–6, 42.
14 Hegel, *The Philosophy of Mind*, 1969, p. 2.
15 *The History of Philosophy*, pp. 22, 176.
16 Hegel, *The Philosophy of Mind*, p. 3.
17 *The Philosophy of History*, p. 26.
18 Hegel, *Phenomenology of Spirit*, 1977, p. 135.
19 Ibid., pp. 294ff.
20 *The History of Philosophy*, p. 76.
21 Ibid.
22 'Contribution to the critique of Hegel's *Philosophy of Right*', in *The Portable Karl Marx*, ed. E. Kamenka, 1983, p. 124.
23 Note to Part 1 of Marx's *The German Ideology*, quoted by L. Kolakowski, *Main Currents of Marxism*, 1981, vol. 1, pp. 172–3.
24 'On the Jewish question', in *The Portable Karl Marx*, ed. Kamenka, p. 105.
25 *Economico-Philosophical Manuscripts of 1844*, in ibid. pp. 136–7.
26 See John Passmore, *Man's Responsibility for Nature*, 1980, pp. 24ff.
27 *Economico-Philosophical Manuscripts of 1844*, in *The Portable Karl Marx*, ed. Kamenka, p. 139.
28 *Irrational Man: A Study in Existential Philosophy*, 1960, pp. 29ff.
29 *Being and Having*, 1949, pp. 11–12.
30 *Cahiers pour une morale*, 1983, p. 514.
31 See, for instance, *The Will to Power*, 1968, section 585.
32 *Cahiers pour une morale*, p. 485.
33 Hegel, *The Philosophy of History*; Kierkegaard, *The Present Age*, 1962.
34 Buber, *I and Thou*, 1937, pp. 58, 115.
35 Ibid., pp. 8, 90.
36 Ibid., pp. 57–8, 107.
37 Ibid., pp. 71–2.
38 Quoted from Buber's *Das Problem des Menschen* by Paul Roubiczek, *Existentialism – For and Against*, 1964, p. 151.
39 Buber, *I and Thou*, pp. 21, 26.
40 Heidegger, *Being and Time*, p. 178H, for instance.
41 'What are poets for?', in *Poetry, Language, Thought*, 1971, p. 108.
42 Heidegger, *The Basic Problems of Phenomenology*, 1982, p. 327.

3

From Phenomenology to Existentialism

'Pure' Phenomenology

One reason why existentialism deserves its name, I explained in chapter 1, is that in its mature forms it is 'existential' phenomenology. The contrast here is with the 'pure' version expounded by the father of phenomenology, Edmund Husserl. In this present chapter I shall first describe Husserl's position and then examine both the Existentialist's debt to, and critique of, that position. The 'existential' alternative to the 'pure' version is the subject of the following chapter.

Brief exegesis of Husserl's phenomenology is no easy task. His style is a convoluted one; and during a long and dogged career his position underwent many revisions, some of them quite radical. The main problem, though, is that his many restatements never succeeded in resolving certain crucial ambiguities. Competent commentators can still, therefore, dispute whether he was a realist, an idealist, or simply unconcerned with the status of the external world. Especially frustrating are the lines like 'For me, the world is nothing but what I am aware of,'[1] which lend themselves equally to a trivial and a dramatic interpretation. Does that line mean that the world as I am aware of it is the world as I am aware of it, or that no world could exist outside of awareness of it?

I do not need to become embroiled in most of the controversies over Husserl's meaning. This is because I am concerned with existentialists' responses to Husserl as *they* understood him. Even if, as he himself believed, they got him wrong in certain respects, this does not detract from the philosophical value of examining the confrontation as they perceived it.

In his final writings during the 1930s, Husserl was anxious to emphasize the spiritual value of philosophy. At the individual level, philosophy is the 'resolve to ... shape oneself into the true "I", the free, autonomous "I" ', and to 'find oneself'.[2] At a more global level, it is the 'heroism of reason' that might yet save Europe from the 'barbarian hatred of spirit' into which it was descending.[3] This emphasis contrasts with his earlier, drier characterizations of philosophy as a 'rigorous science', the only one which, by returning to 'absolute beginnings', could yield knowledge that was without any presuppositions. (Here and elsewhere, one should recall that the German 'Wissenschaft', unlike the English 'science', can apply to such disciplines as history and philosophy as well as to the natural sciences.) Throughout his writings, however, Husserl had a single target, which he called 'naturalism' – the naïve faith in the empirical sciences as the sovereign respositories of truth. Husserl's early complaint had been that these sciences rested on assumptions which a more fundamental form of enquiry, philosophy, must examine. Later the attention shifts to the spiritual damage wrought by 'naturalism'. Not only does it encourage a dualistic picture of 'nature ... alien to spirit',[4] but the manifest failure of the sciences to address problems of value and meaning had led to disillusion with reason itself and the consequent descent into 'barbarism'.

It was not only events on the world's stage – the war, the Bolshevik and Nazi terrors – which prompted this shift in emphasis. By 1930 Husserl was piqued by the popularity of Jaspers and his own pupil, Heidegger – a popularity based, he believed, on the unfair perception that they were addressing 'relevant' issues in a way he had not. Jaspers in particular, he feared, was teaching young Germans to treat philosophy as 'a sort of personal religious faith', instead of as a commitment to reason as the sole resolution of 'the crisis of European man'.[5]

In this chapter I shall be concerned with Husserl's conception of philosophy as a 'rigorous science', to which he gave the name 'phenomenology'. His starting-point is the venerable set of distinctions between the empirical and the a priori, and the contingent and the necessary. The empirical sciences occupy themselves with contingent facts about individual objects (or classes of them). This ought not to be the concern of philosophy, though in practice philosophy has made itself 'contemptible', in the shape of 'positivism', by endorsing the conceit of empirical science that it alone provides genuine knowledge. True philosophy, phenomenology, is not 'a science of facts, but ... of essential being, ... which aims exclusively at establishing "knowledge of essences"'.[6]

It is only in virtue of somehow instantiating essences – man or John Smith – that an object can count as a man, or this particular man John Smith. 'It belongs to the meaning of everything contingent that it should have ... an Eidos [essence, idea] to be apprehended in all its purity.'[7] Phenomenology is the knowledge of these essences, especially those of the greatest generality, like physical object, thought or value.

Three features of essences need emphasizing. First, 'the positing of the essence...does not imply any positing of individual existence.'[8] Thus, although no individual centaurs exist, we can still 'posit' the essence of centaurhood. Second, an essence is not a psychological item, such as a mental concept arrived at via a process of abstraction, like a Lockean 'general idea'. No more than a number does an essence depend for its being on anyone thinking of it. Third, we can only know essences through a non-perceptual type of *intuition*, an 'immediate "seeing"' distinct from the 'sensory seeing of experience'.[9] Once clearly intuited, it is inconceivable that the essence should be other than it is 'seen' to be. It is this manifest, self-evident character of essences which explains why Husserl calls them 'phenomena', for the traditional notion of a phenomenon is of something that cannot be other than it appears to be (hence its application by some philosophers, though not Husserl, to allegedly incorrigible sense-data).

It follows from these three features of essences that the study of them will indeed be disjoint from the empirical sciences. Observation of objects about which it is possible to be mistaken can contribute nothing, beyond illustrative examples, to the intuition of self-revealing essences, which do not even require 'correlates' in the actual physical world. For Husserl, one achieves 'essential intuition' through a process of 'eidetic reduction'. Roughly, this is his name for the time-honoured procedure of imagining various objects, 'seeing' which ones we would count as Xs, and grasping what it is in virtue of which we so count them.

Much more interesting than this, however, is Husserl's insistence that 'essential intuition' first requires a kind of mental purge akin to Descartes' methodological doubt. Our minds are so choked up with factual beliefs and presumptions that unless we first clean out this Augean stable, we shall be unable to gain an unimpeded view of essences: 'the spell of naturalism... makes it so difficult for all of us to see "essences" or "ideas".'[10] Not only do essences not require us to 'posit' actual, physical existence but, as phenomenologists, we must disregard it. This is the famous doctrine of the *epochē* ('abstention') or 'bracketing', to which I now turn.

Husserl calls phenomenology 'a twentieth-century Cartesianism', one reason being the similarity between his *epochē* and Descartes' resolve to doubt everything in which he had hitherto believed – the physical world included. Husserl distinguishes his procedure from Descartes', however. First, the aim is not to *question* belief in the external world but to 'set it..."out of action"..."disconnect it", "bracket it". It still remains there like the bracketed in the bracket.' In the *epochē*, I *debar* myself 'from using any judgement that concerns spatio-temporal reality', but without denying or doubting such judgements.[11] Second, Descartes' aim is to *overcome* his initial doubts, to prove that his natural beliefs were, after all, true. The *epochē*, on the other hand, must be constantly and vigilantly maintained, its purpose being the therapeutic one of concentrating attention on essences.

It helps to compare the *epochē* not with bracketing words, as in Husserl's metaphor, but with putting them inside quotation marks. If I quote 'History is the history of class struggle,' then in one sense I do something quite different from Marx; for I do not make an assertion. Nor do I thereby deny or cast doubt upon his thesis, but put the issue of its truth-value, its relation to reality, 'out of action'. In another sense, I do exactly what Marx did, for I use the same words with the same meanings. Indeed, a likely purpose of putting the words inside quotation marks is to concentrate attention on what is *meant* by them and away from the question of their truth. This attention to meaning has, as we will see, its analogue in Husserl's bracketing of beliefs.

Bracketing is not confined to suspending belief in the existence of a physical world. One kind, which falls short of that, is of special interest to us. This is the *epochē* in which we suspend belief in the *scientist's* world, in order to focus on the *Lebenswelt*. This 'life-world' is 'the world for all of us ... the world that can be commonly talked about'.[12] Husserl was no enemy to science *per se*, but to the pretension of science to provide the one true account of reality. Such, however, is the prestige of science in the modern world that, if we are to carry through the difficult task of 'disconnecting' our natural beliefs, we must first free ourselves from the grip of this 'positivism'. We shall never intuit the essence of *man*, say, if our conception is dominated by the things biologists have to tell us about men.

One way to loosen this grip is to appreciate that the scientific image of the world is parasitic on our common, untutored experiences of our world. Had we not, in the light of our purposes and needs, come to identify and classify things as we have, there would be nothing for science to investigate. Before the accomplishments of science, 'there has always already been a universal accomplishment, presupposed by all human *praxis*.' In the *epochē* from science, we do not of course ignore it, for scientific practice is now an important element in the *Lebenswelt*. What *has* disappeared is any presumption that it is the scientist, and not you or I, who is the authority on how things are. Science is reduced to its proper status as 'but *one* among the many practical hypotheses and projects which make up ... the life-world'.[13]

If this *epochē* is less radical than the bracketing of all physical reality, there is a further *epochē* which is perhaps more radical. In this further *epochē*, 'there exists no "I" ... the natural human ego, specifically my own, is reduced to the transcendental ego.'[14] Roughly, that is, we must bracket belief in the existence of selves or persons, *my* self included. To the extent that the human ego is thought of as necessarily embodied, then it will, of course, be set 'out of action' along with all other physical objects. But Husserl has more in mind than this.

Whether thought of as embodied or as an immaterial Cartesian substance, a person or self is typically conceived of as something which retains identity over the course of time, possessed of a certain character and psyche. A person is a contingently existing individual and the subject of empirical, psychological investigation. Like any contingent, empirical entity, therefore, the person must be bracketed for purposes of 'essential intuition'. As far as the essence of John Smith goes, it matters not a whit whether there actually exists such a person. He could as well be a character from fiction. *Something*, of course, must remain after the human or empirical ego is bracketed – namely, the consciousness which is engaged in the bracketing exercise. This is what Husserl calls 'the transcendental ego', the pure consciousness before which the distilled essences are to be paraded. The word 'I', Husserl notes, is ambiguous, referring sometimes to an empirical self and sometimes to the pure consciousness for which that self is an object of investigation. From the point of view of this second, 'pure I', it is irrelevant whether the first really exists. If everything I believed about myself *qua* empirical ego – my past, my character, my body, etc. – is mistaken, that takes nothing away from the essence which *would* have been instantiated had those beliefs been true.

The net effect of these and other *epochēs* is to have produced a 'purified consciousness', cleansed of any assumptions about the existence or nature of things beyond what is 'immanent' to that consciousness. Reality has undergone a 'phenomenological reduction' to an absolutely autonomous and 'self-contained' realm of essential being. It is self-contained because 'it is essentially independent of all being of the type of a world or Nature, and it has no need of these for its existence.'[15] The phenomenologist has become a 'methodological solipsist' who can now develop 'the theory of the essential nature of the transcendentally purified consciousness'.[16] The key to the resultant theory is the notion of *intentionality*, to which I now turn.

Husserl is not the only philosopher to have postulated a self-contained domain of consciousness. Descartes and the British empiricists spring to mind. Husserl is keen, however, to dissociate himself from these writers. Their mistake is to analyse consciousness into no more than two terms – an ego and its *cogitationes* (thoughts, sensory experiences, etc.). They treat it as a 'title-name for... "bundles" or streams of "sensations"', occurring in, or (as Hume held) constituting the history of, an ego.[17]

These philosophers cannot, Husserl contends, accommodate the fact that it is 'of the perception's essence' to be *of objects*.[18] Either, like Descartes and Locke, they hold that we are perpetually making 'inferences from... cognitive life to an "outside"'; or, like Hume, they treat an object as a complex bundle of experiences which we infer from the ones we are having at present. Both views are unfaithful to the phenomenological fact that we do not *first* experience sense-data or sensory impressions and *only then* infer that we are perceiving, say, a tree. Paying sole attention to impressions is, in fact, a sophisticated feat parasitic on the normal 'holistic' perception of physical objects. (Jean Cocteau tells of a woman who, asked how Debussy's corpse looked, replied, 'I don't know. I didn't see him. *I* see nothing but colours.'[19] She was, I venture, an impressionist painter.) Neither view, moreover, can explain how we ever came to conceive of enduring physical objects in the first place. If, as for Locke, these are necessarily outside all experience, they are at best 'I-know-not-whats'. If, as for Hume, there are only bundles of sense-data, how could we have made the mistake of imagining a single object common to what are, after all, the quite distinct sets of sense-data which make up what we call 'seeing a tree' over a period of time?

Analysis of a conscious 'act' must be into *three* terms – 'ego – cogitatio – cogitatum' – which 'though inseparable from one another, one must pursue...one at a time'.[20] The ego has a cogitatio *directed* towards a cogitatum (an object). Or, as Husserl also puts it, the act *intends* an object. This directedness or intentionality is *the* essential feature of consciousness. 'Every intentional experience – and this is indeed the fundamental mark of all intentionality – has its "intentional object".'[21] Intentionality is fundamental because the directedness of a conscious act cannot be *inferred* from any more parsimonious account – in terms, say, of a passing parade of sense-data.

But what business does Husserl have introducing objects into the analysis when belief in their existence has already been bracketed? Husserl's reply is that, even if the object does not exist, the conscious act is always *as if* it were directed to the object. And, indeed, we are familiar with the idea that in some sense a person can see, think about or want something – a pink rat, say – even though the something is not there. It remains, in Husserl's terminology, an 'intentional object'.

The further ingredients of intentionality are best understood in connection with Husserl's answers to three related questions. How, exactly, can an act be directed towards an object? How, in particular, can this be done when the object does not exist? And how can different acts – different perceptions, say, or a perception and a memory – be directed towards one and the same object? Husserl's answers are in terms of his notions of 'noesis' and 'noema', which are his names for, roughly speaking, the conscious act and its 'content'. Before I elaborate, let me make an apparent detour.

Analytic philosophers will detect structural parallels between those three questions and some central issues about words and their reference. How do puffs of air manage to *stand for* things? How can I intelligibly speak about Cerberus, when no such creature exists? And how can quite different expressions, in different languages perhaps, refer to the same thing? One very influential set of answers appeals to Gottlob Frege's distinction between sense or meaning (*Sinn*) and reference (*Bedeutung*).[22] A word refers to a thing because it expresses a sense which is satisfied by that thing. Since a word may express a sense even when nothing satisfies it, I may still speak intelligibly when I use it. A sense provides a route, as it were, along which to travel in order to identify an object: though, as with 'Cerberus', the route may sometimes lead nowhere. Different expressions, finally, may refer to the same object either because they have the same sense or because, as with 'the Morning Star' and 'the Evening Star', the two routes happen to converge at the same point.

Exploiting the parallels between Frege's and Husserl's questions, Dagfinn Føllesdal has provided an illuminating comparison between a Fregean theory of sense and reference and Husserl's account of the noema and intentionality. Husserl himself wrote that 'the noema is...a generalization of the idea of meaning [*Sinn*] to the field of all acts.'[23] A perception, for example, 'contains' a noema or meaning in virtue of which it 'intends' an object. Experiences 'contain in their own essence this peculiar feature of being related to . . . things through their . . . posited meaning'.[24] A veridical perception, or an accurate memory, is 'fulfilled' by an object in the way a word's sense is satisfied by a referent. Where there exists no such object, the act is still directed since it contains a meaning which *would* be 'fulfilled' *if* the object existed. Perceptions from different perspectives, or a perception and a memory, may be of the same object through containing the same sense. When I perceive something, this sense provides expectations of what I shall perceive from further perspectives, which is why the further perceptions count as being of the same object.

A further aspect of the analogy with the Fregean theory is worth drawing out. Frege saw himself as combating the powerful tendency to equate a word's meaning with its reference – a tendency sufficiently powerful to have encouraged some philosophers, like Meinong, to postulate the 'subsistence' of Cerberus, rather than concede that 'Cerberus', since it is meaningful, might refer to nothing at all. For Husserl, analogously, people have an inexorable tendency to suppose that perceptions and other conscious acts are directly, immediately engaged with objects. The tendency is of a piece with the 'natural standpoint', our absorption in and preoccupation with the natural world.[25] The theory of the noema, therefore, belongs to the more general attempt to get us to 'disconnect' the actual world, so that we may focus on what is 'immanent' in consciousness.

Not the least benefit of this is the realization, suppressed in the 'natural standpoint', of the role played by consciousness, as the repository of meaning, in lending order and coherence to the world as we perceive it. We are no mere mirrors of reality. Rather, 'whatever the world may be...must be represented...by meanings and positings.'[26] These serve to 'animate' the material presented to the senses – material which would otherwise be without significance, but which can now be recognized as 'fulfilling' the schemata of sensory experiences.

To summarize: the concern of the philosopher, the pure phenomenologist, is not with empirical facts, but with the essences in virtue of which objects are the ones they are. To attain 'essential intuition' we must bracket the 'natural standpoint', including the scientist's account of the world, and our beliefs in the existence of an outside world and of our empirical psyches. Once this is done, we are free to focus on an autonomous realm of consciousness, whose principal feature is to 'intend', or direct itself towards, objects. Consciousness does this by casting a net of meanings or noemata for objects to 'fulfil'. It is, roughly speaking, these noemata which are the essences studied by the phenomenologist. In studying them, he lays bare the ways in which consciousness, as the trafficker in meanings, 'animates' and 'constitutes' the world as it is encountered.

The Existentialist Critique

The Existentialist's criticisms of pure phenomenology are bound to seem a bit thin in abstraction from the alternative position he develops. But since that position is developed out of dissatisfaction with Husserl's philosophy, it is with this that we need to begin; though not until we appreciate the Existentialist's debt to Husserl as well.

'So near and yet so far' might summarize the Existentialist's verdict on Husserl. The key to a proper account of the relationship between consciousness and the world is to be found in Husserl's writings but, as Sartre judged, he 'misunderstood [the] essential character' of his insights, and ended up with conclusions as far away from the truth as could be imagined.[27]

It is often suggested that existentialism's main debt to Husserl is one of *method*.[28] I fail to understand this. The two ingredients in Husserl's philosophy which deserve to be called 'methodological' are the 'eidetic' reduction of particular objects to their essences via a procedure of 'free fancy', and the phenomenological reduction of the natural world to the contents of consciousness. Existentialists, to a man, reject both of these reductions. Heidegger, it is true, refers to his own phenomenological reduction, but what he means by 'phenomenon' and by 'reduction' is quite different from Husserl. A phenomenon is not an essence divorced from empirical reality, but simply 'that which shows itself in itself, the manifest'. By a reduction he means 'the leading back of our vision from beings to [their] Being'.[29] This is hardly crystal-clear, but whatever is intended is expressly contrasted by him with Husserl's method. In practice, the reduction is primarily a matter of ridding ourselves of prejudices inherited from science and bad metaphysics. In fact, the word 'method', with its connotations of a systematic *procedure*, is not a felicitous one for Heidegger's philosophical practice.

The Existentialist's real debt is to certain Husserlian doctrines, the master's own misunderstanding of them notwithstanding. The first of these is the insistence on the priority of the *Lebenswelt* over the worlds depicted by the sciences. Only out of a world revealed in our everyday engagement with it can the possibility of its scientific study arise, and this study cannot challenge the prior revelation. A true physics, as Sartre put it, cannot contradict that 'other absolute . . . the world of perception and *praxis*'. For Merleau-Ponty, the geographer's knowledge of forest or prairie presupposes, and cannot replace, the practical understanding of the native or peasant.[30]

A second debt is to Husserl's rejection of the Cartesian *cogito*. Descartes' mistake was to view the *cogito* as 'a small corner of the world', a *substantia cogitans*, related to other substances by 'a principle of causality'.[31] This is to view the relation between consciousness and its objects as contingent. Consciousness might never have been directed, and objects might never have been accessible to consciousness. For the Existentialist, as for Husserl, this view is incoherent. In Sartre's terminology, consciousness is *nothing* apart from its directedness; hence not a *something* which could stand in causal relationships to other things. Nor can sense be made of a world logically independent of our experience. The world as we experience it requires our contribution in order to be as it is, and Nietzsche was right to denounce 'the illusion of worlds-behind-the-scene'.[32]

The deepest debt is to the doctrine of intentionality. Simone de Beauvoir relates how Sartre 'turned pale with emotion' when, in the early 1930s, Raymond Aron, recently returned from Germany, described the doctrine to him.[33] Sartre's pallor was due to two implications he saw in the doctrine. With its insistence that conscious acts must be directed to objects, and its concomitant rejection of sense-datum accounts of perception, the doctrine promised an alternative to the 'alimentary' theory, according to which consciousness can have truck only with its own, inner ingredients. Second, the doctrine requires that our awareness of objects is mediated by *meanings*. It was the apricot cocktail itself, not private visual and gustatory sense-data, which he and Aron saw and tasted. Yet there could only be perceptions of an apricot cocktail through a structure of significance which we have brought to the world. Human being is inescapably *semantic*, or as Merleau-Ponty put it, intentionality demonstrates that 'we are condemned to meaning.'[34]

Finally, we should not ignore existentialist echoes of Husserl's conviction that philosophy is no mere intellectual exercise, but a procedure of self-discovery and self-liberation as well. The Existentialist will not follow him in demanding, for these purposes, an *epochē* from 'the natural attitude', but the idea that the philosopher is engaged in a kind of withdrawal that is also a movement of freedom is an important theme in existentialism. For Marcel, philosophy is part of an endeavour to cure oneself of intellectual and emotional 'sclerosis', while Jaspers tells us that '*Existenz-Philosophie* is the way of thought by means of which man seeks to gain space for [himself].'[35]

Despite these debts, the Existentialist's judgement is that Husserl betrayed his own best insights. Sartre understates his criticism when he writes that 'Husserl has not always been faithful to his first intuition[s].'[36] More bluntly, Husserl was someone who did not know where to stop. The importance of the attack upon 'naturalism', for example, is to return our attention to the *Lebenswelt*, whereas Husserl saw it as the prelude to a global *epoché* in which the *Lebenswelt* itself would be bracketed. Again, the real import of the rejection of the Cartesian *cogito* is that human existence is not to be modelled upon that of things or substances. Husserl, unable to leave well alone, concludes that the self, in the shape of the transcendental ego, must therefore exist somehow outside of the empirical world. Worst of all, perhaps, Husserl betrays his own doctrine of intentionality. The doctrine's true message, that no sense can be made of consciousness except in terms of its engagement with the world, is contradicted by the phenomenological reduction which reduces experience to the 'immanent' contents of consciousness. The result of this reduction, as Sartre puts it, is that conscious acts become like so many 'flies bumping their noses on the window without being able to clear the glass'.[37]

Sartre and some other existentialists go further than this in their criticisms, for they accuse Husserl of being an idealist who, quite simply, denies that there is anything at all beyond the glass. Husserl's ambiguities and apparent inconsistencies allow commentators to disagree wildly on the issue of his idealism. We do not need, fortunately, to become embroiled in this debate because, idealist or not, Husserl was certainly committed to a thesis which is presupposed by idealism, and it is this thesis which the Existentialist wants to attack. I mean the thesis that it is possible, indeed mandatory, to suspend all belief in external reality. Idealism would add insult to injury, perhaps, but the real damage is caused by this thesis, with its implication that the domain of consciousness is a self-sufficient, self-contained one. I suggested in chapter 2 that what is really disturbing in Cartesianism is not the doubt it casts on the external world, but its portrayal of the *cogito* as 'cut off' in logical isolation from the world. Similarly, it is Husserl's initial bracketing of the world, not his subsequent failure to remove the brackets, on which criticism should focus. If the criticism is well taken, then Husserl's alleged idealism cannot get off the ground.

It is important, as we turn to the details of existentialist criticisms, to see them in the light of what the Existentialist discerns as the underlying cause of Husserl's self-betrayal. This is his failure to divest himself of the epistemological premise which has, transparently, underpinned so much traditional philosophizing. This is the premise that knowledge and understanding belong, in the final reckoning, to *spectators* rather than *agents*. Philosophy, wrote Husserl, only attains to its 'proper aim and field of interest' through a 'deliberate *epochē* from all practical interests' which allows the philosopher to become 'the non-participating spectator of [his] acts and life'.[38] It is not denied, of course, that our practical activities in the *Lebenswelt* incorporate beliefs and conceptions. But for Husserl – as for Descartes, Hume and countless others before him – the credentials of such beliefs and conceptions can only be determined by placing them, and the activities in which they are embedded, under the spectatorial gaze of a detached, passive intellect. Phenomenology becomes existential with the denial of this primacy of spectatorial knowledge; with Heidegger's insistence that '[human] existence is indeed more than mere cognition in the usual spectator sense of knowledge and such knowledge presupposes existence';[39] or with Sartre's realization, on reading Heidegger in 1940, that since 'meaning came into the world only by the activity of man, practice superseded contemplation'.[40]

The first product of the spectatorial premise is the transcendental ego, which is, as Husserl emphasizes, *nothing but* 'the disinterested spectator of [the] natural and worldly ego and its life'.[41] This ego is bodiless, moodless, characterless, loveless, since body, mood, character traits and emotions are, like everything else, so many items for its disinterested gaze.

Some of the Existentialist's objections to the transcendental ego are rehearsals of Hume's famous rejection of the self as the unchanging substance in which thoughts and perceptions inhere. Just as Hume was never able, when inspecting his current perceptions, to catch in addition a glimpse of the self, so for Sartre 'the "I" is not given as a concrete moment' to consciousness.[42] He reaffirms Hume's further point, that such a self cannot serve to lend unity to a 'bundle' of perceptions. Unless we *already* have a criterion for uniting the items in the bundle, there can be no call for referring them to a single 'I'.

But if the transcendental ego is both invisible to introspection and 'totally useless' for founding the unity of experiences, is the notion intelligible at all? How, to begin with, are we to *count* transcendental egos? Husserl believed that there are many such egos to be individuated – mine, yours, his, hers and so on. 'Other consciousnesses', as he puts it, are not 'constituted' by a single, solipsistic one.[43] But when the ego is cut loose from all empirical criteria – bodily ones, for example – we are deprived of the means for telling whether John Smith is one ego, a series of different egos, or just one member of an ego-sharing scheme. Again, how are we to conceive of the relationship between the transcendental and the empirical egos? As Heidegger rhetorically asks, 'how is consciousness ... at the same time joined with the unity of a real human that also exists as a real object in the world?'[44] Who is the real Smith – a transcendental or an empirical ego? Or is the suggestion that these two are aspects of one and the same self, rather as different perspectives can be of the very same physical object? The trouble with this suggestion is that the two egos, as described by Husserl, differ in their most fundamental respects. The empirical ego is a *natural* object, related to other objects through causal connections, whereas the transcendental ego is pure intentionality, standing outside the world and its causal network. Husserl is left with no means of bringing together his two stories, transcendental and empirical, into one.

Later we shall see the Existentialist arguing that, in Heidegger's words, intentionality is 'a central possibility of the factual self, the concrete person'.[45] For the present, the point is that Husserl's refusal to regard 'the concrete person' as the locus of intentionality is the result of his spectatorial premise. He cannot allow that the engaged, participating agent is the vehicle of knowledge and understanding. This is because an agent can be an object for reflection, and the spectatorial premise requires that understanding and knowledge are the privilege of the disengaged being which does the reflecting.

Criticism of the transcendental ego is already blending with the Existentialist's rejection of Husserl's version of the doctrine of intentionality, to which I now turn. Part of the objection, we have seen, is that this version destroys the charm of the doctrine. The lesson to be drawn from the intentionality of consciousness is that we are 'plunged into the world' as revealed to us through the meanings of our activities and projects. It is the apricot cocktail itself, and not some inner *ersatz*, which I experience, and I do so through a structure of significance which I deploy. By making the objects of experience 'immanent' to consciousness, and by turning meanings into essences intuited by a pure ego, Husserl betrays the doctrine. Heidegger agrees with Husserl that the relation between a conscious act and its object is not an 'external', causal one, for that would entail that consciousness could in principle exist undirected. But he is equally scathing about Husserl's own 'perverted subjectivization of intentionality', which treats the object as no more than an ingredient of consciousness: 'The idea of a subject which has intentional experiences merely inside its own sphere and is not yet outside it but encapsulated within itself is an absurdity which misconstrues the basic ontological structure of the being that we ourselves are.'[46]

The other element in Husserl's theory of intentionality to which the Existentialist objects is the account of meaning. Husserl, we saw, treats meanings as the essences or noemata via which consciousness is directed towards objects. Understanding of experience is thereby reduced to intuition of these essences and the manner in which they are 'fulfilled'. This, for the Existentialist, is an impossibly intellectualist and spectatorial account.

It will be useful here to exploit further the analogy between Husserl's account and a Fregean theory of sense versus reference. A consequence of the latter dichotomy is that a person could in principle understand a language, the senses of all its expressions, without ever actually *using* that language for such purposes as referring. But this is an implausible consequence. How, to begin with, can we count someone as knowing what 'x' means unless he manifests a capacity to employ 'x' correctly? It is not enough that he says, and truly so, '"x" means...', for we have to be sure that he understands what he is saying. A computer which prints out such truths is not thereby credited with understanding English.

Can we not solve this problem, the Fregean may ask, simply by insisting that *real* knowledge of senses confers a capacity for using words, even though – reference being quite distinct from sense – this capacity may never have the opportunity to be exercised? The difficulty now, however, is whether linguistic understanding can be portrayed as a capacity that might in principle never be exercised. Consider in this connection the favoured analogy between knowing a sense via which one can refer to an object, and knowing a route via which one can reach a destination. To be sure, I can know a route to London without ever taking it, but could I be said to know this or any other route, unless I was a participant in a society where people engage in the activity of going from one place to another? Surely, the very intelligibility of notions like *route* or *destination* presupposes that this is an activity in which people actually engage. It cannot then be adequate to represent the voyager's understanding as a knowledge of routes – for in order to possess that knowledge, he must already enjoy a demonstrated practical acquaintance with the activities which lend intelligibility to what it is he knows. Likewise, it must be inadequate to represent understanding a language as knowledge of senses, since the latter presupposes a practical acquaintance with the employment of words.

The point is reinforced when we reflect on the implausibility of representing linguistic understanding as a sum of separate atoms of knowledge, articulated as '"x" means...', '"y" means...' and so on. For one thing, such articulated knowledge will only generate linguistic ability in conjunction with a vast panorama of unarticulated background assumptions.[47] To respond appropriately to the builder's instruction, 'Bring me a slab!', it is not enough that I can spell out the senses of 'slab' etc., for that would not preclude my bringing him a white-hot slab, or one wrapped in Christmas paper. It would be hopeless to suppose that all such inappropriate responses could be guaranteed to be prevented by ever more precise articulations of the meanings of the words.

The example prompts a further objection to representing linguistic understanding as the knowledge of senses. No one can be guaranteed against making grotesque responses to 'Bring me a slab!' who does not know what slabs are for, and he cannot know that unless he understands something about buildings and their purposes, such as providing shelter and security. Our understanding is, we might say, *holistic*. The mastery which confers the practical ability to use a word correctly belongs, finally, to the grasp of a 'form of life', to cite Wittgenstein's phrase, in which slabs or whatever have their place. As this way of putting it suggests, the point is not confined to the grasp of *word* meanings. Concepts and things will have the meanings they do only through membership of an immense network which, however many of its elements we care to articulate, will remain as a whole *unsurveyable*. This is what Heidegger intends when he writes that 'to disclose such things as "significations"' presupposes our familiarity with a 'relational totality' which he calls 'significance' (*Bedeutsamkeit*).[48] Sartre, too, writes of the impossibility of completely 'deciphering' the world to which 'I adapt myself... in and through action.'[49]

For Husserl and the Existentialist alike, the fundamental feature of conscious existence is its trafficking in meanings. But the effect of the above criticisms of Husserlian intentionality is to relocate the relevant notion of meaning. In Husserl's account, meanings are analogous to the senses of words: but, for the Existentialist, they are closer to the meanings that we speak of actions both possessing and conferring in virtue of their purposive or goal-directed nature. The significance of a slab is not an abstract noema, a slab-essence, but the place held by slabs within a form of life. Husserl is sometimes criticized for employing a vocabulary of 'meaning', 'direction' and the like, which misleadingly suggests he is emphasizing the voluntaristic, purposive dimensions of consciousness. One way of viewing the shift from pure to existential phenomenology is to see that, in the latter, the purposive connotations of that vocabulary are taken in deadly earnest. In Danto's happy phrase, the Existentialist gives a 'Stakhanovite reading' of notions like significance and intentionality.[50]

Husserl is debarred by his spectatorial premise from this 'Stakhanovite reading'. For one thing, the Stakhanovite worker has a *body*, in and through whose actions he manifests his practical understanding of his world. Husserl, for whom the body is bracketed and meanings gazed at by a disembodied ego, makes no allowance for this understanding. It is against Husserl, among others, that Merleau-Ponty writes: 'all meaning was... conceived as an act of thought, as the work of a pure "I"... [but] bodily experience forces us to acknowledge an imposition of meaning which is not the work of a universal constituting consciousness... my body is [the] meaningful core...'[51]

Little needs to be added on the Existentialist's criticism of Husserl's global *epochē*, his bracketing of the 'natural standpoint'. Rejection of this is entailed by what has gone before. The point is not that the *epochē* is a plausible though finally unsuccessful exercise, but that there can be no sense in embarking upon such an exercise. For one thing, who is to conduct it? It cannot be the empirical ego, the 'concrete person', for this is something bracketed along with all other empirical objects. It would, therefore, have to be the transcendental ego – but this has turned out to be a chimera. Second, the *epochē* requires that our understanding take the form of knowledge of essences or noemata, which might fail to be fulfilled or satisfied by anything in reality. But this conception of our understanding, it was urged, is wrong-headed. At the fundamental level, our understanding of the world is a dimension of our practical engagement with it. To be sure, a person can tell a science-fiction story in which the world turns out to be an illusion and we are so many disembodied spirits. But such stories are disingenuous: for they ignore the fact that, were it not for the storyteller's own engagement in the world, he could never have come by that reflective knowledge which he now exploits in order to relate his fantasies. He is like an author who writes of a universe in which language has never emerged. That universe cannot, at any rate, be the writer's own.

Heidegger offers an interesting variant of the argument that we cannot imagine ourselves worldless. To imagine a hammer or a slab as not existing is to conceive of something *absent* from the contexts – building, say – in which it has its place. Only against such contextual backgrounds can we speak of things being missing or absent. It is nonsense, therefore, to imagine the *world* as not existing, for obviously there is no context larger than the world within which the world could fail to occupy its place. 'Nor', as two commentators on Heidegger put it,

> could nonexistence of the world be understood through imagining a totality of nonexisting things. That would have to be a totality of absences; but an absence, like a gap in a fence, only makes sense in terms of what isn't absent. A nonactual world as a totality of nonexisting things is no less absurd than a nonactual fence as a lineup of fence gaps.[52]

In the Existentialist's view, Husserl illegitimately *primes* us to accept the feasibility of the global *epoché* by describing what gets bracketed as the 'natural thesis' or the '*positing* a world as real'. If the natural standpoint really were a mere hypothesis or postulate, it might be one which, with imagination, we could suspend. But, as Heidegger complains, such a hypothesis, far from constituting our natural stances towards the world, belongs at a level of sophistication well removed from our everyday engagement with the world. What Husserl calls 'the natural attitude' is, in effect, 'a well-defined theoretical position', and not 'man's natural manner of experience'. This latter should not be referred to as an *attitude* at all.[53]

We might, in this connection, consider the remarkable passage in Sartre's novel *Nausea*, where Roquentin describes his experience of a chestnut-root. Looking at this root in the gathering dusk, he ceases to see it *as* a root, or indeed *as* anything. Conceptualizing and categorizing are held in abeyance, but this makes Roquentin all the more aware of the root's being 'steeped in existence'. 'Existence,' he muses, 'is not something which allows itself to be thought of from a distance: it has to invade you . . . pounce upon you, weigh heavily on your heart like a huge motionless animal.'[54] I do not know how many people have shared this 'nauseous' sense of brute, irreducible existence, but the philosophical point, perhaps, is that the existence of physical objects is not something we hypothesize, and in which we might therefore suspend belief, but an ineradicable aspect of our experience. The target would then be Husserl's proposal that 'X exists' means merely that certain predictions about the course of our perceptions will be confirmed or fulfilled.

In concluding this account of the Existentialist's critique of pure phenomenology, it is only fair to remark that Husserl is not without possible rejoinders. Indeed, in his last writings, he expressly defends himself against Heidegger and other critics. It will be best to discuss this in chapter 4, for the Existentialist's rejection of this defence will help to clarify his own position, which is the topic of that chapter.

Notes

1 Edmund Husserl, *The Paris Lectures*, 1975, p. 8.
2 *The Crisis of European Sciences and Transcendental Phenomenology*, 1970, p. 338.
3 'Philosophy and the crisis of European man', in *Phenomenology and the Crisis of Philosophy*, ed. Lauer, 1965, p. 192.
4 Husserl, *The Crisis of European Sciences*, p. 154.
5 Ibid., p. 390.
6 Husserl, *Ideas: General Introduction to Pure Phenomenology*, 1962, p. 40.
7 Ibid., p. 47.
8 Ibid., p. 51.
9 Ibid., p. 75.
10 Husserl, 'Philosophy as a rigorous science', in *Phenomenology and the Crisis of Philosophy*, ed. Lauer, p. 110.
11 Husserl, *Ideas*, pp. 98, 100.
12 Husserl, *The Crisis of European Sciences*, p. 209.
13 Ibid., p. 131.
14 Husserl, *The Paris Lectures*, p. 10.
15 Husserl, *Ideas*, p. 142.
16 Ibid., p. 161.
17 Ibid., p. 231.
18 'Philosophy as a rigorous science', in *Phenomenology and the Crisis of Philosophy*, ed. Lauer, p. 114.
19 Quoted in André Gide, *Journals 1889–1949*, 1978, p. 305.
20 Husserl, *The Crisis of European Sciences*, p. 171.

21   *Ideas*, p. 241.
22   See especially 'On sense and reference', 1966. In what follows I shall speak of a 'Fregean' account, rather than of Frege's, since on some points his exact views are a matter of contention.
23   Quoted from Husserl's *Ideen*, vol. 3, p. 89, by Føllesdal, 'Husserl's notion of noema', 1982, p. 74. Husserl sometimes speaks of the meaning as contained, as a 'nucleus', within the noema, which also includes 'the way the object is given' (e.g. perceptually, in memory, or whatever). A bonus of Føllesdal's interpretation is that it encourages further analogies between criticisms of Husserl (by Merleau-Ponty especially) and criticisms of Frege (by Saul Kripke and Hilary Putnam, for example). In this connection, see the useful exchange between Thomas Baldwin and David Bell, 'Phenomenology, solipsism and egocentric thought', 1988.
24   Husserl, *Ideas*, p. 346.
25   Husserl, *The Crisis of European Sciences*, p. 119.
26   Husserl, *Ideas*, p. 345.
27   *Being and Nothingness: An Essay on Phenomenological Ontology*, 1957, p. lxi.
28   See, for example, Mary Warnock, *Existentialism*, 1970.
29   Heidegger, *Being and Time*, 1962, p. 28 H, and *The Basic Problems of Phenomenology*, 1982 p. 21.
30   *Phenomenology of Perception*, 1962, p. ix.
31   Husserl, *The Paris Lectures*, p. 9.
32   Sartre, *Being and Nothingness*, p. xlvi.
33   *The Prime of Life*, 1965, pp. 135ff.
34   *Phenomenology of Perception*, p. xix.
35   'Philosophical autobiography', 1957, p. 40.
36   *Being and Nothingness*, p. lvii. It is a measure of the esteem in which existentialists held Husserl that their critical remarks tend to be muted or disguised. Heidegger's criticisms rarely mention Husserl by name, while Merleau-Ponty presents his own existentialist phenomenology as being what, deep down, Husserl was 'really' trying to formulate. See especially his 'The philosopher and his shadow', in his *Signs*.
37   *Being and Nothingness*, p. 100.
38   'Philosophy and the crisis of European man', in *Phenomenology and the Crisis of Philosophy*, ed. Lauer, p. 168, and *The Paris Lectures*, p. 30.
39   *The Basic Problems of Phenomenology*, 1982, p. 276.
40   Simone de Beauvoir, *Force of Circumstance*, 1987, p. 13.
41   *The Paris Lectures*, p. 15.
42   *The Transcendence of the Ego: An Existentialist Theory of Consciousness*, 1957, p. 50.
43   See especially *Cartesian Meditations*, 1960.
44   *Prolegomena zur Geschichte des Zeitbegriffs*, 1979. For a good explanation of Heidegger's point, see Frederick A. Olafson, *Heidegger and the Philosophy of Mind*, 1987, pp. 18ff.
45   Letter to Husserl of 22 October 1927, *Husserliana*, 1962, vol. 1, pp. 601–2.
46   Heidegger, *The Basic Problems of Phenomenology*, p. 64.
47   On this point, see John R. Searle, 'Literal meaning', 1979, and Hubert L. Dreyfus' editorial introduction to *Husserl, Intentionality and Cognitive Science*, 1982.

48 *Being and Time*, p. 87H.
49 *Being and Nothingness*, p. 200.
50 *Sartre*, 1975, p. 104.
51 *Phenomenology of Perception*, p. 147.
52 Hubert L. Dreyfus and John Haugeland, 'Husserl and Heidegger: philosophy's last stand', 1978, p. 226.
53 Heidegger, *Prolegomena zur Geschichte des Zeitbegriffs*, p. 155.
54 *Nausea*, 1986, pp. 183–9.

4

'Being-in-the-World'

Some of this chapter has already been prefigured, for it was impossible to rehearse the Existentialist's criticism of pure phenomenology without giving some indication of his own account of man and the world. The main task of the chapter is to examine the twin claims that the world is 'essentially human' and that human existence is intelligible only in terms of an engagement with it. These claims, if true, make it somewhat artificial to divide the discussion into two sections, on the world and on ourselves who are 'in' it. But, as Heidegger remarks, the 'unitary phenomenon' of our Being-in-the-world does not exclude paying separate attention, though only provisionally, to the 'constitutive items in its structure'.[1]

World

The Existentialist shares Husserl's ambition to provide a description of the world that is both fundamental and phenomenological. The description must be one presupposed by any other accounts, adequate as these may be for their own special purposes. And it must describe the world as it is 'for us' – as a phenomenon, in the sense of what is *manifest* to us. It will not be a trivial matter to find an account which fills both bills: one which is both fundamental and phenomenological.

In delineating our manifest understanding of the world, the Existentialist is not aiming to produce an account on which everyone will readily agree. Indeed the understanding in question does not, in his view, have the shape of an *account* or a *theory* at all. We should, in fact, be suspicious of people's responses to questions about how the world is, since these are liable to encapsulate a 'folk' version of the bad metaphysics and 'scientism' which have dominated thinking for too long. Moreover, the very fact that the responses will, to a degree, be *reflective* should make one wary of them. This is because the understanding we seek to describe is not that of reflectors, but of people actively engaged in everyday dealings with the world. Such an understanding is not at all apparent to people: it needs to be 'uncovered', made manifest, and the results may be surprising.

It is precisely the reflective, disengaged stance which the Existentialist holds responsible for the 'standard' account of the world against which his own is pitted. On the standard view, the world is essentially a collection of *substances* – of more or less enduring, discrete physical objects. These are identified and distinguished through their intrinsic properties, such as size, colour and density. These substances stand in various relations to one another, pre-eminently spatial and causal ones. They are, however, logically independent of each other, and indeed of anything else. (This is the feature captured by the term 'substance' in its traditional philosophical usage.)[2] It would be a scientific fantasy, but not a logical absurdity, to imagine a world containing nothing but that tree outside my window. To be sure, the world contains things hardly describable as physical objects – events, dispositions, shadows, etc. – but the assumption is that these can be handled as modifications of, or relations between, objects.

This standard account is, of course, a natural bedfellow of the 'spectatorial' premise discussed in chapter 3. If the world is as just described, then our fundamental understanding of it must be the kind we possess *qua* perceivers and observers. Knowledge of the world will be empirical knowledge of substances, their properties and their interrelations. This knowledge will be a mirror of a world articulated prior to and independently of our acquisition of the knowledge.

Sophisticates will no doubt want to offer an account of the world different in some respects from the 'naïve' one outlined. Scientifically educated, they will ascribe various complicated structural properties to things, and they may want to banish some familiar properties from the world – colour and smell, say – because they are too dependent on the perceiver's own make-up. But such moves represent a sophistication, not an abandonment, of the standard, spectatorial account. The scientist is a spectator with more than the naked eye to rely upon.

The Existentialist does not hold that the standard account is false or useless. What he rejects is its pretension to being fundamental and phenomenologically adequate. This account, he argues, is necessarily parasitic on a more basic kind: and the entities it describes are not ones we experience or encounter at all, except during special moments and for special purposes. What the standard account ignores is the degree to which the world is a human one, whose structure, articulation and very existence are functions of human agency. To speak with Sartre, the world is more 'the image of what I am' than I am the mirror of it.[3]

The Existentialist offers three main, and closely related, considerations in support of his alternative to the standard account. The first two, due to Heidegger, concern the 'equipmental' and 'sign-like' character of things in the world. The third, which is owed to Sartre, concerns the place of 'negativity' in the world's fabric. Since the 'equipmental', the 'sign-like' and the 'negative' only come into the world through human agency, and since they are essential aspects of the world, then this world will indeed be a human one.

In Heidegger's terminology, the standard, spectatorial account construes objects as 'present-at-hand' (*vorhanden*). His contention is that there is a prior and more 'proximal' way in which objects are encountered – namely, as 'ready-to-hand' (*zuhanden*). Readiness-to-hand is the kind of Being belonging to 'equipment' (*Zeug*), so it is as equipment that we first encounter the world's contents. For example, we encounter objects, like this inkwell, as serviceable for a certain purpose. Despite some misleading remarks, Heidegger does not think the world contains two kinds of entity, the ready-to-hand and the present-at-hand, since he is insistent that *everything* is 'proximally' encountered as ready-to-hand. 'To the extent that any entity... is discovered in its Being – it is already something ready-to-hand... not a "world-stuff" that is merely present-at-hand.' Even an item of Nature, like the south wind, is 'discovered ... only by the circumspection with which one takes account of things in farming'.[4] Heidegger is equally emphatic that anything at all, once 'discovered', *can* be viewed as present-at-hand – stared at, dissected, inspected and so on.

These two kinds of Being are not, however, mere descriptive devices. We do not only describe, but actually *encounter* things as ready-to-hand in our 'dealings' and 'traffic' (*Umgang*) with them. This traffic, moreover, is 'not a bare perceptual cognition, but... the kind of concern which manipulates things and puts them to use; and this has its own kind of "knowledge"'. So we do not first encounter things and *then* describe or interpret them as ready-to-hand, for the encounter incorporates our 'proximal' understanding. 'The hammering itself uncovers the specific "manipulability" of the hammer.'[5]

The glass is for an inkwell, the inkwell for holding ink, the ink for filling a pen... Eventually, though, things can only be *for* anything, only have an 'in-order-to', and so be ready-to-hand, in virtue of the human projects and purposes which they are 'for-the-sake-of'. It follows that if the world can only be 'lit up' and yield 'access' to itself *qua* equipment, then the world as we first encounter it is intelligible only in relation to human concerns.

These claims of Heidegger's prompt a number of queries. For one thing, granted that the south wind or the sun figures importantly in the farmer's calculations, is it not impossibly strained to describe such natural phenomena as 'equipment' or 'ready-to-hand'? Second, we require further explanation of the knowledge or understanding which, we are told, is actually carried by our active 'dealings' with things. And finally, how, if we are constrained to encountering things as ready-to-hand, do we manage to achieve, as Heidegger concedes we do, a merely 'cognitive' view of them as present-at-hand?

We go some way to answering these queries, and to elaborating Heidegger's insights, by bringing in the second of the main considerations in support of the thesis of a 'human world' – the one concerning things' 'sign-like' character. Not everything, of course, is a sign in the way a car's indicator or a milestone is, but Heidegger holds that 'the sign- structure . . . provides an ontological clue for "characterizing" any entity whatsoever.'[6] This is because signs accomplish in a paradigmatic manner what everything ready-to-hand achieves in less obvious ways – namely, *reference* (*Verweisung*). Reference, directionality and indication are, in only modestly extended senses of these terms, of the very essence of the ready-to-hand, 'that by which readiness-to-hand is constituted'.[7] The world, indeed, is a gigantic 'referential totality', each of whose constituents relates to others in a 'sign-like' way.

This assimilation of objects to signs deepens the criticism of the standard, spectatorial account. On that account, the basic relations among objects are spatial and causal, and between objects and ourselves perceptual. This cannot be right if objects are essentially 'sign-like'. The flashing indicator doubtless stands in many spatial and causal relations to the car and the road, but it is not in virtue of these that it signals a right turn. No doubt, too, drivers can observe and stare at the indicator; but it is not this connection between them that allows us to say that the latter signifies something for the former. If everything ready-to-hand is 'sign-like', then neither the fundamental relation among things within a 'referential totality' (a workshop, say), nor that between these things and ourselves, will be of the kind proposed on the standard account.

To be sure, there are difficulties in explicating the exact nature of the relations between signs, their users and what they signify. This does not detract from the importance of the claim that the essential relations obtaining among human beings and things ready-to-hand are of an analogous nature.

I suggested that such analogies might help us with the queries prompted by Heidegger's thesis of the priority of the ready-to-hand. One query challenged the viability of treating natural objects, like the south wind, as equipmental. Heidegger's response is that objects like these are 'proximally' ready-to-hand through serving as signs. The south wind gets 'accepted' as a sign of rain, and this 'acceptance' is essential to its 'discovery', not 'a bonus' of something already discovered to be present-at-hand – namely, an air flow. More generally, 'in roads, streets, bridges, buildings, our concern discovers Nature as having some definite *direction*.'[8] Nature only gets 'disclosed' at all through our practical activities – as a world of signs (warnings, promises, etc.) seamlessly integrated with the world of artefacts that more directly testify to our practical concerns.

The assimilation to signs also suggests an answer to the query about the nature of our understanding of the ready-to-hand. It will be analogous to linguistic understanding. The latter is itself hardly transparent, but some of its features can be articulated and exploited. To begin with, linguistic understanding is *practical*. No amount of knowledge *about* words constitutes understanding of a language in the absence of a manifest capacity to use them.[9] How this capacity is to be characterized – whether, say, as mastery of rules – is a matter for dispute. The important thing for us, though, is that explication of our knowledge of the ready-to-hand is brought into the orbit of that dispute.

Linguistic understanding also has a *holistic* character. Words and signs are not understood as isolated items, but as constituents within whole languages and systems. When the ready-to-hand is assimilated to signs, this suggests a further contrast with the standard account. On the latter, our knowledge of the world is a sum of individual items of knowledge about this substance, those properties and so on. As Heidegger urges, however, in understanding particular entities 'we have always "presupposed" the world. Even if we join them together, we still do not get anything like the "world" as their sum'[10] – any more than we get a language by adding together previously isolated words. We saw the importance of this holism of the understanding when criticizing the pure phenomenologist's ambition to represent knowledge as a sum of 'essential intuitions', and we shall see it again at the end of this section of the present chapter.

A final aspect of linguistic understanding is that it is not to be separated from understanding of the purposes which language, as a communicative practice, serves. It may be that we can explain what this or that word or sentence means without reference to the particular communicative intentions behind its use,[11] but in the final analysis it can only be in virtue of such intentions that the noises we make have meaning and thereby belong to a language at all. Likewise, for Heidegger, the 'for-the-sake-of', to which explanations of things ready-to-hand must eventually refer us, 'always pertains to the Being of *Dasein*', *our* kind of Being.[12] Assimilation of the world to a language is, therefore, an especially vivid way of rendering it human.

From the pursuits of linguists and semiologists, we are acquainted with the possibility of standing back from everyday traffic in words or signs and examining them as, so to speak, laboratory specimens. There are two features of this retreat which are suggestive for the more general transition from the ready-to-hand to the present-at-hand. First, no one imagines that it is only the linguist, and not we speakers, who 'really' understand language. On the contrary, his knowledge is clearly parasitic upon ours; just as what he studies

– syntactic or phonetic features, say – are abstractions from language as actually used. The linguist's knowledge, valuable in its place, cannot *compete* with our 'proximal' understanding. As Heidegger puts it, 'the sign is not authentically "grasped" if we just stare at it and identify it as an indicator-thing.'[13] So, in the understanding of signs, we have a clear and salutary reminder that it is the encounter with readiness-to-hand which is privileged.

Second, it is not unreasonable to speculate that if communication always went smoothly, then that studious retreat which resulted in linguistics would never have been undertaken. It is because communication does not always go smoothly, because it is only too prone to a variety of breakdowns, that there is a premium on *examining* language – on discovering its 'rules', say – so as to locate and repair the breakdowns. This point, generalized, is Heidegger's explanation of the shift from engagement with the ready-to-hand to observation of the present-at-hand – a shift, we noted (p. 60), which calls for explanation. 'The presence-at-hand of entities,' he writes, 'is thrust to the fore by the possible breaks in that referential totality in which circumspection "operates".'[14] The pen won't write, so I stare at it, take it to bits, examine its structure. So the shift is not an inexplicable abandonment of our practical stance towards the world. Rather, concern with the present-at-hand emerges smoothly from our practical concerns since these require us, where things go wrong, to stand back and take stock. Examining things as present-at-hand cannot then be our fundamental stance towards the world, any more than the surgeon's examination of our bodies can be the primary form of encounter between human beings.

If everything has to be 'proximally' encountered as ready-to-hand, as 'sign-like' if not as 'equipmental', then the world is a human one. The worry must persist, however, that it is a Protean exercise to squeeze everything we experience under such headings. This worry should be borne in mind as we turn to the third of the Existentialist's main considerations concerning the 'human world' – the one, due to Sartre, about the role of *negativity*.

Although Sartre makes such Heideggerian remarks as that the world is 'a world of tasks', in which 'the original relation between things is ... instrumentality,'[15] he contends that instrumentality is a function of a deeper, more pervasive dimension of reality. In order for 'being to order itself around us as instruments,' he writes, 'it is necessary that *negation* rise up ... as the rubric ... which presides over the arrangement ... of being in things.'[16]

Sartre rejects the familiar view that negativity is a feature solely of propositions and judgements, and argues in a series of persuasive examples that negativity belongs to the fabric of reality. 'Nothingness,' in Sartre's picturesque phrase, 'lies coiled in the heart of being – like a worm.'[17] When I go to the café to meet Pierre and fail to find him, his absence, his not-being-there, is as real and vivid a property of the café as the noise, smoke and other 'positive' features. The world, indeed, is *imbued* with negativity. There is 'an infinite number of realities...which are experienced...and which in their inner structure are inhabited by negation'.[18] Sartre coins the term *négatité* to refer to these 'realities', such as Pierre's absence from the café. *Négatités* are by no means confined to what is ordinarily described in explicitly negative terms. The storm *destroys* something, but it can only do this, if we recognize that, by our criteria, something *no longer* exists after the storm. *Cleaning* a room is not, as some wit has it, shifting dirt from one place to another, but removing it from where it should *not* be. This glass is *fragile*, which means 'it carries in its being a definite possibility of *non-being*' when struck.[19] A creature incapable of experiencing *négatités* could not conceive of things being destroyed, cleaned or fragile. It is soon apparent that countless things and properties have negativity as 'a necessary condition of their existence'; or better, perhaps, countless concepts contain a negative element as a condition of their intelligibility and application.

Two questions which arise here concern the relation between all this and, respectively, the claim that 'the world is human' and Heidegger's insistence on the priority of equipment. The answer to the first question is that, while negativity is indeed a dimension of reality, 'man is the being through whom nothingness comes to the world.'[20] It is man who 'causes a world to be discovered' through the negativity he imparts, for Being-in-itself is said to be solid, *massif*. 'Pools of nothingness' can only enter via a creature capable of 'nihilating'. This is the For-itself, or human consciousness. Stripped of the odd terminology, Sartre's point is the reasonable one that our experience of *négatités* cannot be a mirror of how the world is independently of our engagement in it. Pierre can only be absent for someone who expected to find him. The glass can only be fragile for creatures concerned with the conditions under which things break. 'The world is human' because it is one we cannot conceive of except in terms of the *négatités* which we, with our concerns, expectations, hopes and fears, bring to that world.

The link with Heidegger becomes clearer when Sartre refers us to a kind of negativity, 'the one which penetrates most deeply into being', which he calls 'lack' (*manque*).[21] Lacks are the *négatités* which 'appear as the essential conditions of instrumentality'. Something counts as an instrument when it can be used to make good a lack, as when the inkwell is used to cure my pen's lack of ink. Ultimately, as we might expect, lacks are human. It is because *I* lack something – the finishing of this page, say – that my pen can be said to lack something. That human beings are constantly in the position of lacking and trying to make good their lacks is a fundamental aspect of their existence. It is, therefore, because 'I am a lack' that 'the order of instruments in the world is the image of what I am.'[22]

With his thesis that 'the world is human,' the Existentialist presents a challenging alternative to traditional accounts of the basic relation between ourselves and the world. We should, then, examine the main objection traditionalists have to this alternative. The objection is clearly stated by Husserl, especially in his remarks on *Being and Time*.

Husserl complains that Heidegger at best provides 'an individual psychology of the personality', or perhaps an anthropology, and not a 'philosophical world apprehension'. Heidegger describes the world in terms of 'practical interests' and 'significances'; but these 'vary relative to the person'. The philosopher should, however, be concerned with 'what is identical through variation of subjects and their practical interests'.[23] This requires us to 'disregard all the "spiritual" or "cultural" characteristics that make [something] knowable as, for example, a hammer', and focus on the thing as 'given . . . in . . . passive experience'. Far from the present-at-hand presupposing the ready-to-hand, the latter 'presupposes, at the lowest level . . . the object that confronts us as a . . . mere physical thing'.[24]

This restatement of the 'standard' account brings out its basic premise. Things cannot, in the first instance, be equipmental, 'sign-like', etc., since we can identify the self-same objects persisting throughout radical variations in these aspects. The thing itself must be the 'mere physical' one, 'given in passive experience'. 'Cultural' characteristics, values and significance are relatively superficial glosses which we add on to these objects. Husserl does not deny that it may be impossible, practically speaking, to disregard these characteristics, so as to view things 'with their skins off' (as Heidegger puts it). But the crucial issue is whether the difficulty here is solely of a practical kind or, as the Existentialist maintains, one of principle. Nothing would be left, he holds, if we stripped the world of everything cultural or human.

He begins by noting two ways in which Husserl stacks the odds in his own favour. First, he presents the choice as one between a world of 'mere physical things' and worlds inseparable from *personal* interests and interpretations. It would certainly be implausibly anarchistic to hold that things have no identity underlying individual, idiosyncratic perspectives on them. But this is not what the Existentialist holds. Hammers, signs, the storm's destruction, the glass's fragility are what they are in virtue of criteria and interests common to people in a culture, to people who share a form of life. *Pace* Husserl, a 'cultural' object like the hammer, in its standard use, *is* 'there for "everybody"'. That different people can take different interests in it – as a murder weapon, perhaps – does not show that it has no constant significance. One might as well argue that 'dog' has no constant meaning in English because people can put it to various metaphorical or ironical uses.[25]

Second, Husserl takes it for granted that the criteria for identifying and classifying things as present-at-hand must take precedence over those applying to the ready-to-hand. It is true that things which count as the same by the former criteria may be different from one another when considered as 'cultural' or ready-to-hand. Think of the Coca-Cola tins used by some South American Indians as currency. But it is no less true that objects which count as the same by criteria of use and significance may differ from each other very radically in their physical properties. Until recently, I could return the pound I owed you by giving you either a certain lump of metal or a certain piece of paper. Chessmen, bottle-openers, chairs and coffee-makers come in fantastic varieties of shape, size and substance, but retain their equipmental identity. Prejudice aside, it is not clear what permits us to ignore this kind of variation whilst harping, in Husserl's way, on the variety of cultural uses to which the same 'merely physical things' can be put.[26]

It is true, perhaps, that one can think of a physical object having *no* ready-to-hand character, whereas one cannot imagine something ready-to-hand having no physical properties. But the import of this point is unclear. The fact that words have to have *some* physical 'realization' – in sound, ink or whatever – scarcely establishes that language is 'really' a collection of mere noises or scratches.

The crucial question, moreover, is whether one could conceive of a *whole world* stripped of ready-to-hand, 'cultural' features. That any particular object we care to take can be stripped does not mean that *all* objects together can be. For it may be that my ability to strip the hammer down to its 'merely physical' properties presupposes a mastery of a conceptual scheme which I could never have come by had *everything* been encountered by me 'with its skin off'. It is important here to bear in mind the Existentialist's emphasis on the holistic nature of our experience. Were objects encountered as discrete items, global 'disregard' for 'cultural' characteristics might be possible – as the sum of individual acts of 'disregard'. But this is not how things are 'proximally' encountered. They are encountered as elements within 'referential totalities' and we can pick out the hammer and treat it as merely present-at-hand only by keeping in place the referential totality within which the hammer counts as a distinct object at all. Without that totality, why would the 'merely physical' hammer be *an* object at all – rather than, say, a collection of ten, or twenty or ten thousand smaller objects, or perhaps one-half, one-quarter or one-twentieth of a larger object? (Wittgenstein asked why we count a broom as one object and not two – a stick and a brush. His point, similar to the present one, is that individuation of objects makes no sense in abstraction from particular practical interests.)[27] If someone insists that he *can* imagine a purely 'passive experience' of a world stripped of all 'cultural', ready-to-hand characteristics, we must be satisfied that his imagination is not exploiting his *familiar* understanding of the world, for this is something he should have 'bracketed'. It is not clear how he can satisfy us over this.

For one thing, the Existentialist will ask, what *descriptive resources* would be available for describing this world 'with its skin off'? For the reasons given, words like 'hammer', 'south wind', 'destruction' and 'fragile' could not belong to this vocabulary. Indeed, the thrust of the reasoning was that none of our familiar terms for physical objects could belong, since they rely for their intelligibility upon their integration in a conceptual scheme rooted in human practices and interests. Would it, then, be a purely sense-datum vocabulary? Husserl, for one, could hardly welcome that suggestion, for he insists as much as the Existentialist that such a language cannot be phenomenologically adequate to our experience. Moreover, what exactly would this sense-datum vocabulary contain? Does 'hard', for instance, describe a 'passively' experienced feature? How, if it does, do we explain the fact that a hard cheese may feel much less resistant to the touch than a soft metal? 'Hard', in fact, is rather obviously guided in its application by the kinds of practical interests which we are supposed to be disregarding. Even if this vocabulary could be specified, and even if it were adequate to a certain kind of experience we can enjoy – perhaps like that of the woman who could not see Debussy's corpse, only its colours (p. 44) – it is unclear why this kind of experience should be regarded as 'basic' or 'fundamental'. Would it not be more reasonable to regard it, as the Existentialist does, as a peripheral and meagre abstraction from our real encounter with the world? This question raises considerations, of course, about the sort of creatures that we are: and it is to these that we turn our attention in the next section of this chapter.

In order not to complicate matters, I have confined attention so far in this chapter to the writings of Heidegger and Sartre. But I am confident that other existentialists would subscribe to the account which has emerged. The preface to Merleau-Ponty's *Phenomenology of Perception* is an affirmation of the logical priority of the *Lebenswelt*, the world of human significance and praxis, over the present-at-hand worlds of the 'spectator' and scientist. And here is a passage in which Ortega expresses a view whose affinity to the one presented over the last few pages requires no comment:

> What we call nature ... or the world is essentially nothing but a conjunction of favourable and adverse conditions encountered by man ... [it] has no being ... independent of us; it consists exclusively in presenting facilities and difficulties ... in respect to our aspirations.[28]

Human Existence

We are beings-in-the-world. Having discussed the Existentialist's description of the world we are in, we must now look at what he says about the beings, ourselves, who are in it. Like the account of the world, the description of our existence is intended to be 'fundamental', a description presupposed by all those which 'specialists', like anthropologists and psychologists, might offer. In Heidegger's terminology, the aim is to identify the 'existentialia' for our existence, its necessary and *a priori* dimensions.

The present discussion will be limited in two important, and related, respects. First of all, it will ignore the crucial distinction drawn by the Existentialist between 'authentic' and 'inauthentic' modes of existence. That distinction is especially pertinent to his account of the *self* – which is the second topic deferred until later. The views as discussed in this chapter will therefore sound thinner than they will when they eventually emerge.

Some readers will have been complaining that, in contrast to my renditions, neither Heidegger nor, to a lesser extent, Sartre writes for the most part of human existence, man, etc., but, instead, of *Dasein* and Being-for-itself. '*Dasein*' denotes 'the manner of Being' possessed by creatures like ourselves; 'Being-for-itself' the being of self-conscious creatures. Given the need he apparently feels to 'avoid . . . such expressions as "life" and "man" . . . in describing those entities which we are ourselves',[29] Heidegger's choice of '*Dasein*' is not inappropriate. While it is a familiar German word meaning 'being' or 'existence', Heidegger intends to exploit its etymological construction, for he detects in the expression 'Being-there [*Da*]' a clue to the character of our existence. Sartre's choice is also appropriate enough. 'Being-for-itself' is a Hegelian term for self-conscious creatures who, unlike sticks and stones, are something *for* themselves, capable of self-reflection and self-concern.

But why do these philosophers fight more or less shy of familiar terms like 'man', 'life' and, in Heidegger's case, 'consciousness'? The rough answer is that such terms are loaded with unwelcome empirical and metaphysical connotations. 'Human', for instance, conjures up zoological characteristics which distract from the task of laying bare the *a priori* character of our kind of existence. 'Consciousness' carries too much Cartesian luggage to be used in descriptions free from all traditional prejudices. Such warnings about our familiar vocabulary are perfectly in order. But, having noted and absorbed them, the merit in replacing this vocabulary by terms of art is less certain. (One can have some sympathy with Manser's impatience at the In-itself/For-itself vocabulary, if it 'is only a way of saying that the world seems to contain both things and minds'.)[30] I shall continue, therefore, to write of human beings, persons, life, etc., and the more squeamish reader may, if he so wishes, supply his own scare-quotes. (One advantage, though, of the special vocabulary is that it does not prejudice regarding *animals* as having our 'manner of Being'. Since I am sure that some of them do have this, in important respects, let me now disclaim any intention to suggest otherwise.)

One way, it might seem, of enquiring into the fundamental character of our existence is to ask, 'What is our *essence*?' But this way of putting things is generally rejected by existentialists. Among their slogans we find 'There is no such thing as human essence,' 'The essence of *Dasein* lies in its existence' and '[Human] existence precedes essence.'[31] Actually these slogans are, as scrutinized with the eye of a logician, incompatible. For instance, the first denies what is presupposed by the other two – that there is a human essence, 'lying in' or 'preceded by' existence. But it would be as pedantic to scrutinize them in this way as it would be to puzzle about the logical form of an advertising jingle like 'Beanz Meanz Heinz'. They are *slogans*, and as such need to be taken in context and understood in terms of the uses to which their coiners put them.[32] Whatever slogan each of them individually prefers, existentialists would agree upon something like the following: in any traditional senses of 'essence', such as a substance's defining properties, human beings possess no essence. If, in more relaxed senses of the term, we speak of them having essential features, this presupposes – and does not therefore explain – man's having a certain kind of existence. It matters little, in understanding these claims, which of the anti-essentialist slogans we pick upon and try to unravel. So we may as well take the best-known, 'existence precedes essence.'

I make two quick points, though, before we proceed with this. The first is a terminological reminder (see p. 2ff). Some existentialists – and this is one reason they are called that – restrict the word 'existence' to human being. This is partly to emphasize how special they think human being is; and partly because they think the etymological construction of the word ('ex' = 'out', 'stare' = 'stand') suggests something important about the character of that being. Second, we should mention, only to put aside, one construal of the anti-essentialist slogans. Jaspers, following Kierkegaard, makes much of the alleged fact that the individual cannot be fully understood 'under universal categories', since he is 'inexhaustible . . . in the endlessness of his concretion'.[33] An individual's *Existenz* cannot be specified by a list, however long, of essential or any other general predicates. The trouble is that this, if true at all, would apply to *all* objects. Humble as this particular tea-cup may be, there is no finite limit to the number of descriptions that can be made of it. So it cannot be this sort of consideration which explains the special sense in which a person's existence somehow escapes a full characterization 'under universal categories'.

Let us return to 'existence precedes essence.' In a famous passage of *Existentialism and Humanism*, Sartre writes:

> a paper-knife . . . has been made by an artisan who had a conception of it . . . Let us say, then . . . that its essence – that is to say the sum of the formulae and the qualities which made its production and its definition possible – precedes its existence . . . [But] there is at least one being whose existence comes before its essence, a being which exists before it can be defined by any conception of it. That being is man . . .[34]

This makes it sound as if all that distinguishes human from any other existence is that people are not created in order to perform functions laid down in advance. If this is all, we are entitled to some disappointment since, for a start, few of us anyway believe that human beings *per se* have an advance purpose. Only those who take a certain religious line or think, like Hegel perhaps, that we are vehicles for the execution of a grand historical design, believe this sort of thing. Second, it cannot be this absence of an advance purpose which distinguishes us since, in the realm of physical objects, it is only certain artefacts which have an essence in that sense. There have, to be sure, been those who thought that literally everything has its ordained purpose – fleas are there to wake us up, opined Chrysippus – but they belong on the sidelines of intellectual history.

Sartre soon reveals, fortunately, that the slogan is aimed at bigger game: namely, at the idea that a human being has a fixed, given character or nature. Part of the complaint is against the pervasive tendency to employ terms like 'coward', 'criminal' or 'homosexual' for labelling and pigeon-holing people; the tendency to suppose that once Pierre has been classified as, say, homosexual, we have 'summed him up', 'fixed him', 'got to the bottom of him'. The more important complaint is against the idea's implication that a person can do no more about his nature than a snail can. Even if Pierre cannot prevent feeling certain sexual desires (though even here he *could* decide on an operation), he can certainly choose whether to act on them and he can certainly mould his life so as to accommodate, or to defy, these desires. Ortega sums things up thus: 'the stone is given its existence: it need not fight for what it is . . . Man has to make his own existence at every single moment.'[35] Existence now precedes essence in that how a person is at a given time results from the free decisions he has made. This is one of the several messages of Sartre's oft-repeated dictum that 'man is not what he is.' I cannot be defined in terms of what, in one obvious sense, I am (a coward, criminal, etc.), since I can rise above this and direct how I shall become.

All of this is doubtless as important as it is uplifting. It is tantamount to a thesis about man's radical freedom and power to transcend, reject or shape even his seemingly most intractable traits. Several commentators take this thesis to be the core meaning of existentialism's anti-essentialist slogans,[36] but this is a mistake, for at least two reasons. First, the thesis is compatible with, and has often been conjoined with, a doctrine totally at odds with the Existentialist's outlook. According to this doctrine, the reason I am not to be identified with my 'character' is because I am, in essence, an 'inner' self, a soul. The 'real me' is neither my body nor my 'character', both of which I steer, like the captain his ship, from somewhere within. We have seen already in chapter 3 that this is not the Existentialist's doctrine, and we shall see it again when we discuss his account of the self. The second objection to equating 'existence precedes essence' with a thesis about radical freedom is that the basis and the originality of the latter are then disguised. What distinguishes the thesis about freedom from many similar-sounding ones is precisely its roots in a deeper anti-essentialism, which we have yet to uncover.

Clues to this deeper anti-essentialism are found in a battery of metaphors and neologisms to which existentialists are partial. Our existence is called a *light* or *clearing*, even a *hole* or *nothing*. It is characterized as *being-over-there, ahead-of-itself* or *standing outside of itself* ('ec-static' or 'ex-istent'). Man is always *not-yet-being, what-he-is-not* or only *possibility*. His being is that of *care, value* or *lack*. It has the form of a *narrative* or a *vital programme*.

The single negative purpose of all these terms is to emphasize how radically human being differs from that of things or substances. They fall into groups according to the particular differences to which they draw attention. If essence is understood as the essential properties of substances, then we do not have one, since we are not substances. If it simply means the crucial features which distinguish us from things, the 'existentialia', then we do of course have an essence, which it is my job over the next few pages to identify. If by 'essence' we mean, rather infelicitously, important aspects of character, such as cowardice, then people have essences, but an account of how they can have them presupposes their enjoying the kind of existence about to be discussed. Essence in this sense is preceded by existence.

The trouble with nearly all traditional accounts of man, says Ortega, is the whole '*res* business'.[37] We have already met with Heidegger's claim that when people disengage themselves from practical life and reflect, there is an inveterate tendency to construe everything as merely present-at-hand. This is especially disastrous when it is ourselves who are so construed. Yet this is precisely the tendency of the dominant Cartesian tradition, which 'takes the Being of *Dasein* in the very same way as [it] takes the Being of the *res extensa*' – namely, as a substance, whether material or immaterial. The fact is that 'the person is not a Thing, not a substance'; *Dasein* 'does not have the kind of Being which belongs to something merely present-at-hand . . . nor does it ever have it'.[38] Our being, to invoke some of the favoured metaphors, is more like that of a forest clearing, which permits a view of the trees, than like that of the trees themselves; more akin to the light which illuminates than to the sun or lamp which produces the light. I am a 'nothing' (no-thing) more than I am a thing.

But what does this talk of our non-substantiality, our being no-things, amount to in more literal terms? The answer is best given, the Existentialist thinks, in the form of a view about the explanation of human behaviour. We are no-things because the categories in terms of which our behaviour is to be explained are very different from those employed in the case of substances. This is not how most existentialists have themselves tended to put matters, but I hope it will be illuminating to do so on their behalf.

The preferred mode of explaining the behaviour of things is the *causal* mode. Things do what they do partly because of causal processes inherent in their own constitutions, partly because of the effects other things have upon them. The Existentialist's argument for the non-substantial nature of human existence can be gleaned from his objections to using this mode of explanation for human actions. For three related, mutually supporting, reasons, our intercourse with the world is not to be construed as causal.

Causal explanations are contingent. If A is causally responsible for B, as the chicken is for the egg, neither can require the existence of the other as a matter of logic. It must be at least logically conceivable that the egg simply sprang into existence. A and B must, in principle anyway, be separately identifiable; for if they were not, the one could not, in logic, exist without the other. As much is incorporated into Descartes' definition of a substance as 'an entity which is in such a way that it needs no other entity to be'.[39] So one crucial question to ask about ourselves is whether our existence is logically conceivable without that of the world. If it is not, then we cannot be substances among others, with which our traffic is of a wholly causal variety.

While repairing a table, I pick up a hammer – in part because I *see* it lying there. Sitting next to an attractive woman on a train, I move closer to her – in part, at least, because I *desire* her. So my behaviour will only be explained in causal terms if, *inter alia*, seeing and desiring can be construed as causal relations between myself and physical bodies. No doubt causal processes go on in both cases. Light waves affect my retina; something or other is stirring in the glands. But can my seeing and desiring themselves be causal effects in me? If they can, it must be possible at least to *conceive* of my existence in the absence of any objects so affecting me. Seeing and desiring could, in logic, occur in isolation from a world of objects. And why not, indeed? Of course, if the hammer or the woman is not there, I cannot see *it* or desire *her*, but – the old story goes – the *experiences* I have might be exactly the same. Think of hallucinations and erotic dreams. My mental life might be just as it actually is even though nothing exists outside of it. This is what my being a substance entails.

We know from chapter 3 why this story is unacceptable to the Existentialist. It contradicts the claims about intentionality described on pp. 50ff.; it implies that sense can be made of consciousness in abstraction from our actual, active engagement in the world. Seeing a hammer is not to be identified with having visual data which, as it happens, are caused by a certain object. It is to recognize something, and to anticipate that other people would similarly recognize it. This recognition presupposes an understanding of hammers, which in turn requires an acquaintance with a network of human practices in which such understanding is enmeshed. I am, therefore, a 'being-over-there', in the sense that without my engagement in the outside world, in the 'over-there', I could not enjoy anything resembling the actual conscious life that I in fact do. Or consider my desire for the woman on the train. It is impossibly crude to consider this as an inner glow or disturbance triggered by the proximity of her body. For one thing, I shall only desire her if the context or situation is right. The context is not a set of further external, causal factors; rather it is essentially something *understood*, taken in a certain way – as a situation appropriate to making certain moves or to anticipating certain developments. As Sartre puts its, 'desire posits the world and desires the body in terms of the world.'[40] A whole upbringing, a whole culture in which I am an understanding participant, is required for this 'world' or situation to be 'posited' or apprehended by me. Desires, hopes, fears, perceptions – our intentional life, in effect – are incomprehensible outside of this kind of participation and engagement. And we can only conceive of ourselves as creatures who possess such a life. 'The soul,' writes Merleau-Ponty, 'if it possesses no means of expression... no means of actualizing itself – soon ceases to be *anything whatsoever*.'[41]

A second objection to explaining our actions in the causal mode appropriate for substances was hinted at in the references to seeing and desiring as involving *anticipation*. These were but two instances of something deemed to be of the first importance by the Existentialist – the role that the *future* plays in explaining human behaviour, but not that of things. A whole battery of seemingly paradoxical expressions – 'ahead-of-itself', 'not-yet-being', 'what it-is-not' – are designed to convey the idea that a person's existence at any given time is incomplete or 'unsaturated', since the person is always 'on the way' to becoming something in the future. I am at present putting down these words. Why? Because I am writing a book; I am engaged, that is, in a project that carries me well into the future. My current behaviour is not to be explained, nor even identified, except by reference to this orientation towards the future.

But is this not equally true of many mere things? Do we not, to use a Hegelian example, explain the acorn's behaviour in terms of its 'not yet being what it is', an oak-tree? The Existentialist's reply is that, in the case of the acorn, this reference to the future is eliminable. We can fully specify its nature in terms of its current physical properties, including those which are causally efficacious for bringing about its emergence as a tree. In the case of the person, however, the reference to the future that he is 'on the way' towards is not eliminable. But why not? Can my behaviour not be explained by something purely contemporary and causal – namely, my intention to write a book? There are many problems with this suggestion,[42] including this one: the suggestion seems to treat my intention as some inner occurrence which is only contingently connected with my current and subsequent behaviour. The objection to this is that it is a logical nonsense to suppose that a person intends to do something unless, circumstances permitting, he behaves in appropriate ways. My intention to write the book is not something that just happens to issue in my spending time in the library, putting pen to paper and so on. Sartre makes a similar point when he denies that 'the motive causes the act; [rather] the motive is an integral part of the act.'[43] Certainly I do what I do because I intend to write a book; but if this intention can only be ascribed to me in the light of what I am perceived to be 'on the way' towards, reference to the future has not been eliminated.

But can we not explain my writing the book in other terms – the hefty fee I have been offered, the threat to my university job if I don't publish or whatever? Aside from the implausibility of thinking that such factors can sufficiently explain my writing just this book at just this time, the difficulty is merely postponed. For why should the money be tempting or the threat worrying, except in the light of 'projects' for my life which I am 'on the way' towards realizing: the material security of my family, say, or the attainment of status in my profession? The money, the threat and other elements in my present situation may certainly help to explain my actions. This will not, however, render reference to the future redundant if it is only in relation to the future which 'I am not yet' that these elements can be said to belong to my situation. My situation does not comprise just any old facts about myself, but those which take on significance for me precisely in the light of what I am 'on the way' towards. This is part, at least, of what several existentialists have in mind when they insist on the logical priority of a person's future over his past and present. 'The primary meaning of existentiality is the future,' writes Heidegger. It is the future which 'first of all awakes the Present'.[44]

The Existentialist is the first to admit the difficulty in shaking off the conviction that a given stage in an entity's career can only be explained as the outcome of previous stages. He ascribes the difficulty to the grip which the metaphysics of the present-at-hand holds us in, pressing us to model everything on the 'mere physical thing'. It can help to alleviate the difficulty, therefore, if we think of entities other than ourselves to which this model, and the causal mode of explanation, are also inapplicable. Consider, for example, *narratives* – Homer's *Odyssey*, say. To understand an episode is, in large part, to discern how it belongs in the narrative. This is not a matter of the episode, the battle with the Cyclops perhaps, being causally necessitated by what has gone before, but of its being a stage in a story that takes us from a beginning, the embarkation from Troy, to an ending, the reunion with Penelope. The episode must point backwards and, more to the point, forwards. Sense is made of it, in part, by perceiving how it contributes to the future action. It is a bad storyteller who introduces episodes that make no such contribution. They do not, one would say, really belong in the narrative at all.

We might do well, then, to follow Ortega's advice to think of ourselves as having more the kind of being possessed by narratives than by substances.[45] One bonus of this might be to remind us of the central role played by notions of significance and meaning in the explanation of human behaviour. This takes us on to the Existentialist's third and final objection to the imposition of the causal mode of explanation. We have, of course, encountered his emphasis on these notions in several connections. His doctrines of intentionality and of the priority of readiness-to-hand both testified to the pre-eminence of significance in our dealings with the world. The present point is that this pre-eminence also obtains in explanation of our actions, and that, in consequence, a causal mode of explanation is inappropriate. This point has, in fact, been only barely concealed over the last few pages. The reason my 'situation' did not cause my subsequent behaviour was because it was partly constituted by my sense of the significance possessed by certain of my circumstances.

But is the point correct? Why should we not construe the perception of something's significance in terms of its causal impact upon us? Attempts, after all, have been made to construe the meanings of *words* in terms of a causal interaction between things and utterances of the words. 'Food', claimed the semioticist Charles Morris, means food because the presence of the stuff prompts utterances of the word. This is, no doubt, hopelessly crude, but more sophisticated attempts might not be so easily dismissed.[46] The example, though, is instructive. For suppose we grant, for the sake of argument, the feasibility of some such attempt to explain the meaning of 'food'. What now of the significance of its referent – food itself? That the class of foods is deter-mined, at least in part, by the significance its members have for us is hard to deny. Not just any substance we can ingest without harm and can derive nutrition from is a food. In our civilization, at any rate, bluebottles and human eyeballs are not food. To be a food, the stuff has to have for us the significance of *what-is-to-be-eaten*. And when we consider particular foods, it seems obvious that an explanation of how and why we eat them as we do cannot be given without reference to the meanings attached to them. No doubt it is an exaggeration to speak, as do some anthropologists, of foods constituting a language, replete with a grammar.[47] But there is no need to go that far in order to appreciate that our dealings with bacon and eggs, or crumpets and jam, are of a different order from those of the lion with its kill or the maggot with its cheese.

That foods are not mere present-at-hand substances, but 'sign-like', ready-to-hand and articulated with reference to what matters to us as members of a culture, is an illustration, of course, of the thesis about the world urged by the Existentialist earlier in this chapter. Existentialists have proposed various terms in an attempt to capture the general character of our relationship to this world. For Heidegger, our being is one of *care* (*Sorge*). This does not mean that we are constantly worrying about things, or paying solicitous attention to them. The term reminds us, rather, that we are creatures for whom the kind of life to be lived matters and is an 'issue'. The world is made 'accessible' and 'disclosed' to us through the projects and practices whereby we resolve the 'issue'. There is not a world *and* ourselves, standing in a causal relation, for without ourselves there is not that 'referential totality' which constitutes our world. The behaviour of things present-at-hand may be amenable to causal explanation, but this is because for them 'their Being is "a matter of indifference"; or more precisely, they "are" such that their Being can be neither a matter of indifference to them, nor the opposite.'[48]

Sartre, in similar vein, summarizes our general relationship to the world as that of *valuing* – value being what belongs to that which we 'lack' and which we are perpetually in the process of trying to secure. A world only emerges, and things only take on their contours, through the 'upsurge' of value. This means that explanation of our actions, which must appeal to our discernment of value, cannot be a causal one about the impact of things on us; for things may only emerge and be individuated through those of our practices which manifest our sense of 'lack' and value. If the world is human, it is not an external cause of what humans do.

It is important to be clear that, for the Existentialist, 'caring' and 'valuing' are not extra options which human beings happen to have taken up. Heidegger insists that 'Being-in-the-world is essentially care;'[49] and Sartre writes that 'value in its original upsurge is not *posited* by the For-itself; it is consubstantial with it.'[50] Deprive a person of the capacity to 'care' and 'value', and we are not left with someone who enjoys a human existence, albeit an impoverished one. Rather, we are left with no one, for the person has been stripped of that relationship to the world in virtue of which everything distinctively human is possible. The creature which remains left over cannot perceive and desire, nor even eat and copulate, as human beings do.

How, then, might we summarize existentialist denials of human essence, and the dictum that existence precedes essence? My suggestion has been that we should interpret the Existentialist as battling against the endemic tendency to understand human beings on the model of things or substances. This involves him in arguing that the categories in terms of which we explain the behaviour of things are not applicable to human action. In particular, it is a mistake to think of the relationship between ourselves and the objects belonging to our world as causal and contingent. A substance is, so to speak, 'complete' and 'saturated', existing in splendid logical isolation from anything else. For the Existentialist, our existence cannot be like this. Our existence requires that of the world. It is intelligible, moreover, only in relation to the future beings which we are 'on the way' to becoming. Finally, the objects with which our actions engage are themselves intelligible only in the light of the 'caring' or 'valuing' which constitutes our basic relation to them.

To be sure, during the course of our 'upsurge' into the world, we acquire various characteristics, some of them of crucial importance in our biographies.

We become writers, criminals, cowards or whatever. We acquire, if you so wish, essences. But that we can come to acquire them – that we can be anything at all – is not to be understood as the acquisition by substances, already furnished with essences, of further properties. We must first exist as 'unsaturated', future-oriented loci of 'care' and 'value'. And we continue to exist as these even when, in bad faith, we may pretend to ourselves that some of our properties have become definitive of who we are. In these claims, I believe, resides the true interpretation of 'existence precedes essence.'

The Existentialist has a good deal more to say about the character of human existence, particularly in connection with his distinction between 'authentic' and 'inauthentic' existence and with his notion of existential freedom. Before we work towards these matters, however, we need to consider the implications of what he has already said for some of the issues which inspired his reflections in the first place – the issues of alienation.

Notes

1 Heidegger, *Being and Time*, 1962, p. 53H.
2 Ibid., pp. 89Hff., for Heidegger's description of what I have called the standard' account. See E. J. Lowe, 'Substance', 1988, for a very clear account of the term 'substance' in its philosophical career.
3 *Being and Nothingness: An Essay on Phenomonological Ontology*, 1957, p. 200.
4 Heidegger, *Being and Time*, pp. 85, 80–1H.
5 Ibid., pp. 67, 69H.
6 Ibid., p. 77H.
7 Ibid., p. 83H.
8 Ibid., pp. 80, 71H.
9 It is too strong, in fact, to require that I be able to apply a word with some accuracy in order to count as understanding its meaning. It is enough, perhaps, that some people in my linguistic community can do this, and that I recognize their authority in the area, thereby vicariously sharing in their understanding. See Hilary Putnam's discussion of 'the division of linguistic labour' in 'The meaning of "meaning"', 1979, pp. 227ff.
10 *Being and Time*, p. 72H.
11 See Mark Platts, *Ways of Meaning*, 1979, for a useful discussion of the Grice versus Davidson controversy over this issue.
12 *Being and Time*, p. 84H.
13 Ibid., p. 79H.
14 Ibid., p. 76H.
15 *Being and Nothingness*, pp. 199–200.
16 Ibid., p. 24. My italics.
17 Ibid., p. 21.
18 Ibid.

19 Ibid., p. 8.

20 Ibid., pp. 218, 24.

21 Ibid., p. 86.

22 Ibid., p. 200.

23 Unpublished archive material, quoted in Hubert L. Dreyfus and John Haugeland, 'Husserl and Heidegger', pp. 232–3.

24 Husserl, *Carlesian Meditations*, 1960, p. 78. A similar objection was raised by Gilbert Ryle in his review of *Being and Time* in 1929.

25 For this criticism of Husserl, see Charles B. Guignon, *Heidegger and the Problem of Knowledge*, 1983, p. 115. Husserl's point, incidentally, would be a more apt one to make against Ortega, who writes, 'to each individual the world looks different... The world of the businessman obviously is different from the world of the poet.' 'Man the technician', in his *History as a System and Other Essays towards a Philosophy of History*, 1962, pp. 114–15.

26 See Stuart Hampshire, *Thought and Action*, 1959.

27 *Philosophical Investigations*, 1969, para. 60.

28 'Man the technician', in his *History as a System and Other Essays*, p. 114.

29 *Being and Time*, p. 46H.

30 A. R. Manser, *Sartre: A Philosophic Study*, 1966, p. 46. A qualification is needed, however. Sometimes Sartre uses 'Being-in-itself' to refer to something like the formless remainder which would be left if things were stripped of all the categories and *négatités* which we have brought to the world. This, I suppose, is the kind of Being which Roquentin found so disturbing in the park. (See p. 53f above.)

31 Such remarks pepper the writings of, *inter alia*, Ortega, Heidegger and Sartre. See, for example, Heidegger, *Being and Time*, p. 42H, and Sartre, *Existentialism and Humanism*, 1966, p. 26.

32 It is also pedantic and unfruitful to spend the time some commentators do on relating these slogans to Aristotelian and Scholastic debates about *existentia* and *essentia* – for instance, Jean Wahl, *Philosophies of Existence*, 1969.

33 *Philosophy*, vol. 2, pp. 3ff. For criticism of the meal Jaspers makes of this point, see William Earle, 'Anthropology in the philosophy of Karl Jaspers', 1957.

34 pp. 26–8.

35 'Man the technician', in his *History as a System and Other Essays*, p. 111.

36 For example, Mary Warnock, *Existentialism*, 1970, p. 94.

37 'History as a system', in his *History as a System and Other Essays*, p. 190.

38 Heidegger, *Being and Time*, pp. 98, 48, 43H. The italicized words provide the answer to T. L. S. Sprigge's query (*Theories of Existence*, 1984, p. 135) as to why, when they contrast people with things, existentialists often describe the latter in the present-at-hand terms which they elsewhere criticize. The point is that while it is legitimate, for certain purposes, to regard things as present-at-hand, it is *never* legitimate so to regard *Dasein* and the For-itself.

39 Quoted in Heidegger, *Being and Time*, p. 92H.

40 *Being and Nothingness*, p. 386. See also Roger Scruton's 'intentional' account of sexual Desire, in *Sexual Desire*, 1986, especially ch. 1.

41 *The Structure of Behaviour*, 1963, p. 209. Compare Wittgenstein's remark that 'the face is the soul of the body,' *Culture and Value*, 1980, p. 23.

42 See, for example, G. E. M. Anscombe, *Intention*, 1957, and Charles Taylor, *The Explanation of Behaviour*, 1964.

43 *Being and Nothingness*, pp. 437–8.

44 *Being and Time*, pp. 327, 329H. Some of the more impenetrable passages from Heidegger, Sartre and Merleau-Ponty are those concerning man's temporality. Hence, it may be that assertions like 'temporality is constitutive for *Dasein*'s Being' or 'Man *is* temporality' have a depth which eludes me. Alternatively, they may boil down to relatively accessible considerations like the one discussed in the last couple of paragraphs.

45 See also Alasdair MacIntyre, *After Virtue*, 1981, especially ch. 15, for a rather different exploitation of the analogy between lives and narratives; also my 'Life and narrative', 1988.

46 I have discussed the views of Morris and like-minded writers in *Philosophy and the Nature of Language*, 1973, ch. 2.

47 See, for example, Edmund Leach, *Culture and Communication*, 1976. Leach is, of course, inspired by Claude Lévi-Strauss.

48 Heidegger, *Being and Time*, p. 42H.

49 Ibid., p. 193H.

50 *Being and Nothingness*, p. 94.

5
Dualisms Dissolved

In this chapter I want to elaborate the Existentialist's reasons for rejecting a number of traditional philosophical dualisms which, he believes, serve to reinforce a sense of alienation from the world to which we are anyway prone. Several of these reasons have already been at or near the surface, so I can be relatively brief. The four dualisms or 'fissures', to use Jaspers' term, which I discuss are those of subject versus object, mind versus body, reason versus passion and fact versus value.

Two words of warning are in order. In rejecting these dualisms, the Existentialist is not thereby arguing for a number of monisms: for the claim, say, that there is only mind or only matter. In each case, he is rejecting the premises on which the dualisms and their rival monisms rest. Second, he is no leveller of distinctions; his point being, rather, that the dualisms misrepresent these distinctions. But why are his own distinctions – between, say, human existence and the being of things, or between mood and cognition – not to be described as dualistic? The main reason is that the term 'dualism' is generally, and reasonably, restricted to distinctions between kinds of entities which are being alleged to exist in logical independence from one another. The classic case, of course, is Descartes' distinction between mind and body as logically independent types of substance. The anti-dualistic character of the distinctions made by existentialists is sometimes disguised by their terminology. Heidegger's or Sartre's talk of *Dasein* versus the Being of things or of the For-itself versus the In-itself, for instance, belies the anti-dualistic character of their own ways of distinguishing human beings from 'mere' things. I have already recorded my sympathy with critics of a terminology that is both unnecessary and potentially misleading.

Subject versus Object

We have, on several occasions, met with existentialist hostility to speaking of our relationship to the world as that of a subject to an object which stands over against it. Sartre complained that there is something 'magical' or 'fetishistic' in the idea of a human being as a 'subjectivity-object', and Buber's 'I–It' relation was his metaphor for the subject–object dualism. At the root of this hostility there lies the sense, inherited from Hegel, that the subject – object dichotomy is an alienating one. If we are subjects set over against objects, then we are not essential to the being of the world, nor is it essential to our own. Buber describes men as 'shuddering at the alienation between the I and the world',[1] while Gabriel Marcel compares this alienation to 'the nameless sadness we have all experienced in certain hotel rooms' – rooms not 'impregnated' with ourselves and what is ours.[2]

These poetic remarks invite more literal translation. First, however, it is worth mentioning that rejection of this dualism has become something of a cliché among recent writers who are described as 'post-modernist' in outlook. Sometimes, indeed, 'post-modernism' is defined in terms of this rejection, with the 'modernism' of Enlightenment thought being characterized through its attachment to the idea of the rational subject.[3] What is curious in much of this writing is that it is nowhere made clear what is being dismissed or 'deconstructed', let alone why it deserves to be dismissed. The assumption seems to be that, buried in the pages of Derrida, Foucault or Lyotard, there lurks some decisive argument against the subject–object distinction. If so, then I for one have never managed to unearth it.

In the pages of some existentialist philosophers, on the other hand, we do find both a definite interpretation of the distinction and persuasive arguments for rejecting it. The Existentialist construes the dichotomy as being between substances of one kind (ourselves) and substances of another kind ('mere physical things' primarily). The criticism of the dichotomy is, in Heidegger's words, that subject and object so understood 'do not coincide with *Dasein* and the world'.[4] This is because we do not stand over against things in the world as substance against substance at all. It is only possible to think otherwise if one is in the grip of the metaphysics of the present-at-hand and its bedfellow, the spectatorial premise. The former encourages the dichotomy in two ways. First, it blinds us to the fact that the world is, 'proximally', one of the things which, unlike Marcel's hotel rooms, are 'impregnated' with human purposes and concerns. 'If we suspend our ordinary preoccupations and pay... disinterested attention to [the thing],' writes Merleau-Ponty, 'it is then hostile and alien, no longer an interlocuter, but a resolutely silent other... which evades us.'[5] Second, the metaphysics of presence-at-hand gets extended to ourselves, so that we then conceive of ourselves too as substances – things capable, in logic, of existing independently of the world.

The spectatorial premise also encourages the dichotomy, by inducing the idea that we are self-contained cognitive centres. If I am essentially a spectator, then the world is a theatre of spectacles, of things 'stared at'. Their place and significance in relation to our purposes and concerns are then extra, inessential dimensions tacked on later. And if I am a spectating mind, then, as Husserl reasonably concluded, the actual world becomes irrelevant to the description of my experiences, since it is at most a contingent truth that a world is responsible for them. Only if we see, with Merleau-Ponty, that our primary 'relation to the world is not that of a thinker to an object . . . [that] we experience "in action" ',[6] will we appreciate that it is impossible to disengage our existence from that of the world. I am not, as Marcel put it, 'watching a show'.

The Existentialist is doing little more here than translate into the idiom of 'subject' and 'object' the earlier criticisms of Descartes and Husserl. What the criticisms imply, put in a nutshell, is that our Being-in-the world is 'not that of the Being-present-at-hand-together of a subject and object'.[7]

The only query is whether the Existentialist's construal of the dichotomy is a reasonable one. Heidegger notes that there are philosophers, wedded to this dualism, who insist that subject and object are *correlative* in a way that allows no sense to imagining the one without the other. He quotes the neo-Kantian Heinrich Rickert, who insists that 'the concepts of subject and object require each other.' Doesn't Rickert thereby escape the charge of having divided ourselves and the world into two logically isolable realms of being? Heidegger thinks not. All Rickert is doing is to make the verbal stipulation that, in the absence of a world, we could not *call* a consciousness 'a subject'; and that, in the absence of consciousness, things could not be *called* 'objects'. (The *Gegenstand* (object) would have nothing to be *gegen* (against).) Far from denying that consciousness and world might exist in isolation from one another, this verbal point presupposes such a possibility. Rickert, no less than Descartes and Husserl, fails to grasp that 'it belongs to the nature of *Dasein* to exist in such a way that it is always already with other beings.'[8]

The world, in sum, is indelibly human; and humans are indelibly worldly. So if the sense of alienation induced by the subject–object picture is the sense that our being is inessential to that of the world, and that its being is accidental to our essential nature, then it is an illegitimate sense; and the world is more our home than a hotel room in which strangers lodge.

All existentialist writers express disquiet about the subject–object picture, but some of them try to correct it in a manner very different from the 'mainstream' one just described. Consider, for example, the approach of Karl Jaspers. He thinks that a primary urge to philosophizing is the endeavour to 'cope with' the 'shipwreck' (*Scheitern*) which threatens human beings as part of their very condition. This condition incorporates the recurrent sense that an alien world can afford no 'reliability' or 'home' (*Heimat*). This sense, in turn, derives from a picture of ourselves separated from the world as subjects from objects. Unlike the Existentialist, however, Jaspers does not believe that thinking in terms of subject and object is an eliminable mistake. On the contrary, this 'fissure' (*Spaltung*) is one that 'we are constantly within . . . whenever we are awake and conscious.' Despite this, we are to admire those mystics who attempt 'to overcome the . . . fissure in favour of a complete oneness of subject and object through the disappearance of objectivity and the extinction of the ego'. For what mystics perceive is that 'Being-as-a-whole can be neither object nor subject, but must be the "encompassing" [*Umgreifende*] which comes to appearance in the form of the fissure.'[9] They grasp, moreover, that this 'encompassing' cannot be rationally thought about, since only objects can be thought about. (Incidentally, Jaspers' argument for the conclusion that Being-as-a-whole can be neither subject nor object, but some kind of 'ground' on which this distinction appears, is startlingly feeble. He seems to think that since not everything is a subject and not everything is an object, then everything is neither. One might as well argue that since not everyone is male and not everyone is female, then everyone is neither male nor female.) If Being-as-a-whole cannot be thought or spoken of, one might expect Jaspers to remain silent about it. But he seems to think that we are able to 'read' certain 'signs' or 'ciphers' which somehow indicate its character. At any rate, he tells us that 'the "encompassing" is thought of as being itself, transcendence (God), the world, and that which we ourselves are: life, consciousness in general, spirit and *Existenz*.'[10]

This does not, I think, provide a wholly intelligible substitute for the Existentialist's attempt to dissolve the dichotomy. What he does is to describe the world and ourselves in ways that are free of the dichotomy, and to show us how we may think of our Being-in-the-world in less erroneous terms. Jaspers, however, holds that our thought and speech are necessarily constrained by the subject–object distinction. Escape can only be found in obscure intimations furnished by the 'ciphers' which, with Jaspers' help, we might hope to 'read'. I doubt that most of us are able to place sufficient confidence in this 'reading' skill to suppose that here lies a cure for our 'homelessness'.

Mind versus Body

It is reasonable to think of this venerable dualism as a special instance of subject–object dualism. At the core of the latter was the idea that human beings and objects in the world are substances between which the relation can only be contingent. It is this same idea which defines mind – body dualism. Cartesian doubt and Husserl's *epochē* both allow that the *cogito* or 'pure ego' can exist in a world without bodies.

Doubtless it is not the thesis of contingency by itself which induces the sense of alienation from one's body that for many people at various periods has been an acute one. As Hegel's discussion of the 'unhappy consciousness' indicates (p. 28), it also requires a perspective, typically a religious one, from which the body is seen as a hindrance to the realization of one's true, 'spiritual' being. Still, this perspective could only emerge on the assumption that mind and body are logically separable. It is worth remembering that early Christian versions of the afterlife postulated the resurrection of the body. The belief that only a soul enjoys eternal life required the victory of Plato's doctrine of disembodiment over Christianity's Judaic inheritance.

The Existentialist's criticisms of Descartes and Husserl, and his own account of human existence, make his hostility to the present dualism predictable. It comes as no surprise to find Marcel declaring, 'I *am* my body'[11] nor Sartre denying that 'the union of soul and body is the contingent bringing together of two substances.'[12]

To speak of mind is, at a minimum, to speak of understanding. A creature has a mind if and only if it has a capacity for understanding. Now one thing on which the Existentialist insisted was the priority of practical understanding. We must exercise our 'operative intentionality', to use a favourite expression of Merleau-Ponty's, before we can sit back and indulge in theoretical judgement and reflective knowledge. Rodin's *Le Penseur* would have nothing to ponder had he always been frozen, hand to brow, and never engaged in purposive action. 'Consciousness is in the first place not a matter of "I think that" but of "I can".'[13]

We could treat the point here as a generalization of Wittgenstein's view of linguistic understanding. This understanding, he argues, is not some 'inner' process or occurrence, but resides in the capacity to use words appropriately, and to respond appropriately to their use by others. Such a capacity must be manifested through behaviour and can only belong, therefore, to an embodied creature. The behaviour which manifests understanding of a given word cannot, moreover, be isolated from one's life at large. To understand words requires understanding of a language, and 'to imagine a language means to imagine a "form of life".'[14] We saw as much, indeed, in our discussion of understanding the word 'slab' on p. 51 (Wittgenstein's own example, in fact). We also saw how the Existentialist extends the point to understanding in general. To understand what a hammer is, is to manifest in one's behaviour a grasp of the activities, and of the 'form of life' in which they are embedded, to which hammers owe their significance. This behaviour is not a dispensable symptom of an 'inner' process which 'really' constitutes the understanding. 'I really do think with my pen,' said Wittgenstein, 'because my head often knows nothing about what my hand is writing.'[15] Likewise, for Merleau-Ponty, our primary mode of knowledge is 'knowledge in the hands'.[16]

As with several of the views which he criticizes, the Existentialist spends as much time on calling attention to the misleading pictures which encourage mind – body dualism as on directly assaulting it. One such picture, as we might expect, is due to the spectatorial premise. Is my body not something which, like any other object, I can look at and inspect? So how can it, the inspected, be confused with me, the inspector? But another picture is also at work. My body, surely, is not simply an object that I can inspect. Is it not also an instrument I use – one which, moreover, is peculiarly under my direct control? I have only to will that my mouth open, and open it does. So how can it, the instrument, be confused with me, its user?

These two pictures – the mind as the spectator of its outer shell, and as the pilot at the controls of its ship (to use Descartes' metaphor) – conspire towards the idea of a mind which is only contingently connected to a body. The response of the Existentialist is to draw a distinction between what Merleau-Ponty calls the 'objective' body and the 'lived' body. It is only my 'objective' body – a certain complex of flesh, nerves, bone, etc. – which could have a merely contingent relation to myself. My 'lived' body is not separable, even in thought, from my existence. Such labels can mislead, if they suggest that each body has a kind of *Doppelgänger*, at once coextensive with it, yet different from it. This is not, however, the point of the distinction. Part of its point is that, under normal circumstances, my knowledge of my own body's doings is quite different from my knowledge of what other people's bodies are doing. I do not have to look in a mirror to tell that my mouth is opening and closing.

More important, though, is the following consideration. That I have a body, considered as a particular physiological–anatomical complex, may be a contingent matter. What is not contingent, however, is that I am an embodied 'vehicle' of intentions, understanding and perception. As Merleau-Ponty puts it, I am necessarily an embodied 'point of view'.[17] This, my 'lived' body, might have taken a different form from the particular 'objective' body which I have – though it would have to have been sufficiently like it actually is in order to serve as a 'vehicle' for the 'operative intentionality' which confers on me my status as a human being. To take an analogy: the carburettor in my car might not have been the particular metallic object it is, but it could not have been too different without ceasing to perform the function which identifies it as a carburettor. It is not, then, that I have two bodies, an 'objective' one and a 'lived' one. My 'lived' body is my body considered as an embodied 'point of view', a 'vehicle' of 'operative intentionality'. My 'objective' body is my body considered as a particular flesh-and-blood complex. What is necessary is that I am a 'lived' body; what is contingent is that this 'lived' body has the 'objective' form it does. I might, after all, have been composed of a different stuff. In a sense, therefore, the person who stares at his body in a mirror and denies that he is seeing himself is right. For he is not viewing himself as a 'lived' body. The reason is not that the 'lived' body is too gossamer-like, but that a 'point of view', an 'intentionality', is not the kind of thing that shows in the reflection of a mirror: no more than the carburettor's function is visible in its metal.

A further reason, perhaps, why the person fails to find himself in the flesh which he stares at is that he is looking at a static body, one that could almost be a corpse. Sartre, it is worth remarking, holds that the dehumanization of the body which we call *obscenity* has to do with the cessation of motion. 'The obscene appears when the body adopts postures which . . . reveal the inertia of the flesh.'[18] When I look at a film of myself laughing, chatting and eating, I do not feel the same resistance to the thought that I am watching an intelligence, a mind, at work.

The picture of the body as an instrument also rests on the failure to distinguish the 'objective' from the 'lived' body. For it portrays the body as an object which needs to be galvanized into action, with the mind doing this job instead of Baron Frankenstein's bolts of lightning. But this is a bad picture for several reasons. Unless blessed with psychokinetic powers, I can no more get my mouth to open by willing it to than I can the door of a safe. That, generally speaking, I do not do something unless I want to does not mean, as we have seen, that my wanting it is an 'inner' occurrence which happens to cause the act. Moreover, the idea of my body as an instrument, of which I am the user, is not cogent. As Marcel notes, instruments are 'extensions' of the body, which are put to use through it, and so 'presuppose' it.[19] I cannot, in general, therefore, be using my body as an instrument, since that would require that it too be put to use through my body. An infinite regress is then under way. There are, to be sure, occasions when it is reasonable to speak of a person using his body as an instrument. A dwarf once described to me his unedifying employment as a kind of human broom when, brush attached to his head, he would be pushed through drainage pipes to scour them out. The case has only to be described for its deviance from the normal role of the body in action to be apparent.

But how, if not as the spectator of my outer shell or the pilot of my ship, am I related to my body? There are existentialists who, agreeing that the 'lived' body is no mere object or instrument, conclude that it is a mystery, which cannot be further analysed or explicated, since language is designed only for the articulation of the objective world.[20] But the Existentialist's more considered judgement is that the question is badly posed, for it implies that, having described our Being-in-the-world, a riddle still remains. If this description provides, as it must, for an account of our physical engagement with things and with one another, and if it brings into relief, as, it should, the embodiment demanded by our kind of understanding and 'operative intentionality', one wonders what the residual puzzle could be. After all, the puzzle as usually formulated presupposes just that conceptual isolation of mind from body which the Existentialist denies.

It would, incidentally, be mistaken to describe the Existentialist as a *materialist* on the basis of the foregoing. Materialism, as usually formulated, is the thesis that the mind is the brain, or some suitable part of the 'objective' body. It should be apparent by now that the Existentialist can be no more receptive to this thesis than to the suggestion that the mind is an immaterial object or stuff. When Simone de Beauvoir forbids us 'to reduce the mind to matter... or to merge them within a single substance', she is not reverting to dualism, but reminding us that the mind is not a substance at all.[21]

Reason versus Passion

This is an umbrella heading for a number of contrasts familiar in both philosophical and 'folk' psychology. These include: belief versus desire, judgement versus feeling and cognition versus affectivity. At one level, no one could object to such distinctions. My desire to be rich is distinct from the belief that I am rich. To draw a conclusion is distinct from the pleasure my reasoning may give me.

There is a long tradition, however, in which such distinctions have been worked up into a dualistic account of the human psyche. Reason and passion are distinct 'parts of the soul', or the business of separate faculties of the mind. In this tradition, moreover, they are not merely contrasted but, for the most part, set at odds with one another. In Plato's metaphor, wisdom and appetite are horses pulling the chariot in different directions. Such conflicts are only to be resolved by the mastery of one faculty over the other. With rare exceptions, the tradition's preference is for the victory of reason over passion. A person should not, perhaps, be a cold fish, but his temperature must be regulated by his rational faculty.

Hegel saw this tradition as contributing to men's sense of alienation, the more so when it encourages people to identify with their rational selves and to regard their passions as unwelcome invaders. This sense culminates in the 'unhappy consciousness', in which passion figures as an 'enemy' or an 'embarrassment'. Hegel found the contemporary expression of this tradition in Kant's contrast between the 'noumenal' self, which heeds the call of reason, and the 'phenomenal' self, which is subject to the mechanics of desire. The task of ethics, as Hegel saw it, was to delineate conditions in which no such split could be experienced. In the Hegelian state people will identify emotionally with what they also perceive as the rational demands made upon them by their community.

The traditional dichotomy has been the target of more direct criticisms. Attention has often been drawn, for example, to the so-called 'rational passions' like love of truth, which, far from pulling in the opposite direction from reason, serve to keep it in motion. While this point may go some way towards dissipating the combative tenor of the traditional contrasts, it does nothing to dispel their dualistic character. More significant, therefore, is the recognition that many passions necessarily incorporate an element of judgement and appraisal. Fear of an aggressive dog is not simply an inner sensation, but the appreciation that one is confronted with danger. Jealousy at my girlfriend's conversation with my handsome colleague requires that I judge her behaviour to be flirtatious, not just friendly. Otherwise it would be impossible to assess fear and jealousy, in the ways we do, as appropriate, unwarranted and so on. Such feelings are, in the phenomenologist's sense, *intentional*. My fear of the dog is not an inner disturbance prompted by the presence of the dog (which might after all turn out to be a toy or a shadow). Rather, it is directed towards an intentional object – an object, that is, under an interpretation.

It is upon this dimension of feelings, desires and so on that the Existentialist concentrates when making his two main claims about the relation between reason and passion. The first is that we could not be creatures of reason and understanding unless we were also ones of passion (desire, mood, etc.). As Heidegger puts it, 'mood is a primordial kind of Being for *Dasein* . . . *prior to* all cognition.'[22] Desire, far from being necessarily an obstacle in the way of knowledge, is a precondition for the latter. The second claim is that some passions are themselves forms of understanding, through 'disclosing' features of the world and ourselves.

The first claim follows more or less directly from the thesis of the primacy of readiness-to-hand. The world is 'proximally' understood as one 'lit up' in relation to our purposive activities. But these are the purposes of creatures with desires and concerns, who experience the joys and frustrations consequent upon the outcomes of their activities. Beings who only stand and wait, stop and stare, would have no world to understand and reason about. All of this is encapsulated in Heidegger's use of a term from the vocabulary of affectivity, 'care', to designate our fundamental relation to the world.

Important here is the earlier consideration that neither understanding nor desire and feeling are to be construed as mere accompaniments to our activities. These activities are not the visible products of distinct inner processes, but the vehicles of a 'caring' engagement with the world. It is permissible to decompose that engagement into bodily, cognitive and affective components only when it is appreciated how artificial and provisional this procedure is.

Sartre, it is worth recording, has an ingenious suggestion for accommodating emotions like anger, which seem less amenable to this approach. He construes such emotions as a kind of action distinguished by its 'magical' character. These emotions are attempts to transform recalcitrant situations when, for some reason, we are unable to cope with them in a practical manner. 'The impossibility of finding a solution to the problem ... provides the motivation for ... experienc[ing] the world differently ... Emotional behaviour tries to confer on the object ... another quality, a diminished existence etc.'[23] The child's new toy will not work. Unable to repair it, he flies into a temper, proclaiming that he never wanted it in the first place. The toy is thereby transformed 'magically' into something not worth repairing.

Whether or not this functionalist explanation of emotions is right, Sartre's account also involves the second of the Existentialist's main claims about the passions. For he is drawing attention to the manner in which an emotion serves to reveal aspects of a situation for us. This point is made much of by Heidegger. Human being is characterized, as one of its *a priori* 'existentialia', by *Befindlichkeit* – an untranslatable term which might be rendered roughly as 'a sense of how one is faring'. ('Wie befinden Sie sich?' = 'How are you feeling/getting on/faring?') This sense is also described as 'mood' or 'being-attuned'. (The German word *Stimmung* means both mood and the tuning of a musical instrument.) Heidegger writes that *Befindlichkeit* 'implies a disclosive submission to the world, out of which we can encounter something that matters to us ... we must as a general principle leave the primary discovery of the world to "bare mood".'[24] For example, it is only through *Befindlichkeit* that the world can be disclosed to us as being threatening. Or, to take a very Sartrean example, a hill can only be disclosed as steep through an 'attunement' that accompanies activities like hiking. A steep hill is not one with a certain angle of elevation, but one experienced as daunting, whose conquest is cause for satisfaction and the like.

Someone will object that the features alleged to be disclosed in relation to how one 'fares' are not properly features of the world at all. Steepness, as just understood, is no more a property of the hill than pleasure is a property of the ice-cream I enjoy. The Existentialist's reply is that while steepness is not, of course, a property of that 'dimmed down' world of the present-at-hand, nor are *any* of the properties encountered in the world we are proximally 'in' – the world of readiness-to-hand, significance and *négatités*. If 'steep' is to be described as 'subjective', so must the vocabulary of destruction, fragility, solidity and so on (see p. 63 above). And the proper conclusion to draw from this is that the 'subjective' label is an unhappy one.

When we combine Heidegger's explanation of the shift to the perspective of presence-at-hand (p. 62 above) with Sartre's functionalist account of emotions, we obtain as a bonus an interesting explanation of our tendency to pit reason against passion. Examination of objects present-at-hand and indulgence in emotions like anger have the same origin – the recalcitrance of the world. Confronted with the broken toy, one child takes it to bits to examine it while another flies into a temper. The first deals with the recalcitrant object practically, the other 'magically'. So reason and passion can come to seem incompatible strategies for coping with the world. The mistake of the dualist who seizes upon this and speaks of separate faculties or 'parts of the soul' is a failure to appreciate that, when things run smoothly, there can be no factoring out and isolation of the elements of understanding and mood, belief and desire, which are integrated in our engagement with the world.

The steepness of a hill is an undramatic example of something disclosed through mood. An important and distinctive feature of existentialist writings, however, is the demonstration that some moods and passions disclose matters of great moment. It is this which prompts one commentator to remark that the existentialists' 'phenomenology of the emotions... will prove to be one of their most valuable and lasting achievements'.[25] An obvious instance is *Angst*, which is taken by several of our writers to intimate to us our radical freedom and individuality. I shall return to this and other examples including, by way of further initial illustration, the disclosive character imputed to sexual experience. 'There is no doubt,' writes Merleau-Ponty, 'that we must recognize in modesty, desire and love in general a metaphysical significance.' Shame and shamelessness, for example, together reveal the 'ambiguous' character of the body. In shame, it is revealed as an 'object', victim of the gaze and inspection of another. In shameless behaviour, a 'subject' – the dancing Salome, say – seeks to captivate another person, turn him into an 'object'. More generally, Merleau-Ponty concludes, sexual experience is 'an opportunity... of acquainting oneself with the human lot in its most general aspects of autonomy and dependence'.[26]

Whether Merleau-Ponty's particular suggestion is plausible does not matter for present purposes. What does matter is the plausibility, given the Existentialist's view of our Being-in-the-world, of supposing that sexual and other feelings should have 'metaphysical significance'. If our Being-in-the-world is an embodied engagement with a world that 'opens' itself to us through our concerns and projects, there can be no reason to think that it will be disclosed only when we take stock and reflect. On the contrary, unless its features are revealed in a more 'proximal' way, there would be nothing to take stock of and reflect upon. If so, it must be wrong to suppose that reason is the faculty which discovers how the world is and passion merely the arena in which our subjective reactions to this discovery are played out.

Fact versus Value

The Age of Enlightenment, thought Hegel, was that of 'self-alienated spirit', because its spokesmen denied to the world any intrinsic significance and value. With the demise of 'superstition', these would be revealed for what they are – projections onto the world of 'subjective' desire and sentiment. The effect of this message, Hegel believed, was to render the world 'foreign' to people hitherto accustomed to experiencing it as a place of meaning and value. If that experience is illusory, if nothing in the world is important or trivial, worthwhile or worthless, then the 'real' world becomes the one studied by the cool, detached scientist. 'Ours' turns out to be, in the main, a subjective veneer superimposed upon reality.

Some existentialist writers explicitly concur in Hegel's judgement. Buber thinks that, by imprisoning meaning and value in a subject or self opposed to a world of facts, the 'I–It' dichotomy is secured.[27] Heidegger writes that 'with the being of values a maximum of... *uprootedness* was achieved.'[28] His point is that the notion of value arises out of an illicit bifurcation of Being and 'the Ought' (*Sollen*). This is illicit because the sense of 'Being' which can be contrasted with 'the Ought' is that of presence-at-hand, Being as captured in 'mathematical–physical thinking'. The fact/value dichotomy will be dissolved once we recall that our 'proximal' experience is of a world ready-to-hand, replete with significance, utility and worth. 'In interpreting, we do not... throw "signification" over some naked thing which is present-at-hand, *we do not stick a value on it.*'[29]

Why is it, then, that in both the popular imagination and serious comment-aries, existentialism is seen as wedded to an absolute distinction between fact and value? (In one commentator's opinion, indeed, it is the existentialists' insistence on this distinction which was the main cause of the break with Husserl.)[30] The main reason is some remarks by Sartre in his hastily prepared lecture, *Existentialism and Humanism*. I mean such remarks as these: 'there disappears with [God] all possibility of finding values in an intelligible heaven'; '[Man] chooses without reference to any pre-established values... moral choice is comparable to the construction of a work of art'; and 'You are free, therefore choose – that is to say, invent. No rule of general morality can show you what you ought to do.'[31] It is remarks like these which lead Mary Warnock to declare that Sartre is 'perfectly familiar with the truth', known to analytic philosophers like R. M. Hare, that describing and evaluating are disjoint activities.[32]

If Sartre's remarks are correctly interpreted as announcing an unbridgeable gap between fact and value, or between describing and evaluating, then they are in direct contradiction to the Existentialist's account of man's relation to the world presented over the last few chapters. This is so for two closely related reasons. First, as we have just been reminded by Heidegger, our 'proximal' encounter is not with things present-at-hand on to which we subsequently 'stick' values. Rather, we experience things as ready-to-hand, imbued with significance, utility and value. A medicine, for example, is not a stuff to which we consequently, as a bonus, attach a value. It only counts as a medicine because of an important role it has in our lives. If this corresponds to anything in recent analytic philosophy of value, it is to the insistence by writers like Philippa Foot that our vocabulary is replete with terms – 'polite', 'cruel', 'courageous', etc. – in which descriptive and evaluative elements are inextricably interwoven.[33]

Second, the Existentialist claims that it is only through the goals and values that inform our activities that anything can get 'disclosed' or 'lit up' in the first place. There can be no question of first describing how the world's contents are and then placing them on a scale of values: for there would be no world of facts to describe in the absence of projects that matter to us. Sartre himself is explicit on the implication of this for the nature of value. We are constantly in the business of making good the 'lacks' by reference to which the world, encountered as a 'world of tasks', is articulated. Value is what belongs to that which makes good our 'lacks'. Far from the 'positing' of values being some extra, optional exercise in which the For-itself engages, valuing is 'consubstantial with it – to such a degree that there is no consciousness which is not haunted by its value'.[34]

How might the apparently dualistic remarks from Sartre's lecture be made consistent with all of this? A main purpose of that lecture was to defend existentialism against charges of despairing quietism and abdication of moral responsibility. Sartre counter-attacks by claiming that it is existentialism's enemy – the spirit of 'seriousness' – which in fact has such consequences. Because Sartre's concern is a practical and moral one, the impression is easily gained that the 'serious' man's mistake is solely about values, which he takes to be imposed on us by the will of God, the intrinsic nature of the world, or whatever. Other writings of Sartre make it plain, however, that the mistake is to take *anything*, not just values, as pre-given and independent of human engagement. So-called 'brute facts' about the past, for example, are not really such, since 'it is finally impossible for me to distinguish the unchangeable brute existence from the variable meaning which it includes.' A 'thousand projects', including my adoption of a social order in which a person's existence is deemed to begin at birth, are involved in my holding it for a brute fact that I had whooping cough at the age of four. It may be that, in some sense of 'choose', we choose our values; but in that sense we also 'choose the world'.[35] Moral choice may be comparable to the construction of a work of art, but so is the 'choice' of our past, our situation, our world.

A comparison can be made here with the care needed in construing some of Nietzsche's remarks on values, such as 'There are no moral phenomena... morality is merely an interpretation of certain phenomena.'[36] It is quite wrong to read this as proclaiming a divorce of facts from values, since according to Nietzsche facts too only emerge from the interpretations or perspectives which we bring to the world. 'Facts is precisely what there is not... only interpretations.'[37] Physics, no less than ethics, is a perspective, and if the Overman's valuations are akin to the artist's creations, so are his descriptions and theories. The Overman makes worlds as much as he makes values.

We shall be returning to Sartre's discussion of values, but in the meantime I conclude that it simply bypasses analytic philosophers' discussions of the fact/value relation. He neither asserts nor denies – like the moral 'cognitivist' and 'non-cognitivist' respectively – that evaluative judgements can be derived from purely factual premises. This is because he does not think there is a domain of the purely factual, in the sense of a world describable independently of human engagement with it. If he dissolves the fact/value dichotomy, it is not by assimilating values to facts, but by showing that facts, like values, are unthinkable except in relation to the actions which permit the world to be articulated.

I am not suggesting that, for Sartre, there are not important differences between, say, describing someone as French or as a doctor, and judging him to be a coward or an honourable man. As his lecture shows, he certainly thinks it more urgent to emphasize our responsibility in the making of these latter, moral judgements. 'Seriousness' about moral value is of a particularly pernicious kind. For one thing, so much turns, by way of our treatment of each other, on our moral judgements, so that it is especially irresponsible to take them unreflectingly for granted.

In his *Cahiers*, written a few years after his lecture, Sartre uses the term 'value' in a pejorative sense: and in doing so, he sounds a theme which will occupy us a good deal in the rest of this book. He writes:

> Values in the spirit of 'seriousness' . . . are posited by a consciousness which is not mine and which oppresses me . . . I regard my project with the eyes of the Other . . . value is therefore necessarily an alienated project.[38]

Value, in this special sense, is something a person places not upon the actions and goals which he authentically adopts, but upon those which he sees demanded of him by others. The pursuit of these latter goals, of values, is then described as 'alienated'.

This species of alienation is clearly different from the one upon which the Existentialist has so far concentrated. He has been concerned to dissolve a number of dualisms which, like Hegel, he believes to be partly responsible for a sense of alienation from the world. Sartre, it seems, is suggesting that there may be other, perhaps grimmer, forms of alienation. It is to this possibility that the Existentialist now turns.

Notes

1 *I and Thou*, 1937, p. 70.
2 Quoted in Joe McCown, *Availability: Gabriel Marcel and the Phenomenology of Human Openness*, 1978, p. 19.
3 This is how Jürgen Habermas, for example, defines the terms. *The Philosophical Discourse of Modernity*, 1988.
4 *Being and Time*, 1962, p. 60H.
5 *Phenomenology of Perception*, 1962, p. 322.
6 'The primacy of perception and its philosophical consequences', 1974, p. 196.
7 Heidegger, *Being and Time*, p. 176H.
8 Heidegger, *The Basic Problems of Phenomenology*, 1982, p. 157.
9 Karl Jaspers, *Einführung in die Philosophie*, 1985, pp. 25–8. See also his *Reason and Existence*, 1975.
10 Ibid., p. 28.
11 *Being and Having*, 1949, p. 12.
12 *Being and Nothingness: An Essay on Phenomenological Ontology*, 1957, p. 309. It is sometimes charged that Sartre's insistence that the For-itself is 'wholly body' is incompatible with his contrast between the For-itself and the In-itself. See, for example, Alphonse de Waehlen's preface to Merleau-Ponty's *The Structure of Behaviour*, 1963. But this charge takes too seriously Sartre's admittedly misleading remarks in the introduction to his book, and anyway ignores his insistence that the body which the For-itself 'wholly' is does not belong in the order of the In-itself. My remarks on the distinction between the 'objective' and the 'lived' body later in this section should make clear the position Sartre adopts. See also the discussion in the appendix.
13 Merleau-Ponty, *Phenomenology of Perception*, pp. 429, 137.
14 Ludwig Wittgenstein, *Philosophical Investigations*, 1969, p. 8.
15 *Culture and Value*, 1980, p. 17.
16 *Phenomenology of Perception*, p. 143.
17 'The primacy of perception', p. 200.
18 *Being and Nothingness*, p. 401.
19 *Being and Having*, p. 14.
20 See, for example, Gabriel Marcel, 'On the ontological mystery', in his *The Philosophy of Existence*, 1948, pp. 8–9.
21 *The Ethics of Ambiguity*, 1948, p. 7.
22 *Being and Time*, p. 136H.
23 Sartre, *Sketch for a Theory of the Emotions*, 1962, p. 60.
24 *Being and Time*, pp. 137–8H. For a useful account of Heidegger's view, see Frederick A. Olafson, *Heidegger and the Philosophy of Mind*, 1987, pp. 104ff. One thing he points out is the inadequacy of the rendering of '*Befindlichkeit*' as 'state-of-mind' in Macquarrie and Robinson's translation of *Being and Time*.
25 John Macquarrie, *Existentialism: An Introduction, Guide and Assessment*, 1973, p. 155.
26 *Phenomenology of Perception*, pp. 166–7.

27   *The Eclipse of God*, ch. 5.

28   *An Introduction to Metaphysics*, 1959, p. 198.

29   Heidegger, *Being and Time*, p. 150H.

30   Frederick A. Olafson, *Principles and Persons: An Ethical Interpretation of Existentialism*, 1967, ch. 4.

31   *Existentialism and Humanism*, 1966, pp. 33, 48, 38.

32   *Existentialism*, 1970, p. 123. See also Arthur C. Danto's ascription of 'a qualified non-cognitivism' to Sartre, in *Sartre*, 1975, p. 140. I found most of Danto's account of Sartre on values very illuminating, however.

33   See her paper, 'Moral Beliefs', 1967.

34   Sartre, *Being and Nothingness*, p. 94.

35   Ibid., pp. 498, 463.

36   *Twilight of the Idols*, 1954, Part VII, section 1.

37   Nietzsche, *The Will to Power*, 1968, section 481.

38   *Cahiers pour une morale*, 1983, pp. 15–16, 465. My italics.

6
Self and Others

With the dissolution of the dualisms of the previous chapter, it seems that the Existentialist has done as much as a philosopher can do to overcome the sense of alienation from the world which was his starting-point. But if his journey were to end here, it would be impossible to understand why topics which have hardly surfaced so far should be so closely associated with the name of existentialism. I mean topics like *Angst*, absurdity, authenticity and commitment. The explanation is that these topics loom large in discussion of a different issue of alienation, one which it is in the very nature of the Existentialist's account of our Being-in-the-world to give rise to.

In Hegel's metaphysics, *Geist*'s alienation from Nature is at the same time *Geist*'s alienation from itself. This is because *Geist* is the whole of reality, Nature included. Once Hegel is 'brought down to earth', however, and talk of *Geist* is replaced by that of human beings, no such identification of alienation from the world with self-estrangement can be made. In the Existentialist's view, not only is there a distinct phenomenon of self-estrangement, but it can only be appreciated in the light of his account of Being-in-the-world. One has to accept something like that account to see that self-estrangement is a real and pervasive phenomenon. Interestingly, it is usually in the sense of self-estrangement that existentialist writers have used the word 'alienation'. Heidegger, for example, writes that our everyday existence 'drifts along towards an alienation', and this in virtue of our being estranged from our 'ownmost potentiality-for-Being'.[1] The alienation to which Sartre refers is that which obtains when anything is 'estranged from itself'; and I am estranged from myself, in the shape of a 'Me – ego', when this 'has been taken hold by others'.[2] In this chapter we begin the task of understanding remarks like these.

Some False Starts

The best place to start is with a view of self-estrangement which is very definitely *not* the Existentialist's. Elsewhere I have criticized what I dubbed the 'Polonian' account of self-estrangement and inauthenticity.[3] Polonius, recall, told his son, 'To thine own self be true.' Perhaps he had no particular philosophy of the self in mind, but such words can conjure up a familiar image. A person is composed, in this image, of a number of selves – a 'real', 'true' or 'inner' self, *plus* other 'false', 'illusory' or 'superficial' selves which can and often do silt over the first one. A person is self-estranged or inauthentic when his life accords with the dictates of one of these 'false' selves, instead of the 'true' one which has yet to be excavated.

One might also refer to this view as the 'Californian' one. To judge from the success of various gurus and cults which trade in this imagery, it is one for which the inhabitants of that state appear to have a peculiar predilection. Until recently, at least, slogans like 'Get into yourself' or 'Be your real self' were the currency of those on the journey to 'self-discovery'.

This image of the 'true', 'inner' self from which a person can become estranged has, unfortunately, been associated in the popular imagination with existentialism. No doubt the 'jargon of authenticity', as Adorno called it, which accompanied the image did belong to the vernacular of those black-clad, café existentialists from whom Simone de Beauvoir was so keen to dissociate herself and Sartre. But did not Nietzsche write, 'Be yourself: you are not at all what you now do, think or desire'? He did, but this seemingly Californian pronouncement is immediately followed by the words, 'Your true nature lies, not concealed deep within you, but immeasurably high above you or at least above that which you usually take yourself to be.'[4] The true self, for Nietzsche, is not an inner self somehow occluded by a false, superficial one, but a self you should strive to become. The self-estranged person is not distanced from a self he actually possesses, but from a goal which he should be pursuing.

Like Nietzsche, the Existentialist emphatically rejects the Polonian image. As much might be predicted, indeed, from his criticisms of Descartes and the notion of the ego as a kind of 'subjectivity–object'. For if Polonian talk is to be taken seriously, it requires the existence of something uncomfortably like a 'soul-thing' which can get blocked from view by an imposter self.

It is not only the metaphysically unappetizing flavour of the Polonian account which draws the Existentialist's criticism. What the Polonian encourages is, in Sartre's sense of the term, 'sincerity'. The 'sincere' person believes he has a true, fixed essence, in accordance with which he must try to live. Such a person 'puts himself out of reach: it is an escape'. That 'self-recovery' of his being, in need of which the self-estranged person stands, is in fact 'corrupted' by the 'sincere' attitude.[5] For one thing, the 'sincere' man takes it that, deep down, he has a nature or character which determines in advance how he should be. This misunderstanding of his existence as a human being is compounded by dissociating himself, his 'real' self, from his 'external' behaviour. Since a person is 'nothing else but the sum of his actions',[6] this dissociation is a form of bad faith, an attempt to escape judgement for what one does. Sartre's point here recalls Nietzsche's derision of the manner in which the 'botched and the bungled' bolster their self-esteem by pretending that their actions are no reflection of what, *au fond*, they are really like.[7] Nietzsche and Sartre would subscribe to the comment which the eponymous hero of Rilke's *Ewald Tragy* makes on the Polonian talk of a friend. ' "True to oneself", it suddenly came to Tragy during the night: how ready-made, how clear, how worn-out!.'[8] (Existentialist fiction itself contains several Polonian figures, like the pathetic Paula in Simone de Beauvoir's *The Mandarins*, who is partial to lines like 'I won't permit you to be turned away from your true self,' much to the exasperation of her lover, Henri.)

A final criticism of the Polonian image is that it encourages an exclusively introspective approach towards self-understanding. Heidegger's hostility to this may be gauged from his reference to the 'extravagant grubbing about in one's soul' which it implies.[9] He does not, of course, deny the need to pause and take stock of oneself: but this is the need, not for 'inner perception', but for awareness of the things, and my engagement with them, which constitute my 'environing world'. The shoemaker understands the man he is by seeing himself – replete with his sense of what matters to him and his ambitious for the future – reflected in the shoes he makes, the workshop in which he makes them, and the home in which he lives. *Dasein 'finds itself... in things* because, tending them, distressed by them, it always ... rests in things'.[10] For Sartre too, self-reflection is conducted not by switching on an inner searchlight, but by observing how one is reflected in that 'world of tasks' which is the 'image of myself'.[11]

How, indeed, could matters be otherwise, given that 'each of us is what he pursues and cares for'[12] or a 'sum of actions' or a 'vital programme'? This latest criticism of the Polonian is, therefore, but an extension of the rejection of Cartesian and Husserlian accounts of consciousness as a self-enclosed, autonomous realm which might be inspected in isolation from a real world. If consciousness is 'plunged into the world of objects' and 'the ego is ... outside, in the world,' then it will be there, and not in the inner recesses of a 'soul-thing', that I find myself.[13]

Unsatisfactory as it may be, Cartesianism in the form of its rococo Polonian variation does at least essay an answer to the question of how self-estrangement is possible. The Cartesian also offers solutions to some of the most persistent worries about the self – the problems of the unity of consciousness and personal identity, for example. What alternatives does the Existentialist have to suggest?

Every experience is 'owned', in that it can and must be attributed to an 'I'. In Kant's terminology, each experience is accompanied by an 'I think'. The problem is to understand how it is that different experiences are attributable to a single 'I'. The Cartesian answer is simple: each of them is an occurrence in the history of a single substance, a self. For the Existentialist, we know, this is no answer at all. 'The unifying role of the "I",' writes Sartre, is 'totally useless'.[14] Unless we have prior reason to think that a consciousness is unitary, we have no justification for locating it in a single underlying substance.

At the time he made these remarks, Sartre seemed to think that the unitary ownership of consciousness might be a dispensable notion. Not 'I have consciousness of this chair' but 'There is consciousness of this chair' reports the 'certain content' of the experience.[15] If I understand his later position, it is that while all of Pierre's experiences must be ascribable to a single 'I', the unity of Pierre's consciousness thereby guaranteed is an uninteresting, trivial affair. This certainly seems to be Heidegger's position. That an 'I think' attaches to experiences shows nothing significant about the nature of the thinker. 'I' is to be understood here only as a 'noncommittal *formal indicator*'.[16] Its use by Pierre no more entails an interesting unity among his experiences than his use of 'here' to indicate his various positions entails geographical proximity among them. Certainly the triviality that Pierre's consciousness is unitary, in the sense that each of his experiences is his, does not imply that there is any 'constancy of the self' in Pierre's life. It is Heidegger's view that a self need not be at all unitary in the sense of being constant. Indeed, it is only the 'authentic' individual, whose life manifests 'steadiness and steadfastness', who is self-constant.[17]

But surely Pierre, however 'non-self-constant', remains one and the same person, Pierre? Or if perchance he does not, this will surely be due to something more dramatic than lack of 'steadfastness' – to something like a brain-transplant or the swallowing of one of Dr Jekyll's potions. Either way, must we not possess a criterion for personal or self-identity prior to that for 'constancy', since we must first identify a person before judging his 'constancy' or lack of it? The Existentialist will reject the suggestion that this criterion is to be found in the continuity of a 'soul-thing', but is it not then incumbent upon him to furnish an alternative?

The Existentialist's response is that nothing of the sort is incumbent on him, and that the obsession with providing a criterion of self-identity betrays a failure to be rid of the traditional view of the human being as a substantial subject. The demand for a criterion of self-identity suggests that there is a true or false answer to the question of whether Pierre is the same person after the brain-transplant or after imbibing the potion. But the suggestion is mistaken, for what would be called for in the event of such bizarre occurrences are *decisions* on how to describe them. Such decisions need not, of course, be arbitrary. A host of reasons, including legal considerations about responsibility, can influence whether we describe Jekyll/Hyde as two persons or as a peculiarly dislocated single person. What must be avoided, however, is the pretence that the decision taken is really a discovery of a deep fact about the nature of the self.[18]

Nor need the Existentialist deny that, in the normal course of events, we follow a perfectly workable practice for distinguishing one person from another and for telling if the person we meet today is the one we met last year in Marienbad. Human existence is embodied Being-in-the-world, so persons may be identified through their bodies. The important thing, once more, is to resist the temptation to treat the continuity of Pierre's body as *evidence* for a further, deeper identity of his person or self. Rather, our practice determines the – or, better, *a* – sense of his remaining the same person. Certainly we are not entitled to infer anything concerning Pierre's 'self-constancy' or the integrity of his 'vital programme' from the spatio-temporal continuity of his body.

I referred just now to *a* sense of Pierre's self-identity. Analytic philosophers often distinguish between 'strict' or 'numerical' identity and the 'qualitative' identity or similarity obtaining between the ways a person is at different times. Is the disintegrating Baron de Charlus the same person as the one described in the early volumes of Proust's novel? Yes, in the sense of being 'numerically' identical; no, in the sense of being 'qualitatively' the same. In the 'qualitative' sense, the animal-loving, mystical family man, Heinrich Himmler, was a different person from the cold-blooded Himmler who oversaw the Holocaust, while in the 'strict' sense there was just one Himmler.

The Existentialist makes a similar distinction, but differs from most analytic philosophers in being more interested in something like the 'qualitative' sense than in the 'strict', 'numerical' sense. Heidegger writes:

The *Dasein* is not only . . . identical with itself in a formal–ontological sense – everything is identical with itself – . . . Instead, the *Dasein* has a peculiar selfsameness with itself in the sense of selfhood. It is in such a way that it is in a certain way *its own*, it *has itself*, and only on that account can it *lose* itself.[19]

This implies that while Pierre may remain the same person in a 'strict', 'formal –ontological' sense, there is a more momentous sense (called 'self-hood') in which he may fail to remain himself. He may 'lose' himself. In this more momentous sense, perhaps Charlus is not the self he was, and perhaps Himmler was not *a* self.

What, however, is this sense of 'self' in which a person may 'lose' his self? Before we try to answer, let us reflect on why the Existentialist regards this as the more interesting sense. His reason is that this is the sense at issue in self-reflection, self-understanding, self-integrity, self-constancy, self-creation, and a host of other hyphenated notions, including self-estrangement. Someone seeking to understand himself is hardly concerned with the criteria by which he is 'strictly' the same self as the one he was on the day of his birth. The man who ponders if he is the same person as of yesteryear is not asking if his body is spatio-temporally continuous with the old one. (This is not to say that his ruminations will not concern his body. One reason he may feel he is no longer his old self is that his increasingly decrepit body forbids him the activities – athletic and sexual, say – which were once so important to him. This may be part of what Merleau-Ponty had in mind by saying, 'it is essential to me not only to have a body, but to have *this* body.'[20] If I am a 'lived' body, do I remain the same person when my body no longer allows me to live as I once did?) The person, finally, who wonders if he has 'lost himself' is not puzzling over whether the law of identity has been suspended. He is not wondering if he is who he is.

The question remains: what is this sense of 'self' at issue in self-understanding, self-integrity et al.? Or does it remain? We have been assuming that notions like self-estrangement and self-constancy require analysis in terms of the self. We have looked for a sense of 'self' which would, for example, allow talk of a person's losing his self. Perhaps we have been getting things back to front, however. Perhaps any sense given to the notion of a self must be derived from prior understanding of concepts like self-estrangement. Arguably, it is the uses of 'self' as a prefix and in reflexive pronouns which are the logically primitive ones. Certainly it is not universally true that such uses require reference to a self. A self-monitoring computer is not one with a self that it monitors, and when my dog scratches itself, it is not its self which itches.

Examples like these show that 'self', in such uses, is not 'semantically primitive'. It is 'syncategorematic' in the sense of having no meaning in isolation, but only by way of its contribution to the meanings of longer expressions. And the same, it might be urged, applies, though less obviously, to the substantive noun 'self'. Perhaps this noun in 'Pierre is estranged from his self' has no more of an independent meaning than has 'behalf' in the sentence, 'I did it on Pierre's behalf.' ('On X's behalf' is, logicians would say, 'semantically indivisible'.) If all this is so, then the way to understand Pierre's self-estrangement is *not* by converting it into the idiom of his estrangement from a self, and then pondering the nature of this self. Rather, we should convert references to a self into talk about self-estrangement and the like, and ponder what this talk amounts to.

Such is precisely the approach of Heidegger, who writes: 'When we say that...*Dasein* understands itself, its own self...we must not rest this on some fabricated concept of soul, person, or ego but must see in what self-understanding the factical *Dasein* moves in its everyday existence.'[21] It is self-understanding or understanding oneself which must be grasped first, and not as the result of an earlier grasp of the ego or self. Sartre makes a similar point, I think, when he criticizes the 'hypotatization' which construes the For-itself's capacity for self-reflection as a 'return to the Ego as to its *self*'.[22] The logically primitive notion is that of self-reflection, and we add nothing beyond confusion by translating it into the notion of a self reflecting on a self.

The results of this section of the chapter are negative, but instructive. We began with the Existentialist's contention that our existence is threatened with self-estrangement. The obvious thing, it seemed, was to establish what he means by the self here. It was easy to tell what he did not mean, but harder to tell what his own account could be. It now turns out that the 'obvious' strategy was misguided. In a good sense, the Existentialist does not have, and is not interested in having, a concept of the self. Indeed, the very expression 'the self' is an unhappy one, contributing to the very hypostatization of a human substance against which he warns us.

Elucidation of the idea of self-estrangement will be a matter of describing the ways in which human existence can be carried on, and of showing how some of these ways deserve the epithet 'self-estranged'. Having done this we may, if we insist, refer to people who live in those ways as being estranged from their selves. But this latter idiom will add nothing significant to the descriptions already offered, and it is certainly not the one with which we should begin examination of what is at issue.

'Being-with' and 'Being-for'

The Existentialist's concept of self-estrangement is virtually equivalent to what he calls 'inauthenticity'. When *Dasein*'s 'ownmost potentiality-for-being is hidden from it,' writes Heidegger, 'this alienation *closes off Dasein* from its authenticity.'[23] Sartre's authenticity is the 'self-recovery of being' which is lost during self-estrangement. Both concepts are, crucially, to be understood in terms of a person's relations to others. 'My Being-for-others,' says Sartre, 'is a fall... towards objectivity... this fall is an *alienation*.'[24] Inauthenticity, Heidegger tells us, is 'a kind of Being-in-the-world... which is completely fascinated by the "world" and by the *Dasein*-with of others'.[25]

To explore self-estrangement, then, we need to examine the Existentialist's account of the general relation between an individual and others. His starting-point is that 'the problem of other minds', as traditionally posed, is a pseudo-one. It has been posed as follows: I am aware, in my own case, both of various bodily states or behaviour and of mental states or processes correlated with the former. I know myself, that is, as a body *plus* a mind. Since I am confined, in my experience of others, to perception of their bodies, what justifies my inference that in their case too there are mental states 'behind' the physical phenomena? Might not everyone else be a mere automaton, no more possessed of consciousness than a computer? It would be risky, to put it mildly, to infer from a single case, my own, that the conjunction of body with mind obtains in several billion other cases. Worse, this risky guess is incapable in principle of being confirmed, for I cannot put myself inside your skin and experience your desires and thoughts, if such there be. Is not solipsism, while itself unprovable, a more sober bet than the risky and unverifiable hypothesis that there are minds other than my own?

The Existentialist's first response to the 'problem' is that, as just set up, it is even more intractable than the solipsistically inclined sceptic supposes. For the sceptic at least assumes that inference to other minds, by way of analogy with my own case, is a sensible, though of course uncertain, one. But is he entitled to this assumption? Faced with initially puzzling behaviour, I can certainly ask what *I* would have to be feeling or thinking to behave like that, and then conclude that this may be why the other person acts as he does. But such an inference by analogy assumes that I am confronted with an intelligent, feeling person. As Merleau-Ponty remarks, 'reasoning by analogy presupposes what it is called on to explain' – the existence of other minds.[26] If my *sole* acquaintance with intelligence and feeling is confined to my own case, it is hard to see what sense I could attach to there being others who also think and feel. My only understanding of pain, for example, could be that it is *this*, the kind of feeling I am now having – and what sense could there be in supposing that *this* could be detached from me and belong to someone else? It is no good saying that I can suppose others to have a feeling *similar* to mine since, on the account in question, my grasp of what it is for one feeling to be similar to another – a toothache and a headache, say – would also be confined to my own case. The upshot is that while resemblances between my behaviour and that of others may help in the 'attempt to know others . . . on occasions where direct perception fails . . . they do not teach me the existence of other people.'[27]

Fortunately, for those of us who hope that we are in the company of other people, the 'problem' has been wrongly posed. As much might be guessed from the Existentialist's rejection of the Cartesian view of the mind as an inner domain which happens to be joined with a body. Rather, we are embodied intelligences, whose thoughts and feelings are only intelligible through our physical engagement in the world. Now 'if my consciousness has a body,' Merleau-Ponty rhetorically asks, 'why should other bodies not "have" consciousness?' What I encounter are 'lived' bodies, not the inert lumps of meat inspected by a surgeon; and a 'lived' body is not 'a mere fragment of the world . . . [but] a certain "view" of the world'. A person does not face a 'problem' of inferring a consciousness 'behind' what might be a mere puppet. Even to the young baby, its father's jaw is '*immediately*... capable of the same intentions' to bite and eat as its own is.[28]

Sartre provides a vivid example to distinguish perception of a mere object from that of a person. I am in a park, whose objects organize and orientate themselves around my purposes. That bench is one to sit on; that tree is partly hidden from me, one to get a better view of. Suddenly I see another man, and the park immediately loses the unique distribution it had for me and groups itself around him too. The bench is one he avoids; the tree one he approaches. I see him, that is, quite differently from the way I see objects – as a centre of purposes and perspectives which rival my own. 'The other is ... the permanent flight of things towards a goal which ... escapes me inasmuch as it unfolds about itself its own distance ... [It] has stolen the world from me.'[29]

But how can it be guaranteed that the baby is correct in seeing its father's jaws as stuffed with intentions, or that the man spied in the park really is a 'point of view' and a source of purposes? Such questions are akin to ones about the external world of objects. Granted that we experience things as if they existed beyond our perceptions of them, how can this be validated? We already know the Existentialist's way with this question. While any given perception can be checked for its verdicality, such investigations presuppose the reality of the world; and the character of our conscious, intentional life requires that this be the life of beings 'in' that world. The scandal of philosophy, remarked Heidegger, is not the failure to furnish proofs of the external world, but that 'such proofs are expected and attempted'.[30]

There cannot, for the Existentialist, be a problem about the existence of other minds over and above the problems, themselves unreal, of the existence of the external world and of myself. Knowledge of the external world and of myself incorporates knowledge of others. Let us begin with the first half of this claim.

Heidegger writes: 'In our "description" of that environment which is closest to us – the work-world of the craftsman, for example – ... those others for whom the "work" is "destined" are "encountered" too.' This is but one example of how my 'proximal' experience of the world refers me to other people, intelligent and purposive like myself. I see a suit, which has 'an essential ... reference to possible wearers'; or a boat, which 'indicates' those who might voyage in it. This is because we encounter things as ready-to-hand, and not as things present-at-hand to which the existence of other people must be 'somehow added on in thought'.[31] The ready-to-hand, the equipmental and the sign-like constitute a public, social world in which things are available for use by people at large, not just by me. Things exude an 'atmosphere of humanity', as Merleau-Ponty puts it.[32] It follows that a person cannot first exist alone and then later enter into relations with others. '*Dasein* in itself is essentially Being-with.' A person can, of course, become a hermit, but in such a case 'even *Dasein*'s Being-alone is Being-with in the world.'[33] The loner does not dispense with the existence of others, but chooses to live at a distance from them: hence it remains a life led in relation to others. The solitary rock out at sea is not a loner or hermit.

If Being-with is not a matter of being spatially alongside others, nor is it primarily one of observing and perceiving them. Heidegger gives the name 'solicitude' (*Fürsorge*) to a person's general relation to others. This is the analogue of the 'concern' which is the basic relation to things in the world. Together they constitute the 'care' which is *Dasein*'s defining mode of existence (see p. 74 above). In 'concern' I encounter things in the light of my purposes, which manifest how my life is an 'issue' for me. In 'solicitude' I encounter entities as ones with purposes of their own, as ones which are 'issues' for themselves – in short, as people. Just as 'concern' for things can take the 'deficient' forms of smashing them or letting them rot, so 'solicitude' can also take deficient forms, like indifference or callousness. But I can only be callous towards a being I recognize as one to whom things matter.

One implication of this which Heidegger draws takes us on to the second half of the Existentialist's claim that there is no extra problem about the existence of others. He writes, 'knowing oneself is grounded in Being-with.'[34] But it is to Sartre's account of 'Being-for-others' that we should turn for elaboration of the point. This account is sometimes taken, by Sartre himself for example, as a critique of Heidegger's view, but they are best taken as complementary.

'Except for Jean and Michèle,' muses a character in one of François Mauriac's novels, 'no living creature was altogether real to me. Those who could be collectively described as "the others" were, for me, a mere anonymous crowd.'[35] Sartre's complaint against Heidegger is that the others whose existence is guaranteed are left as 'a mere anonymous crowd'. Sartre's interest is going to be in my encounter with Jean and Michèle. And his point will be that only through my 'concrete' relations with others could I come to that sense of myself as a distinct individual which I undoubtedly have.

Sartre is willing to concede the possibility of 'a For-itself which would be wholly free from all For-others', but he quickly adds that 'this For-itself simply would not be "Man"'.[36] To count as 'Man', a For-itself must be self-conscious in more than the bare sense of being aware that it is aware of things. It must also have a sense of itself as an individual, a distinct presence in the world. Without this sense, a For-itself would be incapable of a vast array of emotions central to our notion of being a person. But this sense is impossible without a concomitant awareness of others. In shame, for instance, '*I* am ashamed of *myself* before the *other*' and so 'confer on the other an indubitable presence'.[37]

Modesty, pride, shyness, loss of face and dignity equally require a person's sense of himself in distinction from others.

The source of such quintessentially human experiences is what Sartre calls 'the Look' (le regard). It is this which 'has revealed to us the indubitable existence of the Other for whom we are'. He illustrates 'the Look' with his usual dramatic flair. I am kneeling by a door, peeping through a keyhole: 'But all of a sudden I hear footsteps in the hall. Someone is looking at me ... I am suddenly affected in my being ... and essential modifications appear in my structure.' The crucial modification is that 'I now exist as myself,' for I have been made into 'an object for the Other'. 'The Look' at once reifies and individuates me. 'Behold now I am somebody.'[38]

Sartre's example can mislead if it suggests that I only become aware of others and of myself in embarrassing and unedifying situations. (Though it might be a truth of child psychology that the child first becomes fully aware of its distinct existence through the disapproving stares of its parents.) 'The Look' is at work whenever I am made aware of myself as an object for the attention of others: creatures who can 'transfix' me in the way I 'transfix' objects about me.

As a 'proof' of the existence of others, this may sound circular. For unless I already know that the creature is another conscious person, why should I think it is really 'looking at' me? But this objection misconstrues Sartre's point. I do not first discern the presence of others and then surmise that they 'look at' me. In the first instance, the other is nothing but 'the Look'. The logically primitive experience is that of subjection to 'the Look', whose source may well be unknown, as when I hear a rustling in the bushes. I do not first observe a pair of 'ocular globes' and then infer to a consciousness 'behind' them. Only when I am already aware of 'the Look' do I come to recognize that it is the owners of these 'ocular globes' who are the primary source of 'the Look' (primary, but not necessarily the only source; for the believer, an eyeless God is also a source of 'the Look').

Becoming apprised of 'the Look' is, for Sartre, only the beginning of one's sense of distinctive selfhood. This sense, once born, becomes 'reinforced' in roughly the ways described by Hegel in his famous dialectic of the master/slave relationship. The rough idea is that being subject to 'the Look' is a disturbing experience because, being a free, spontaneous For-itself, I cannot be the mere object — the squatting voyeur at the keyhole — to which 'the Look' threatens to reduce me. Hence, by way of self-defence, I engage in 'a refusal of the Other'; and in the ensuing battle, during which I reaffirm my subjectivity against the other, 'I ... obtain an explicit self-consciousness [through] a negation of the Other.'[39] This is the key to Sartre's unromantic account of sexual relationships as an almost Hobbesian 'war of everyman against everyman', in which each partner struggles to retain the sense of freedom threatened by 'the Look' or the embrace of the other one. I return to this battleground in the final chapter.

To summarize: the problem of other minds is an unreal one, for as traditionally posed it rests on the mistaken assumptions that mind and body are only contingently related, and that sense can be made of a person's experiences in a world devoid of other consciousness. The latter assumption fails on two counts. I experience the world as a 'referential totality' of things having uses and significances for others whom I am 'with' in that world. Second, it is only through being 'for' others that I can enjoy those emotions and that sense of individuality which partly constitute my being a person. Whether my 'primordial' experience of others is 'Being-with' them in a public world, as Heidegger thinks, or 'Being-for' them as an object of their attention, as Sartre holds – this issue is less important than the single conclusion to which these experiences attest: that I am in a world in which others must also be present. (I have mentioned only the views of Heidegger, Sartre and Merleau-Ponty, but this conclusion is one in which other existentialists also concur. Jaspers, for example, writes that 'I am only in communication with another,' and Marcel holds that 'I cannot think of myself as existing except in so far as I conceive of myself as not being the others.')[40]

We are now in a position to tackle the question of how, in the Existentialist's view, these basic structures of a person's relationship to others give rise to the possibility, or necessity even, that the person's life is for the most part an inauthentic one, a life of self-estrangement. In keeping with the conclusion of the first section of this chapter, the thing to do is not to fasten on a definition of 'self' and deduce what it is for a man to be estranged from his self. Instead we should look at the descriptions the Existentialist offers of what he calls self-estranged or inauthentic existence, and see why such labels are not inappropriate.

Notes

1   *Being and Time*, 1962, p. 178H.
2   *Cahiers pour une morale*, 1983, pp. 429, 433.
3   *Authenticity and Learning: Nietzsche's Educational Philosophy*, ch. 1.
4   Nietzsche, 'Schopenhauer as educator', 1983, p. 129.
5   Sartre, *Being and Nothingness: An Essay on Phenomenological Ontology*, 1957, pp. 65, 70.
6   Sartre, *Existentialism and Humanism*, 1966, p. 41.
7   Nietzsche, *The Genealogy of Morals*, 1968, Essay 1.
8   Rainer Maria Rilke, *Ewald Tragy*, 1980, pp. 47–8.
9   *The Basic Problems of Phenomenology*, 1982, p. 160.
10   Ibid., p. 159.
11   *Being and Nothingness*, p. 200.
12   Heidegger, *The Basic Problems of Phenomenology*, p. 159.

13 Sartre, *The Transcendence of the Ego: An Existentialist Theory of Consciousness*, 1957, p. 49.

14 Ibid., p. 40.

15 Ibid., p. 54.

16 Heidegger, *Being and Time*, p. 116H.

17 Ibid., p. 322H.

18 Some readers will detect a similarity here with influential views of Derek Parfit on personal identity. See especially his *Reasons and Persons*, 1984.

19 *The Basic Problems of Phenomenology*, p. 170.

20 *Phenomenology of Perception*, 1962, p. 431.

21 *The Basic Problems of Phenomenology*, p. 160.

22 *Being and Nothingness*, p. 103.

23 *Being and Time*, p. 178H.

24 *Being and Nothingness*, pp. 274–5.

25 *Being and Time*, p. 176H.

26 *Phenomenology of Perception*, p. 352.

27 Ibid.

28 Ibid., pp. 351ff.

29 Sartre, *Being and Nothingness*, p. 255.

30 *Being and Time*, p. 205H.

31 Ibid., pp. 117–18H.

32 *Phenomenology of Perception*, p. 347.

33 Heidegger, *Being and Time*, p. 120H.

34 Ibid., p. 123H.

35 *A Woman of the Pharisees*, 1988, p. 51.

36 *Being and Nothingness*, p. 282.

37 Ibid., pp. 289, 275. This point about shame is a good example of the existentialist tendency, discussed in ch. 5, to find metaphysical significance in emotions. There is an excellent discussion of such 'import-carrying', 'subject-referring' emotions by Charles Taylor, 'Self-interpreting animals', in his *Human Agency and Language*, 1985.

38 Sartre, *Being and Nothingness*, pp. 282, 260, 263.

39 Ibid., p. 287.

40 Karl Jaspers, *Philosophy*, vol. 2, 1970, p. 47; Gabriel Marcel, *Being and Having*, 1949, p. 104.

7
Modes of Self-estrangement

John Macquarrie asks:

> How do we reconcile the fact that existential analysis reveals the fundamentally communal character of existence with the equally plain fact that existentialist philosophers are in many cases individualists?[1]

What this question really exposes is not so much a tension within existentialist thought as one within human life as described by the Existentialist. We have found him asserting, on the one hand, that a person is a free, meaning-giving 'existing individual'; and, on the other, that a person is necessarily a participant in a public, social world where he is the object of 'the Look', judgements and categorizations of others.

This tension is a crucial dimension of the 'ambiguity' of human existence to which Merleau-Ponty and de Beauvoir frequently refer. It is the tension which yields the possibility, or worse, of the self-estranged or inauthentic life. For this is the life of someone who resolves his 'ambiguity' by identifying too much, and too easily, with the 'communal character' of his existence. In doing so, he 'loses' what is unique about himself, and in that sense 'loses' his very self. He no longer 'owns' himself since, in one way or another, he has succumbed to a take-over by others. In that sense, he is not authentic; for 'authentic' here echoes with the meaning of the Greek word from which it derives, namely 'one who does a thing himself'. The German word which is translated by 'authentic' is still more revealing. '*Eigentlich*' comes from '*eigen*', meaning 'own', as in 'my own house'. The character of authenticity in the relevant sense is not badly captured, therefore, in such colloquialisms as 'doing your own thing' and 'being your own man'.

It is helpful to reflect that the 'communal character' of existence, our Being-with and -for others, which the Existentialist has emphasized, is for many thinkers the *whole* essential truth about human existence. These thinkers come in many shapes and sizes. They range from those who take with sinister seriousness Hegelian and Marxist utterances about the individual being a mere 'accident' of his nation or class to those contemporary 'communitarian' critics of Enlightenment for whom anyone standing outside the traditions and loyalties of a community is a ghost of a person. These thinkers also include sociologists like Erving Goffman, who thinks that a person is *nothing but* the intersection of a number of 'social roles'. Even the most personal recesses of life are 'almost as much subject to role analysis as the core tasks [for example, one's work] themselves'; and it is merely a 'touching tendency' of romanticism to suppose otherwise.[2]

The Existentialist cannot accept that life's 'communal character', such as the playing of 'social roles', is even approximately the whole story about human existence. As Jaspers puts it: 'Although my social I is...imposed upon me, I can still put up an inner resistance to it...Although I am in my social I at each moment, I no longer coincide with it...I am not a result of social config- urations...[for] I retain my own original potential.'[3] What the Existentialist does accept is that people are only too liable to live *as if* the 'communal character of existence' were the whole story. It is precisely when they do that that their lives are self-estranged. Far from 'inner resistance' to the 'social I' being the mark of 'touching' romanticism or of the 'rootless' man's dissatisfac- tion with contemporary society, it is failure to put up such resistance which constitutes loss of self.

It would be wrong to portray the issue between the Existentialist and the wiser of his opponents in too stark a manner. The issue is a complex one, a recent chapter indeed in the perennial debate as to how a person must live in relation to his fellows in order, put grandiosely, to realize his humanity. But before we can tackle the issue head-on we need to describe in some detail those modes of existence which, according to the Existentialist, are ones of inauthenticity or self-estrangement. These modes are made possible by our Being-with and our Being-for others.

Public, Herd and the 'They'

A persistent theme in existentialist writings is the contrast between the life of the authentic individual and the life which is immersed in the anonymous 'public', 'crowd', 'herd' or 'mass', to cite only some of the favoured epithets. Some remarks from Kierkegaard's pamphlet *The Present Age* set the tone:

[A] public is...an abstract void which is everything and nothing...the most dangerous of powers...the public is also a gruesome abstraction through which the individual will receive his religious formation – or sink...More and more individuals, owing to their bloodless indolence, will aspire to be nothing at all – in order to become the public.[4]

Even less flattering are Nietzsche's comments on what he calls 'the herd'. The main purpose of his diatribes against democracy, Christianity and traditional morality is that 'the mentality of the herd should rule in the herd, but not reach out beyond it.' There must be an 'end to its tyranny' over those capable of becoming 'higher men'.[5] For Jaspers, the individual must struggle against 'mass-existence'; while the title of Ortega's best-known book, *The Revolt of the Masses*, indicates where he thinks that the danger for the individual lies. For Heidegger, as we shall see, the inauthentic person is precisely the one who lives under 'the dictatorship of the "they"', the anonymous others.

It is not surprising that many commentators construe such pronouncements as exercises in social criticism. On this construal, existentialists are concerned, first and foremost, to rail against social and political conditions in which there is little or no scope for individual self-expression and idiosyncratic taste and opinion. Their main targets are, in consequence, the mass media, the levelling ideologies of socialism and consumerism, and the elevation of 'the common man'. Existentialists are thereby portrayed as elitists, unable to stomach a society in which individuals of special talents, tastes and genius go under beneath the dead-weight of the masses. Critics of existentialism thus discern, even (or especially) in the plebeian poses of Sartre and de Beauvoir, an 'intellectual snobbery...an exaltation of positions open only to intellectuals'.[6]

This interpretation of existentialist attitudes towards the 'public', 'herd' or whatever is not without some foundation. Most of our writers certainly think that their discussion is particularly applicable to 'a present age' when an egalitarian ideology drives out those pursuits in which only the few with sufficient cultural attainment can engage, or when powerful mass media and advertising or entertainment industries promote the victory of the lowest common denominator. Not a few of our writers hark back to a distant past – Ancient Greece being the favourite – where, in Kierkegaard's words, 'the value of the outstanding individual' was espoused.[7] As those words indicate, moreover, it is not difficult to find an elitist strain in many existentialist writings. This elitism, or 'aristocratism' as he called it, received its fiercest expression in Nietzsche's elevation of the 'Overman', a special 'breed' of individuals, cut out by nature to stand above the rest, who resists the levelling pressure exerted by the 'herd' and its contemporary henchmen – democrats, socialists and their relatives.

Nevertheless, the Existentialist's attitude towards the 'public' is not to be equated with elitist social criticism, for it goes deeper than that. If this equation is made, it would be difficult to see how the Existentialist's position differs from that of countless other elitist critics of modern society – Charles Maurras,

T. S. Eliot and Evelyn Waugh, for example – none of whom is reasonably described as an existentialist. As soon as the positions of, say, Kierkegaard and Nietzsche are examined more closely, it is apparent that something more profound is at stake. What 'the power of the public' or 'the tyranny of the herd' suppresses is not so much 'the outstanding individual' or 'the higher man', but the very possibility of a distinctively human existence. Kierkegaard's and Nietzsche's 'elite' figures are less members of a special breed, superior to the rest of us in talent or virtue, than the paradigmatic manifestations of the truly human. Thus it is humanity, so to speak, which suffers when these figures are kept under by the 'public' or the 'herd'. (One is reminded of Marx's contention that humanity as such is harmed through the oppression of the proletariat.) In the case of Kierkegaard, what is threatened by the 'public' is a person's 'individual religious isolation', his capacity to enter, alone and unaided, into that personal relationship to God which is the highest human aspiration.[8] For Nietzsche, the Overman is distinguished by the power he manifests in lending 'sense and value' to his life and his world. In so doing, he represents in the most vivid way the essentially creative and interpretative character of human existence. 'We have to realize to what degree we are the *creators* of our value feelings – and thus capable of projecting "meaning" into history.'[9]

It is to Heidegger's account of the 'they', however, which we should turn in order to appreciate the distance between the Existentialist's real objective and mere elitist social criticism. ('The "they"', incidentally, is the usual translation of '*Das Man*', an expression coined by Heidegger from the indefinite pronoun '*man*' (the French '*on*'). In English, a variety of indefinite terms – 'one', 'you', 'people', 'we' and 'they' – perform the job of '*man*'.)

According to Heidegger 'the extent to which ["their"] dominion becomes compelling and explicit may change in the course of history';[10] and we are left in no doubt that this 'dominion' is especially pronounced in our time. Technology provides 'them' with hitherto unparalleled means – mass media, mass production and so on – for 'levelling down' and placing individuals in 'subjection' to 'them'. Heidegger is insistent, however, that in describing people's 'fallenness' or 'absorption in the publicness of the "they"', he is not 'expressing] any negative evaluation', not presenting a 'night view' of *Dasein*.[11] It is not easy to reconcile these disclaimers with the heavily loaded pejorative vocabulary Heidegger employs; nor with his insistence that the inauthenticity of life 'in the "they"' is, within limits, something we can, and presumably should, resist and 'modify'. His point, though, is that inauthentic existence is not a characteristic of passing social conditions 'of which, perhaps, more advanced stages of human culture might be able to rid themselves'. 'Fallenness', life 'in the "they"', is, in his terminology, an 'existentiale': a necessary, *a priori* feature of Being-in-the-world. It is inconceivable, therefore, that inauthenticity be done away with – and for that reason it would be silly to decry it as 'bad and deplorable'. Authentic existence cannot replace inauthentic life 'in the "they"'. It can only be 'a modification of the "they"', through which people do not 'float above falling everydayness' but somehow come to grips with or 'seize upon' it.[12]

For an explanation of why life must, for the most part, be 'in the "they"', we need to recall the account of our Being-with-others. A person is necessarily 'with' others, because the world he encounters is already articulated into things ready-to-hand, in virtue of the publicly available uses and significations they have. In utilizing things, I do not act in a way which individuates me, but as 'anyone' acts. 'Anyone' could be using the seat I happen to occupy in the train, or be flicking through the newspaper I am reading. In making use of such things, each person is 'like the rest', part of the 'they'.

Going about as a member of the working, travelling or reading public is by no means the only respect, however, in which a person's life is 'absorbed' in the 'they'. Very generally, 'the "they" itself articulates the referential context of significance', and this for a good, almost Hobbesian, reason. Because his various projects and ambitions intimately involve others, a person is bound to 'care about the distance' between himself and others.[13] He may be jealous that others succeed where he fails, or be concerned to maintain the social distance from others which his kind of life requires. Such concerns are 'disturbing to Being-with-one-another', and it is essential to the smooth running and even the survival of a society that 'distances' between people be 'inconspicuous' relative to a sense of shared, common forms of existence. There is a premium, therefore, on an 'averageness' in which the 'they' 'keeps watch over everything exceptional', and on a 'levelling down' of individual possibilities. As a result, 'We take pleasure and enjoy ourselves as *they* take pleasure . . . we find "shocking" what *they* find shocking. The "they", which is nothing definite . . . prescribes the kind of Being of everydayness.'[14] A passage like this can give the impression that 'the dictatorship of the "they"' is found only in drably uniform, censorious societies of the Stalinist ilk. Yet it is Heidegger's claim that this dictatorship may be equally real in a society where the 'averaging' and 'levelling down' by the 'they' is hidden by a veneer of variety and idiosyncrasy; where people indeed 'shrink back from the "great mass"', but only 'as *they* shrink back'.[15] Indeed the very 'inconspicuousness' of the 'they' can make 'subjection' to 'them' all the more thorough.

In unpacking this claim, we encounter the crucial aspect to Heidegger's insistence that, in everyday life, a *Dasein* is 'not itself', has 'lost itself', and that 'the Self of everyday *Dasein* is the *they-self*,' not that of the authentic individual.[16] Unfortunately Heidegger does not bring out this point with any great clarity. So, having looked for a couple of clues in his text, I shall leave it to my Existentialist to develop the point.

What a person loses to the 'they', says Heidegger, is his 'ownmost possibilities of Being'. This cannot mean that, in the 'they', there is no opportunity for self-expression, originality, personal opinion and a kind of self-exploration. On the contrary, the 'they' often encourages a busy 'versatility', 'curiosity' and 'exaggerated self-dissection'. One clue to Heidegger's meaning is his reference to the way that, in the 'they', a person comes to see himself and others as things present-at-hand. Another is his emphasis upon a particularly insidious kind of 'levelling down', where people become 'insensitive to every difference of level and of genuineness'; and where 'all the possibilities of its [Dasein's] Being will be secure, genuine, and full.'[17]

How might the Existentialist take up these clues and develop an account of inauthenticity and loss of self in the 'they'? A person's existence is an 'issue' for him, and in confronting it he must develop beliefs, values and interpretations of his situation, which will direct the shape he gives to his life. He must determine, for example, the place that work, pleasure or religion will occupy in his life; or the significance for him of, say, his membership of an ethnic group or a profession. To be sure, there is no shortage of opinions, values and interpretations on the market, and a person may simply take a bundle of these on board with minimal reflection – perhaps the ones closely pressed upon him by family or peers. Like the 'aesthetic' figures described in Kierkegaard's Either/ Or, he may drift with the prevailing breeze. In that event, there is a clear enough sense to the contention that the person is failing to make his life his own, that it is an inauthentic one.

But this cannot be the whole story, for the Existentialist holds that we live for the most part 'in the "they"' even in societies where a premium is put on 'self-assertion', 'having one's own opinions' and 'making up one's own mind'.

Let us call those beliefs, values and interpretations which serve to lend shape to a person's life his 'directives'. We know from Heidegger, or from Hobbes for that matter, that people's differing 'directives' can be 'disturbing' to their Being-with-one-another. Unless muted or 'levelled down', the differences lead to jealousies, arguments and conflicts. A famously brutal way of dealing with particularly unwelcome 'directives' is the Soviet practice, until recently, of treating them as symptoms of insanity. This is dehumanizing as well as brutal, since beliefs and values which may be most integral to a person's conception of himself are treated as mere manifestations of something from which he suffers – excrescences on his being, rather than its substance. The seriousness and gravity of his 'directives' are denied by regarding them as fit, not for discussion and appraisal, but only for treatment. (I shall speak of gravity rather than of seriousness in order to avoid confusion with 'seriousness' in Sartre's pejorative sense; see p. 91 above.)

Now there are analogous ways – more common and less brutal – of dehumanizing a man by refusing gravity to his 'directives'. 'He would say that, wouldn't he?' has become a favourite, and revealing, ploy by which an audience absolves itself from taking seriously the beliefs and values of a person. They are simply manifestations of his character, predictable symptoms of his ethnic or class membership, or whatever. What is revealed here is the tendency to treat 'directives' as *expression*. Even, or especially, over the deepest issues, disagreements between people have no more gravity than conflicts of taste. Each person's 'directives' are as 'valid', as 'genuine and full', as the next's. In the sciences, no doubt, there should be real critical appraisal of opposing hypotheses, but in the arena of religion, morality and everything else that is most germane to the shaping of one's life, all is 'opinion', 'commitment' and 'ideology'. The first principle laid down in the Collège de France's report of 1985 to the French President on education for the future runs: 'A well attuned education has to bring together the universalism integral to scientific thinking and the relativism which characterizes the human sciences, sensitive as they are to the wide variety of ways of life, understanding and culture.'[18] Outside of the sciences, education is to be a 'multiculturalist' Cook's Tour through the world's religions and literatures, visited only long enough to be noted, not appraised. Both the author who lambastes a religion, and the faithful who respond by burning his book, are only 'expressing' their respective cultures or commitments. (With considerable prescience, Heidegger wrote: 'the opinion may now arise that understanding the most alien cultures and "synthesizing" them with one's own may lead to *Dasein*'s becoming for the first time ... enlightened about itself. Versatile curiosity and restlessly "knowing it all" masquerade as a universal understanding of *Dasein*.')[19]

Whether brutal or subtle, the ways in which the 'they' has levelled down 'directives' by depriving them of gravity are not, in essence, new. Each society deploys a strategy for quelling the 'disturbance' that conflicting 'directives' introduce into our Being-with-one-another. It is not inappropriate to describe the strategy I have sketched as a 'reifying' one, in which people are treated as present-at-hand. For a person is not being allowed to exist in the sight of the 'they' as he does for himself. He is put in the position of a man who finds himself at a party of indefatigable psychoanalysts, who take what he says and does not at face value, but only as indications of his mental health.[20]

Neither is it inappropriate to invoke a terminology of 'loss of self' and 'inauthenticity'. To 'lose one's self', for Heidegger, is for the 'they' to have 'taken hold of one's ownmost possibilities of Being'. These 'possibilities' are the projects for lending shape to a life which a person determines in accordance with the beliefs and values that matter most to him. When these 'directives', and the 'possibilities' which they inform, are deprived of gravity by being treated as symptomatic of the person's group, class or character type, they are no longer his 'ownmost'. He is rendered, for example, one of those who, in Régis Debray's words, is no longer his own 'personal possession but a patrimonial construct'.[21] Seen from the 'inside', his 'directives' are what give meaning to his life; viewed by the 'they', his 'directives' furnish meanings in the way hairstyles and jewellery do. His 'ownership' of his 'possibilities' is treated by the 'they' as akin to owning the watch or the wig that goes with his station or type.

The self is only truly 'lost', however, when the person comes to view his 'directives' and 'possibilities' with the same lack of gravity as the 'they' does. Now he can speak like the 'they', but in the first person as well. 'I would say that, wouldn't I?' He, too, can soothe the 'disturbance' caused by opposing 'directives' by regarding his own, as well as others', as so many symptoms. Even in his own eyes, he has become no more than the intersection at which a variety of character traits, roles, and social affiliations have chanced to meet.

A villain of the piece, in the Existentialist's view, is the idea of beliefs and values as self-expression. It is ironic, therefore, that existentialist authenticity is often portrayed by commentators in terms of just that. Is the authentic figure of existentialist literature not the one whose words and deeds express himself, rather than what others expect of him or the predilections of the crowd? To be sure, the Existentialist prefers that expression be self-expression in this sense. Who doesn't? What he objects to is the idea that in stating and acting upon the beliefs and values which matter to him most, a person is merely engaged in expressing himself. For it is precisely this idea which inspires one of the strategies of the 'they' for depriving beliefs and values of the gravity which they possess, or should possess, for the person who has come to hold them.

Someone will point out that the Existentialist himself faces a difficulty with respect to the status of 'directives': for it is not obvious how one reconciles their gravity with the idea, encouraged by the way some of our writers talk, that a person 'creates' or 'chooses' his beliefs and values. This and other difficulties will occupy us in due course. Meanwhile we need to introduce a mode of self-estrangement related to, but further to, the one which the Existentialist has developed from Heidegger's remarks. This time the source will be Sartre.

Bad Faith and 'the Predominance of the Other'

Sartre would not take issue with the claims of the previous section. Like Heidegger, he thinks that each of us tends for the most part to be a 'docile instrument of a family, of a social group, of a profession *etc.*', saying and hearing what '*anyone* would have said and heard'.[22] But the mode of self-estrangement he emphasizes is a different one, and due to 'the predominance of the Other in the coupling of Other and Self'. A person gets 'taken hold of by others', in the sense of coming to construe himself as he is for others. He 'conceives his own consciousness on the model of the Other', as if he were to himself as he is to others and they to him.[23]

This theme is richly illustrated in Sartre's fiction. When Lucien, the budding fascist of 'L'enfance d'un chef', finally 'sells out', he adopts, as his 'first maxim', no longer to 'look into himself'. 'The true Lucien ... had to be found in the eyes of others.'[24] He thereby joins the ranks of the *salauds* in *Nausea*, with their ambition to fit perfectly the solid, respectable image which others have prescribed for them. In *The Reprieve*, Daniel gives up the struggle to escape the mould in which others have cast him, proclaiming: 'I am myself for all eternity paederast, villain, coward ... I need no longer bear the responsibility of my turbid and disintegrating self: he who sees me causes me to be. I am as he sees me.'[25] A recurrent figure in the novels is the man who *impersonates* himself, by identifying too completely with the role in which others see him. The young Lucien 'plays at being Lucien'. Mathieu, in *The Age of Reason*, observes a 'barman ... impersonating a barman', and reflects that 'perhaps one has to choose between being nothing at all, or impersonating what one is.'[26] This barman may well be a colleague of the waiter from *Being and Nothingness* who – a little too eager and polite, his step a little too quick – is 'playing at *being* a waiter in a café'.[27] Significantly, this waiter features in the chapter on 'Bad Faith'; for self-estrangement through 'the predominance of the Other' is indeed one of Sartre's 'patterns' of bad faith. When others view me in a certain way and 'I resign myself to *being only that*,' this is 'a reaction of ... bad faith'.[28]

Bad faith takes other forms, including the opposite sin of paying no heed at all to how one is for others. Or it can take the form of identifying with one's 'objective' body as something to which things simply happen – as in the example of the woman who pretends that the hand which she leaves in an admirer's clasp, 'neither consenting nor resisting', is a mere thing. Again, there is bad faith in the form of identifying too closely with how one *has* been, with one's past, thereby divesting oneself of responsibility for one's future.

Of all existentialist concepts, bad faith has most attracted the attention of analytic philosophers. This is because it smacks of logical paradox, and discussion has accordingly focused on solutions to the alleged paradox. The difficulty arises from Sartre's description of bad faith as 'self-deception'. For Cicero to deceive Catiline about the political situation, there must be something which the former knows of which the latter is ignorant. The same, it seems, must obtain if Cicero is deceiving Tully. The trouble is that, in this case, the deceiver and the deceived are the same person, 'Cicero' and 'Tully' being his alternative names. So self-deception appears to require that a person know something that he is ignorant of.

I shall not join in discussion of this apparent paradox, for it is clear that Sartre, despite his initial description of bad faith as self-deception, is concerned, once he gets on to his 'patterns of bad faith', with a phenomenon that is not in the least paradoxical. It matters little whether we elect to describe this phenomenon as a special kind of self-deception. If we do, it is obviously not to be modelled on the puzzling, Cicero/Tully example of a person intending to believe the opposite of what he already knows to be true.

Bad faith has to do with self-identity, in the sense of a person's reflective conception of who he is and what he is like. Some such reflective concern is inevitable, given that a person's existence is an 'issue' for him; or, as Sartre puts it, given that a consciousness is a 'being such that in its being, its being is in question'.[29] The trouble is that the various activities describable as 'self-reflection' have a variety of objects. Convinced of his imminent death, a person may reflect on his life in the sense of taking stock of how he *has* lived, of his past achievements and failures. Cured of his illness, this past may become so much water under the bridge, and self-reflection will now focus on the future possibilities open to him. Or self-reflection may veer between concerns for what Sartre calls 'facticity' and 'transcendence'; between, say, examination of one's present physical circumstances and musing on one's ideal, 'spiritual' destination. Finally and especially relevant to the present discussion, 'upon any one of my conducts it is always possible to convey two looks, mine and that of the Other.' Because of this, I may exclude from my self-rumination any help that others may provide, convinced that they are 'possessed only of a deformed image of me'.[30] Alternatively, I might focus exclusively on how I am for others, in the belief perhaps that any solo feats of self-analysis would be a wayward exercise in narcissistic introspection.

Bad faith is at work, roughly speaking, when instead of balancing these various styles of self-reflection, I identify myself too fully with one or other of the competing objects of my reflections – with my past at the expense of my possibilities for the future, say; or with my body to the exclusion of my 'spirit'; or with my image for others instead of a more solipsistically formed self-image – and so on.[31]

Sartre makes this point sound unnecessarily paradoxical by writing that what is revealed by the possibility of bad faith is that 'human reality [is] a being which is what it is not and which is not what it is.'[32] I tried to defuse this kind of remark when discussing the slogan 'Existence precedes essence' in chapter 4. The thrust of the remark in the present context is that no single perspective of self-reflection can pretend to yield a complete story. Pierre *is* the person who has lived a certain life; but he *is not* to be simply and wholly identified in terms of this past. He *is* the person that others see and judge; yet he *is not* to be equated with how he is for others, since he has it in him to transcend and confound the image they have of him. Human existence, in short, is 'ambiguous', many-sided. Bad faith operates when a person, instead of facing up to his inevitable 'ambiguity', resolves it by ignoring or denying some of the poles between which his existence stands. Such denials are in bad faith, and not simply intellectual errors, because there are bound to be moments of self-awareness when each of the many poles of one's 'ambiguous' existence asserts itself. However dogged, for example, a person's attempt to identify himself with the view that others have of him, there will be 'occasions of failure' when a sense of 'solitude' reminds him of the 'subjectivity' that persists despite his 'objectivity for others'.[33] In this manner, bad faith always involves denial of something which, at times at least, we know to be true of ourselves.

There are at least two reasons for lending pride of place to that pattern of bad faith and inauthenticity in which a person identifies too fully with his Being-for-others. First, it is the pattern which Sartre himself accentuates, both in the later sections of *Being and Nothingness* and in several subsequent writings. It is a main theme in *Cahiers pour une morale*, and *the* theme in his book on his protégé, the author of *The Thief's Journal*, Jean Genet. Labelled at an early age as an inveterate thief, Genet is for Sartre a paradigm of the person whose life proceeds to embody the image which others have thrust upon him. 'Genet the thief will await himself as others await him, with *their* expectations.' In language doubtless inspired by Genet's own prose style, Sartre describes him as having 'shat himself so as to appear as excrement on the table of the just'.[34] (There is a twist to the tale, however. Genet eventually becomes a paradigm of authenticity, in Sartre's view, when he begins to play a game with 'the just', by *ironically* accepting the part for which they have cast him. An English reporter sent to interview Genet presumably experienced this irony when he was greeted at the door by the words, 'I am a paederast – and you?')

The predominance of the Other is also the main theme in the most widely read of existentialist tomes, Simone de Beauvoir's *The Second Sex*. Woman, the argument goes, conceives of herself on the model of the other person which she is in the eyes of men. Feminist disciples of this book, like its author, perhaps, sometimes conveniently forget that people who model themselves in this manner were supposed to be guilty of bad faith, and not the innocent victims of machismo.

The second reason for accentuating this pattern of bad faith is that other patterns, while not reducible to it, virtually entail it. This means that the person who refuses this particular pattern will also effect a 'self-recovery' from the other forms of bad faith. Consider, for example, a man like Daniel in *The Reprieve*, who equates himself with his villainous, cowardly character. A point made by several existentialists is that this kind of identification is tantamount to identification with one's past. For to speak of a person's character is to summarize the tendencies of his life as so far lived. If by a person's 'being' is meant a fixed nature or character, then, writes Ortega, 'the only element of being... in man is what he has been.'[35] For Sartre, this identification of oneself with one's past is, in its turn, tantamount to handing oneself over to the verdict of others. These, if only because of their number, are in a better position to recognize the patterns which run through one's past life.

All of this is illustrated in Sartre's play *Huis Clos* and by its famous line, 'Hell is other people' ('L'enfer, c'est les Autres'). The self-pitying Garcin reflects how during his life he has 'fallen into the public domain' and let others 'weigh him up' ('faire le bilan'). Thus he lived in bad faith. The irony of his words is that since he is now dead, so that the whole of his life is past, he really *is* in 'the public domain'. When Inès, one of his companions in hell, says, 'Garcin, you are a coward because I want you to be,' he can make no reply, for his 'bolt is shot', so that his complete life is now transparent to the view and judgement of others. (He cannot rebut Inès in the way an admirably existentialist old man in a certain lager commercial responds to a presumptuous youngster. 'So you've drunk this stuff the whole of your life then?' asks the latter. 'Not yet,' replies the old man.) If Garcin does reply, it is only to say, 'No need for the rack. Hell is other people.'[36] His point is not, of course, that others are inveterately unpleasant but that, deprived of the capacity to act in the future in a way which will confound their judgements, he has as surely lost his freedom to them as he would to the torturing demons in more Dantesque visions of hell. Garcin's is the hell of bad faith, of the person who, entirely at one with how he *has* been, is by that token solely a Being-for-others. To experience this as hell is, to be sure, to recognize one's bad faith – a recognition which, in Garcin's case, but not yours or mine, has come too late.

Some of the illustrations of 'the predominance of the Other' might suggest that it threatens only certain people under certain circumstances – the spineless Garcin, women in a macho world, Jews in an anti-Semitic society or the young thief in a community of 'the just'. But it is Sartre's contention that this pattern of bad faith 'can be the normal aspect of life for a very great number of people', and that susceptibility to it is 'essential to human reality'.[37] This is because the tendency to such bad faith is inherent in the very fact of our Being-for-others.

To begin with, people in any society whatsoever are eager to classify and pigeon-hole one another, and this for the very good reason that it facilitates the prediction, and hence modification, of behaviour: 'how reassuring for me is a statement such as "He's a paederast," which removes a disturbing freedom from a trait and which aims at henceforth constituting all the acts of the Other as consequences following strictly from his essence.'[38] Second, it is only a fool, wallowing in his own brand of bad faith to boot, who *ignores* how others regard and assess him. Especially when it is a matter of taking stock of how I have been so far, others are typically in a better position than myself. 'To know ourselves,' remarked Salvatore Satta in the last words he ever wrote, 'we need someone to gather us up, to revive us, to speak about us both to ourselves and to others, as in a last judgement.'[39] The line between paying proper heed to what others say to us and about us, and surrendering before the view they take of us, is a thin one. Too many of us, if Sartre is right, really do take the words of others as the last judgement.

Finally, everyone has the following motive to 'flee' into bad faith: by conceiving of himself as something In-itself, a person is relieved of a sense of responsibility for his life, and of the *Angst* and feeling of 'groundlessness' which are coeval with that sense. The main direction of this 'flight', whereby a person 'gives to himself the type of being of the object', is to 'think of himself from the position of the Other'.[40] This was the strategy used by Daniel, so that he 'need no longer bear the responsibility of [his] turbid and disintegrating self'. What Sartre means by giving to oneself 'the type of being of the object' is best gleaned from his contention that, submitted to 'the Look' of others, 'my possibility becomes a *probability* which is outside me.'[41] Others cannot stand to my decisions and commitments in the way that, if authentic, I myself do. For me, these are the taking up of 'possibilities' which lend meaning to my existence. For others, they are only indicators of my probable future behaviour. The difference between the authentic first-person perspective and the third-person one is nicely brought out in the following little dialogue:

'I swear to you that I will do it.'
'Maybe so. You tell me so. I want to believe you.
It is indeed possible that you will do it.'[42]

The promise that is for me a commitment, a taking up of one of my 'possibilities', is for you only an event which happens, allowing a more or less probable prediction of future events. In the pattern of bad faith which has most concerned us in this section of the chapter, a person comes to adopt this third-person perspective upon himself. He comes to view himself as a series of events in the world, no different in principle from the series of events that constitute the causal histories of physical objects. We know from chapter 4 and the interpretation offered there of the slogan 'Existence precedes essence' that this person is viewing himself as a 'substance', and not as an 'existing individual' for whom causal, probabilistic modes of explanation are inappropriate.

A Problem

There is nothing to prevent the Existentialist weaving the two modes of self-estrangement discussed into a comprehensive account. These modes are not only consistent with one another but complementary. One way, for example, to become Heidegger's 'anyone' is, like Sartre's waiter, to assume too completely the roles one happens to occupy. Depriving a person's 'directives' of their gravity by treating them as symptoms is a way of transforming a person's 'possibilities' into 'probabilities', noted by Sartre. In both cases there is the dehumanizing refusal or incapacity to appreciate how things are for the person himself.

Whereas Heidegger, however, denies making any 'negative evaluation' of inauthentic life, Sartre is vitriolic in his comments on the *salauds* and various other creatures in bad faith. This difference stems from a further one. Heidegger speaks of authenticity as something to be won in struggling out from a natural condition of inauthenticity; while Sartre's reference to authenticity as 'self-recovery' implies that *it* is the original condition, later lost through bad faith. This difference, in turn, reflects the more constant emphasis in Heidegger's work on our Being-with-others in a public world of shared meanings and activities. We start in the hive, so to speak, whereas Sartre sometimes makes it sound as if we begin outside it.

These differences are real ones which will matter to the later discussion of existential freedom, but they should not be exaggerated. It is disingenuous of Heidegger to disclaim all critical intent, and his vocabulary of 'fallenness', 'seduction' and 'inauthenticity' is poorly chosen if neutral description is his aim. Conversely, Sartre, for all the vitriol, is insistent that bad faith is 'essential to human reality' and the 'normal aspect of life' for most of us. Moreover, in sections of *Being and Nothingness* too often skipped over (for example, on 'instrumentality'), as well as in his *Cahiers*, Sartre is as adamant as Heidegger that the individual is 'thrown' into a public and already articulated world.

So adamant is this insistence on the 'communal character of existence' among existentialist writers that we are returned to the problem with which this chapter began. Why, if we are creatures so entwined with one another, should life in the 'they' or under 'the predominance of the Other' be described as inauthentic, self-estranged or in bad faith in the first place? Why, some of the sociologists and 'communitarians' mentioned earlier might ask, is the inauthentic person not the one who, misguidedly and with 'touching romanticism', professes to be above or against the 'they' and the Other?

We have been treated, to be sure, to some interesting descriptions of allegedly inauthentic modes of existence. But if these are what the descriptions really are disclosing, then a certain account of the fundamentally individualistic character of human existence is surely presupposed. It is important, of course, to recognize how the 'they' deprives a person's 'directives' of the gravity they may have for him, and how the Others transform his 'possibilities' into more or less probable eventualities. But if we are to speak here of dehumanization and alienation, we must be certain that the first-person perspectives which are overriden in these ways really do have priority. We must be certain, in other words, that treatment of 'directives' as symptoms of character or group allegiance, and the construal of commitments as useful indicators of future events in a person's history, are misguided or deficient. It is unclear that the Existentialist has yet afforded us this certainty. It is no good, for example, being told by Heidegger that our everyday, 'fallen' lives are 'elemental evidence *for*', not against, '*Dasein*'s existentiality'[43] – for this presupposes that our everyday existence deserves to be called 'fallen'.

The problem is compounded when we reflect on an important difference between self-estrangement and the alienation from the world which occupied us earlier. In the case of the latter, no distinction was to be drawn between *being* alienated and, roughly speaking, *believing* oneself to be alienated. This cannot be so in the case of self-estrangement. Indeed, the more effective one's strategies of bad faith, the more complete one's unreflecting 'absorption' in the 'they', the less capable is one of recognizing the state of inauthenticity. Like Kierkegaardian 'despair', existentialist self-estrangement is all the more entrenched to the degree that it is unaware of itself as such. But just as one wants to ask Kierkegaard how people can be in 'despair' even when they seem to be as happy as larks, so one must ask the Existentialist to justify the notion of a self-estrangement of which people can be without an inkling.

But has the Existentialist not provided a solution to the problem, through his account of human existence in chapter 4? This account urged that human being is radically different from that of things. It is ex-istent, intentional, meaning-giving, 'ahead of itself', 'not what it is', an 'issue' for itself and so on. The force of these epithets was to indicate the various respects in which human behaviour is not susceptible to explanation through the categories applicable to objects or substances. But it is difficult to see how this account solves the problem at hand and thereby justifies reference to life in the 'they' as inauthentic or self-estranged. The reason is that, as it stands, there is nothing distinctively *individualistic* about the account. Heidegger himself emphasizes that, for the most part, it is the 'they' which is the source of meanings and values, and whose existence is an 'issue' for itself. So, if the 'they''s way of being is inauthentic, this cannot be because it fails to satisfy the terms laid down in chapter 4 for characterizing human existence.

Imagine the most thoroughly 'communal' society you can – an exaggerated version, perhaps, of the traditional tribal societies of which anthropologists speak. In the imagined tribe, there is minimal scope for autonomy of belief and action. Tradition is so powerful that people do not think of challenging the interpretations and norms which it dictates. No one dares, or even desires, to dispute the reckoning which others make of him. Each person fits smoothly and without question into the roles which the tribal ways prescribe for him. Here we have people as 'absorbed' in the 'they', and as subject to 'the predominance of the Other', as one can imagine. Yet it will be as true of the tribal life as of any other that people's behaviour cannot be explained through the exclusively causal categories appropriate for the behaviour of things. The Existentialist's various epithets for distinguishing human existence will also apply to this tribe. Tribal behaviour will, for example, only be explicable by reference to the meanings attached to situations and to the tribe's conception of what matters to it.

Moreover, the tribal dissident, if such there can be, will hardly be greeted by his fellows as a hero of authenticity. More likely he will be pitied as a man whose very identity is disintegrated by his attempt to stand out against the traditions which define a person's place in the cosmos. The opinions which he voices in opposition to the tribal traditions are likely to be taken as symptoms of a sickness, or perhaps of pernicious foreign influences. On what grounds can the Existentialist challenge the tribal verdict on its rebel? Unless he can provide grounds, it looks as if his notion of authenticity may reflect little more than a relatively recent predilection in Western thought for the priority of the individual conscience. In the next chapter we examine the concepts with which he will attempt to respond to this criticism.

Notes

1   *Existentialism: An Introduction, Guide and Assessment*, 1973, p. 118.
2   Erving Goffman, *Where the Action is*, quoted by Jonathan Glover, in *I: The Philosophy and Psychology of Personal Identity*, 1988, p. 122.
3   *Philosophy*, vol. 2, 1970, p. 30.
4   Kierkegaard, *The Present Age*, 1962, pp. 63–4.
5   *The Will to Power*, 1968, sections 287, 361.
6   Mary Midgley, *Beast and Man: The Roots of Human Nature*, 1979, p. 329. Similar remarks are made by Iris Murdoch in *The Sovereignty of the Good*, 1985.
7   *The Present Age*, p. 52.
8   Ibid., p. 54.
9   Nietzsche, *The Will To Power*, section, 1011.
10   *Being and Time*, 1962, p. 129H.
11   Ibid., pp. 175, 179H.
12   Ibid., pp. 176, 179H.
13   Ibid., pp. 129, 126H.
14   Ibid., pp. 126–7H.
15   Ibid., p. 127H.
16   Ibid., p. 129H.
17   Ibid., pp. 130, 127, 177H.
18   Quoted in Alain Finkielkraut, *The Undoing of Thought*, 1988, p. 95. This book skilfully catalogues many examples of the deprivation of gravity I am describing.

19   *Being and Time*, p. 178H.
20   The analogy with victims of the psychoanalysts may indicate to some readers a similarity between the 'reifying' attitude of the 'they' and the 'objective' attitude described by P. F. Strawson in his fine essay, 'Freedom and resentment', in *Freedom and Resentment and Other Essays*, 1974.
21   Quoted in Finkielkraut, *The Undoing of Thought*, p. 94.
22   Sartre, *Saint Genet: Actor and Martyr*, 1968, p. 407.
23   Sartre, *Cahiers pour une morale*, 1983, pp. 429, 444. But see Sartre's 1948 essay *Truth and Existence*, in which bad faith is treated primarily as a form of willed 'ignorance'.
24   Sartre, 'L'enfance d'un chef', in his *Le Mur*, 1939, p. 243.
25   Sartre, *The Reprieve*, 1986, pp. 116, 345.
26   Sartre, *The Age of Reason*, 1961, p. 173.
27   Sartre, *Being and Nothingness: An Essay on Phenomenological Ontology*, 1957, p. 59.
28   Ibid., p. 290.
29   Ibid., p. 47.
30   Ibid., pp. 57–8.
31   My remarks on Sartre's concept of bad faith owe a good deal to a perceptive paper by Phyllis S. Morris, 'Self-deception: Sartre's resolution of the paradox', 1980.
32   *Being and Nothingness*, p. 58.
33   Sartre, *Saint Genet*, p. 408.
34   Ibid., pp. 389, 402.
35   'History as a system', in his *History as a System and Other Essays towards a Philosophy of History*, 1962, p. 213.
36   Sartre, *Huis clos*, 1947, pp. 174, 180, 182.
37   *Being and Nothingness*, p. 50.
38   Ibid., p. 64.
39   *The Day of Judgement*, 1988, p. 299.
40   Sartre, *Cahiers pour une morale*, pp. 484–5.
41   *Being and Nothingness*, p. 265.
42   Ibid. Sartre's point is similar to the one urged more recently in many places by Thomas Nagel. See, for example, his 'Subjective and objective', in his *Mortal Questions*, 1979.
43   *Being and Time*, p. 179H.

8

Angst, Death and Absurdity

We now reach a number of related topics which, in the popular imagination, constitute the very stuff of existentialism. We have reached them late in the book, not because the popular image is entirely mistaken, but because, isolated from the movement of thought I have tried to describe, such topics can easily appear eccentric and morbid predilections, marginal to the central enterprise of philosophy.

Angst

I begin with a phenomenon whose place in existentialist thought is indeed pivotal – one to which Kierkegaard devoted more than one book and which, in Heidegger's grandiloquent words, 'provides the phenomenal basis for explicitly grasping *Dasein*'s primordial totality of Being'.[1] This is the phenomenon of *Angst.* Generally, I shall stay with the German word in preference to either the various English words offered as translations ('anxiety', 'dread') or other expressions favoured by some existentialists (Sartre's 'anguish', Jaspers' 'metaphysical fear'). The German word has the advantage, for English readers, of being known only in its fairly technical uses, so that it lacks the misleading connotations of the various English words. (German readers are, presumably, in a less happy situation.) 'Dread' is too suggestive of impending disaster, and 'anguish' of people tearing their hair out. 'Fear', as we shall see, is explicitly contrasted with '*Angst*' by most of our writers. The best of a bad bunch is 'anxiety', but this ordinarily refers to something more familiar and commonplace than existentialists have in mind.

To appreciate the strategic importance of *Angst* for the Existentialist, we need to recall the problem with which he was faced in the previous chapter. He had described everyday life as lived, for the most part, in bad faith, sunk in the 'they' and under the sway of the Other. Such descriptions presupposed an authentic existence from which average, everyday life is a 'fall' – an 'individualized' existence in which a person recalls himself from bad faith and the 'they'. But two questions immediately loomed. If this Promethean-sounding existence is our true one, how is it that we so persistently manage to avoid it? Second, what warrant is there in the first place for regarding this 'individualized' existence as authentic, and not as a self-delusive and perhaps pathetic endeavour to deny the essentially collective character of human life?

The charm of *Angst* for the Existentialist is that it provides an answer to both these questions. It is in the very nature of *Angst,* hardly a pleasing feeling, that people should generally endeavour to avoid it by 'fleeing' into bad faith and the comforting embrace of the 'they'. At the same time, it is a mood which intimates or attests to the 'individualized' nature of genuine existence. The answer to the first question relies to a degree on the answer to the second. Even if average everyday life is continued in a way that minimizes onsets of *Angst,* we could hardly describe it as 'flight', let alone as 'bad faith', unless the *Angst* which is suppressed is held to testify to the truth of human existence. Otherwise, our invidiously described 'tranquillized' life will be a way in which people sensibly protect themselves against gloomy and unfounded misapprehensions.

Partly because *Angst* can only explain the 'flight' into bad faith if it also testifies to why this *is* bad faith, I shall make only one point in connection with that first role. Clearly, the explanation could only work if *Angst* is an unwelcome, disturbing experience of which people want to be rid. Yet we sometimes find it described so that it sounds like none of these things. Heidegger refers to a 'sober anxiety' which can be accompanied by an 'unshakeable joy',[2] while there are passages in Sartre where *Angst* is made to sound positively exhilarating – the kind of sensation sought perhaps by Mlle de la Mole, whose cure for boredom was to 'play heads or tails with her whole existence'.[3]

The tension apparently created by these descriptions can be relaxed by distinguishing two stages of *Angst.* In the first instance, *Angst* is the disturbing and 'uncanny' mood which summons a person to reflect on his individual existence and its 'possibilities'. It is this which people are more than ready to pass off as a 'funny turn', returning with relief to the 'tranquillizing' ways of the 'they'. But suppose a person 'faces up' to his *Angst,* accepting the truths about his existence which it intimates. Then a number of options appears, including modulation into that resolute, sober and 'joyful' *Angst* to which Heidegger refers. But possible, too, is the derring-do of Mlle la Mole, or of Gide's Lafcadio in *Les Caves du Vatican,* who celebrates his escape from the 'they' by committing shocking *actes gratuits.* In this chapter I am concerned with the first, 'disclosive' stage of *Angst.* More precisely, my main concern is with the significance which our writers are agreed on ascribing to *Angst,* and not with various extra interpretations which some of them have, more idiosyncratically, added. Kierkegaard, for instance, sees a link between *Angst* and both sin and faith. In *Angst,* a person dimly discerns his potential for sinning against God, but also his potential for making an ungrounded 'leap of faith'.[4] In *Existentialism and Humanism,* Sartre understands it as the sense of 'complete and profound responsibility' which belongs with a person's 'fully realizing that he is not only choosing what he will be, but... deciding for the whole of mankind'.[5] The religious and moral meanings with which *Angst* is here being endowed are not, of course, without interest, and I discuss some of them in the final section of this chapter.

It should be no surprise that existentialists attribute an important disclosive role to *Angst,* for they are insistent that the world is revealed not only through 'cognitive' operations, but through action and mood. Without the *Befindlichkeit* (see p. 88 above) which gives us our stances towards the world, there would be nothing to think and have beliefs about. It is important here to be rid of the bad old habit of treating moods as mere inner tweaks and stirrings. One reason why this a bad habit is that moods are individuated by the ways in which objects appear to people – as threatening, say, or promising pleasure.

This raises a problem, however, for many existentialists are agreed that *Angst* is distinguished from ordinary fear precisely by its *lack* of particular objects. I fear a certain thing, like that rabid dog, whereas *Angst,* says Heidegger, often ' "does not know" what that in the face of which it is anxious is'. It does not follow, though, that it is ever undirected: in fact, it is always 'anxiety *about* something'.[6] There is no puzzle here if we distinguish between two different notions of 'object'. *Angst,* like any mental state, has an object in the sense of being *towards* or *about.* What it is directed towards, however, is not 'thing-like', not an 'entity within-the-world', such as the dog. It is not an object in the sense of a spatio-temporally located particular.

What, then, is the object of *Angst?* The problem now is not that the literature provides no answer, but a seemingly embarrassing abundance of different ones. Among the candidates are: myself, my freedom, nothingness, emptiness, the world, Being-in-the-world, finitude and death. This plethora, however, disguises a single, central thesis – one I shall now try to explain.

Let us begin with Sartre's low-key, and potentially misleading, illustrations of *Angst.* The first is the experience of vertigo, where 'I am afraid not of falling over the precipice, but of throwing myself over.'[7] The second is the ex-gambler's realization of the 'total inefficacy' that his vows of abstention have to stop him returning to the roulette wheel. In both cases there is 'anguish before myself', rather than fear of external events. And in both, a 'nothingness has slipped into the... relation' between different moments of a person's existence.[8] Nothing now present prevents the climber from throwing himself off the cliff the next minute, and nothing in the gambler's past – a 'boneless phantom' – determines that he will not now buy some chips.

The examples can wrongly suggest that Sartre's main concern is with the experience of freedom to choose a particular act. In fact, they are only clues to the bigger game which he is after. We get closer to this when he writes that *Angst* 'means that man is always separated by a nothingness from his essence', or that the 'self... exists in the perpetual mode of detachment from what is' or, finally, that I can always 'disengage myself from the world where I had been engaged'.[9]

The vertigo example was not accidental since vertigo has always provided existentialists with their favourite metaphor for *Angst*. Kierkegaard refers to it as the 'dizziness of freedom', while Jaspers describes metaphysical fear as 'the vertigo and trepidation of freedom facing a choice'.[10] Vertigo requires the presence of an abyss, the absence of a supporting ground. *Angst* likewise is the experience of groundlessness, the absence of anything holding one in place and anchoring one's actions. At a micro-level, it is the ex-gambler's realization that nothing 'secures' his vow to abstain. At a macro-level, it is Virginia Woolf's 'tragic' sense of life as 'a strip of pavement over an abyss'.[11] It is, then, the appreciation that none of the exigencies, values and commitments with which we find ourselves embroiled in everyday life furnishes sufficient grounding for the attitudes, interpretations and behaviour we adopt. In the 'disengagement' or 'detachment' of *Angst*, a person apprehends that exigencies and values – the summons of the alarm-clock, the need to get to work, the imperative to feed a family – only have the force which that person, unconstrained, grants to them: 'it is I who confer on the alarm-clock its exigency – I and I alone ... who makes ... values exist in order to determine [my] actions by their demands.'[12] At its deepest and most dramatic, *Angst* discloses 'a being which is compelled to decide the meaning of being'.[13]

For Sartre, then, *Angst* testifies to a freedom to be moved only by those 'appeals of the world' which a person *permits* to move him. The freedom thereby intimated deserves separate treatment (chapter 9). I want, in the meantime, to focus on an obviously related, but apparently distinguishable, dimension of *Angst*'s disclosure – its 'individualizing' message. This will relate the discussion to the problem encountered by the Existentialist at the end of the previous chapter. For this dimension of *Angst*, it is Heidegger to whom we turn.

Heidegger displays a greater awareness of the strategic importance of *Angst* than any other of our writers. If *Dasein* is not doomed to 'lose' itself in the 'they', there must be 'a way of disclosure in which *Dasein* brings itself before itself.'[14] This way is *Angst* which, in the now familiar manner, Heidegger distinguishes from fear of particular objects and events. Far from fearing these, the 'anxious' person experiences them as 'insignificant', 'not relevant'.

In *Angst,* says Heidegger, all 'entities within the world . . . *sink away*', so that the familiar world becomes 'uncanny' (*unheimlich*). This has the crucial consequence that a person's understanding of himself and his world can no longer be in the familiar 'terms of how things have been publicly interpreted'. It is for this reason that Heidegger can write that '*Angst* individualizes *Dasein* and thus discloses it as *solus ipse*.'[15]

This abstraction of, and by, an individual *Dasein* from the public world which has 'sunk away' is, however, very different from the one rehearsed by Descartes at the beginning of the *Meditations* or in Husserl's *epochē*. There the world is truly suspended, leaving only a disembodied, solipsistic *cogito* or 'pure' ego. For Heidegger, of course, there can be no question of abstracting myself from my Being-in-the-world, since no sense can be made of a person not engaged, through 'care', in a world. Indeed, it is precisely my Being-in-the-world towards which *Angst* is directed. This needs explaining.

What 'sinks away' in *Angst* is the world as interpreted by the 'they'. The usual meanings of things and actions fade as the everyday framework within which they have their slots becomes 'uncanny'. Heidegger puts this by saying that we are brought before 'the "nothing"', but is quick to add that this 'nothing' is 'the world as such'.[16] We know already that there can be no world except in relation to *Dasein*'s engagement and 'disclosure'. So Heidegger cannot mean by 'the world as such' some transcendent realm beyond any disclosure. 'The world as such' is not the public world of the 'they', but nor is it a different, more 'real' one. Rather, it is the world *considered as* a world; as the totality of what *Dasein*, through being 'in' it, discloses and is responsible for. The 'they' forgets and disguises the 'worldly' character of 'their' world. That it is but one, not especially privileged, product of a 'way of disclosing' is masked by 'their' inveterate tendency to pass off a system of meanings as inevitable – or, worse, to pretend that the world is not 'sign-like' at all, but a mere collection of things present-at-hand. It is this, the 'worldly' character of the world I am 'in', which is intimated by *Angst*. The strategic importance of *Angst* is that it is the experience of 'the possibility of a disclosure which is *quite distinctive*: for *Angst* individualizes.'[17]

There are for Heidegger further, somewhat Kierkegaardian, respects in which *Angst* 'individualizes'. If *Angst* intimates my potential for an individual, 'distinctive' disclosure of the world, it follows that I am not to be identified with the 'publicly interpreted' persona which I present to the 'they', with an 'anyone' whose identity is exhausted by the social roles I happen to occupy. In *Angst*, these aspects of myself 'sink away' into 'insignificance' as much as the things around me. To be sure, I am not therefore a 'soul-thing' who might be disengaged from social existence. But I come to appreciate that the shape and significance of my life do not have to be stamped upon it from the outside, but can belong to it in virtue of the ways in which, I, as an individual, take up the 'issue' which my existence is for me. This is getting close to the thought that to be an individual is to lend a 'wholeness' and integrity to one's life, and not to be 'dispersed' in the roles furnished by the 'they'. This is a thought I shall take up in the next section of this chapter, since it is one peculiarly related, for Heidegger, to a person's anticipation of death.

Another matter postponed until the next chapter is the crucial one of whether the radical freedom and authentic potentiality which the Existentialist takes *Angst* to intimate are in fact possible. Does *Angst* reveal something genuine or illusory? We do need, however, to consider a prior question. Is the Existentialist correct in his interpretation of *Angst* as the dark apprehension (even if finally illusory) of freedom and individuality? Unless he is, he has not found even the *prima facie* evidence he seeks, in the shape of a distinctive mood, for his claim that our lives are mostly inauthentic, self-estranged and in bad faith.

Iris Murdoch has suggested an alternative to, indeed a complete reversal of, the Existentialist's interpretation of *Angst*. What is disturbing about *Angst*, she argues, is not its awakening a person from the slumber he enjoys in the bosom of the 'they' and in the condition of bad faith, but on the contrary its indication that one does not enjoy the freedom in which it has become fashionable, not least through the popularity of existentialism, to believe: 'the heart of the concept...I would describe as a kind of fright which the conscious will feels when it apprehends the strength and direction of the personality which is not under its immediate control...the will is dismayed by the feeling that it ought now to be everything and in fact is not.'[18] I suffer *Angst*, then, not when I realize that the freedom and responsibility I have sloughed off to the 'they' is really mine, but when I discern that I am not in control of myself in the way I would like to think.

Murdoch's point is harmless if she is doing no more than draw attention to a mood, different from the one which concerns the Existentialist, which is reasonably described by words like '*Angst*' and 'anxiety'. (Indeed, it is one of which he himself speaks in discussion of modes of bad faith.) He can happily concede that Murdoch's mood is one to which such words, in their ordinary usage, may apply. None of this damages his description of the mood *he* has in mind under the heading of '*Angst*'.

It is clear, though, that Murdoch is objecting to more than the hijacking of a word and is challenging the Existentialist's diagnosis of what he has in mind. That mood is not an intimation of freedom but of hidden forces that preclude freedom. The Existentialist's reply will begin by pointing to a crucial ambiguity in this objection. Is Murdoch simply saying that the freedom and 'ownmost' potentiality intimated by *Angst* are illusions; that whenever people seem to apprehend them, they are really in the grip of unseen forces or motives? If so, she is denying that *Angst* has the impact of a demonstration of freedom and authentic potentiality, and hence preempting the question which is deferred until the next chapter. Or is she saying, in addition, that *Angst* is never even the illusion of freedom, but rather a discernment of our subjection to latent forces? Construed in this second way, the Existentialist will not find the point intelligible. El Dorado was an illusion, but that does not mean that the Spaniards did not search for it, nor that they could have been mistaken in thinking that this was what they were doing. Similarly, how could Sartre's gambler, say, have been *mistaken* in supposing that the intentional object of his *Angst* was his freedom, despite his past vows, to play at the roulette table? The Existentialist is describing an intentional state, and one cannot show that description to be mistaken – or even open to the possibility of mistake – merely by arguing that what it is directed towards has no actual existence. Perhaps the sense of authentic potentiality for 'distinctive' disclosure of which Heidegger speaks is a sense of what cannot be: but that is no objection to his describing *Angst* as constituted by such a sense. If people sometimes have such a sense – and nothing Murdoch says begins to show they do not – it will be this which warrants the description, and not the veracity of what is sensed.

Death

Most existentialist writers have devoted attention to the topic of death. This is not, as popularly supposed, out of preoccupation with the gloomier side of the human condition, nor due to a belief that death renders life pointless. The attention is explained, rather, by the conviction that the phenomenon of death reveals authentic possibilities of human existence.

The Existentialist's discussion of death continues that of *Angst.* For one thing, it is in relation to one's death that *Angst* is peculiarly liable to arise. 'Being-towards-death,' writes Heidegger, 'is essentially *Angst.*'[19] This mode of *Angst* testifies in an especially vivid way to what *Angst* in general intimates – the free, individualized character of existence. 'From this nothingness [i.e. death] alone can I obtain my assurance of true *Existenz,*' as Jaspers puts it.[20] Death is not itself the object of *Angst*: rather, its prospect occasions *Angst* towards its usual object, my Being-in-the-world and the issue this is for me. *Angst* is therefore to be distinguished from ordinary fear of death, its painful prelude and possibly hellish aftermath.

In at least two senses, it is not death as such which concerns the Existentialist. First, like Jaspers, he distinguishes 'existential' from 'vital non-being'. The latter ensues with clinical death, since I am no longer alive. But I could remain alive, yet cease to 'ex-ist': if, for example, I am rendered a hopeless vegetable by brain damage. The Existentialist is concerned with the finitude of existence, the fact that it ends, and not with the particular way – clinical death

– in which that end normally comes. Second, he is not concerned with the event – death, brain damage or whatever – which ends my existence, but with my life in relation to the prospect of that event. This is what Heidegger means by calling death an 'existential phenomenon', and by saying, 'when we speak of death, [it] does not signify *Dasein*'s Being-at-an-end, ... but a *Being-towards-the-end*... Death is a way to be.'[21] These remarks will occupy us later.

We will also need to clarify the several remarks by existentialists which give the impression that death is what gives meaning to life. De Beauvoir, for instance, notes with apparent approval Montaigne's dictum that 'the continuous work of life is to build death,' while Jaspers refers to death as 'throwing us back upon the fulfilment of *Existenz*'.[22] In a special sense it does turn out that, for the Existentialist, death or finitude is responsible for existence having meaning. But it is important, straightaway, to distinguish this from other senses. Jaspers, for example, makes it clear that death should never be thought of, in the *Liebestod* tradition, as the triumphant 'perfection' of the otherwise drab business of living. Nor, even with religious existentialists, is death the aim of life in the sense of a gateway to something better. The sentiment is not at all Mozart's, who wrote to his father: 'As death... is the real purpose of our life... [its] image is very soothing and comforting! And I thank God for affording me... the opportunity... of realizing that [it] is the key to our real happiness.'[23] The sense in which, for the Existentialist, death may confer a meaning on life comes closer, as we shall see, to the thought attributed by Anthony Kenny to Wittgenstein: 'If death has meaning, it is precisely as an end, a final end, of life. Wittgenstein described his father's death as beautiful, as a death worth a whole life. Perhaps, indeed, the test of a good life was that it was one that issued in a good death.'[24]

The main business is to explain why the Existentialist thinks the phenomenon of death – death as a prospect for each of us – reinforces and elaborates the testimony of *Angst* to the free, individualized character of existence. He has, I think, three points, the last of which is the most important one.

The first point is that a person's finitude is at least a necessary condition of his freedom and individuality. Sartre puts it unequivocally:

Death is the limit, but also a constituent of freedom... If a being were endowed with temporal infinity, he could realize all his possibilities... he would disappear with respect both to individuality (the realization of some possibilities to the exclusion of others) and to freedom (dangerous and irremediable choice of certain possibilities).[25]

If we lived for ever, each of us would eventually take up the same possibilities, so that no one could be individuated by the choices peculiar to him. Each of us would eventually taste everything on offer, so no real weight would attach to choosing this now rather than that later. 'Our lives would merge into universal indifference,' writes de Beauvoir, and 'there could be neither projects nor values.'[26]

Put like this, the point requires us to speculate on how things might be for us if we lived for ever – a requirement that the Existentialist may be advised to avoid. However things may be for immortals, he can argue, our actual sense of ourselves as free individuals is tied to recognition of our finitude. Not all choices need be 'dangerous', but it would damage our image of our freedom if nothing of final moment ever turned on the choices we make. Now the idea of choices being of moment and weight would not arise, arguably, if our lives had no temporal limit and every decision could one day be remedied and replaced. Nor is it clear that notions deployed in characterizing a person's individuality – the *shape* of his life, say, or the *story* to be told of it – could gain purchase if lives never ended. Shape demands boundaries, and a story which *could* not end is not a story. To be sure, a novel, *Nausea* for example, may have no end in that things are 'left in the air'. But the reader knows that Roquentin is not going to turn into a frog, nor go backwards in time, nor live for ever. Without that silent knowledge, the story – the coherence and direction of the episodes – falls apart. We should have no way of identifying episodes as significant, for we should have no grip, however loose, on what is significant in the characters' lives. In fiction and in fact, we must assume that a person's life is going in some directions and not others, and that whatever the direction, it will come to an end.

The second of the Existentialist's points is that attention to a particular aspect of a person's fate after death throws into sharper relief how things stand with him when alive. Put differently, the error of some ways of thinking of human life is brought out by recognizing that they are properly true only of people whose lives are ended. The point was already encountered in a different context when we were discussing Sartre's *Huis clos*. The bad faith in Garcin's whine that his life had 'fallen into the public domain' is made apparent by the irony that now, since he is dead, the complaint is indeed warranted. The crucial significance of death, for Sartre, is that it is the 'transformation into otherness of the whole person'. Death, he nicely puts it, is the act of 'supreme generosity', whereby I place myself totally at the disposal of others.[27] The dead man no longer has the opportunity, through future action, to give the lie to the Other's summation of him, nor to pit his own interpretation and evaluation of his life against the Other's. Without further possibilities, his freedom and individuality are absolutely alienated in favour of those who remain. It is this which is at the heart of Sartre's and de Beauvoir's horror at '*my* utter non-being'.[28] This particular kind of horror of what happens at death would be inexplicable if, as some of those writers mentioned in chapter 7 maintained, we were always, even when alive, constituted by the place we occupy in the schemes and categorizations of others. An appreciation of the way that, at death, we are delivered over to others carries with it the perception that this is not how matters stand before that event.

The last of the Existentialist's claims is encapsulated in Heidegger's remark that 'anticipation [of death] utterly individualizes *Dasein.*'[29] This individualization has two merging senses already encountered during the discussion of *Angst.* A person is individualized to the extent, first, that he withdraws from immersion in the world of the 'they' and, second, that he lends a wholeness and integrity to his life.

It was Kierkegaard who first focused on, and connected, these senses – not in relation to death, but to the 'despair' attendant on the 'aesthetic' way of life. By this last expression he does not have in mind only, or mainly, the kind of life led by an Oscar Wilde or Aubrey Beardsley. The 'aesthete' – whether in the shape of a dilettante, a Don Juan, or a busybody hopping from one activity to another – is a person 'sunk in immediacy'. He blows with the wind: following the latest fashion, chasing the latest girl, or indulging in the latest pursuit to cure his boredom. His is a life of 'despair', not because he is buried in gloom, but because his life 'hinges upon a condition outside of itself'.[30] Fashion, caprice, public opinion, external stimuli dictate the course of this life. The worst aspect of such an existence is that the person is dissolved into a 'multiplicity', and has lost 'the inmost and holiest thing of all in a person, the unifying power of personality'.[31] So the person who fails to follow Kierkegaard's imperative, 'Be an individual!', through drifting with the prevailing breeze which blows from the 'public', also fails to follow it through the absence of a 'unifying power' in his life.

Kierkegaard's conclusion, now in relation to death, is taken up by Heidegger and Jaspers. In anticipation of death, writes Heidegger, one is 'wrenched away from the "they"' and 'liberated from one's lostness in those possibilities which may be accidentally thrust upon one'. Only through this anticipation, furthermore, 'can it be made plain to what extent *Being-as-a-whole* ... is possible in *Dasein* itself'.[32] That is, I am 'individualized' through the prospect of my death, since it enables me both to 'wrench' myself away from the 'they' and to lend a wholeness to my life.

But how is this? By what process does anticipation of death enable this dual 'individualization'? An answer is suggested by Heidegger's badly misunderstood pronouncement, 'Death is *Dasein*'s ownmost possibility.'[33] Many critics have objected to both terms in this description. Death is 'ownmost', Heidegger seems to argue, because it is not 'delegatable'. 'Dying is something that every *Dasein* must take upon itself.'[34] This, his critics argue, is either false or trivial. That it is false, taken one way, is shown by cases like Sydney Carton's 'standing in for' Charles Darnay at the scaffold. To be sure, Carton could not die

Darnay's death in the sense that he could wear his hat, but nor, in that sense, could he have gone through Darnay's marriage or bout of flu. So, taken another way, it is trivially true of my death – as it is of my marriage and flu – that it is not 'delegatable'. Second, is it not absurd to describe death as a 'possibility' – unless one asserts as Heidegger does not, that there is also a possibility of immortality?

What these critics ignore is that the 'death' Heidegger describes as my 'ownmost possibility' is not the event of my demise, but what he calls my 'Being-towards-death'. And the 'dying' which cannot be 'delegated' is defined as a *'way of Being* in which *Dasein* is towards death'.[35] So it is a way of *living* in relation to the prospect of death, and not my execution or heart-attack, which is my 'ownmost possibility' – a possibility, in fact, which most people fail to take up, preferring as they do to be 'distracted' from and 'anaesthetized' against the prospect of their deaths.

This 'ownmost possibility' is none other than my living so as to become a totality, a Being-as-a-whole – a possibility whose realization requires a 'wrenching away' from those provided by the 'they'. But how, quite, is this possibility related to death, and why is it my 'ownmost'? The suspicion must lurk that Heidegger is punning on two senses of 'wholeness' or 'totality': that of having finite boundaries and that of being an integral unity. But the suspicion is not, I think, warranted. Heidegger is not punning, but trying to forge deep conceptual connections between the finitude and potential integrity of a life.

To begin with, it is my knowledge that there will be a final 'not yet' which enables me to range before it and order my other future and potential 'not yets'.[36] And it is in virtue of this ability that I can stand back from my present passing embroilments. For without a sense of a future direction and pattern, I should be without a perspective for assessing the significance of what I am about at present – my work, say, or a romantic involvement. It is an irony that an immortal creature, lacking an idea of its possible demise, could not take the long-term view which, as Heidegger puts it, 'liberates' a person from immediate embroilments. Because a day will never come for such a creature when it can say, *'This* is how I judge the significance of my life as a whole, its direction, its success or failure,' there cannot be a time when it stands back from its situation so as to assess the place it might occupy in that final judgement.

But we are still left without an explanation of why this possibility of wholeness is uniquely 'ownmost'. We get some help from Charles Guignon's remark: 'there is one possibility each of us has which is *not* delegatable . . . Although all the concrete roles I take over are public and not unique, there is one possibility that is mine alone: my Being-towards-death as the possibility of appropriating these public meanings in an integrated and coherent way.'[37] I suggest we understand the point in the following terms. There is nothing I ordinarily do of which I can say, 'It is impossible that anyone else, however suitably placed, should have done that.' Someone else might have written this book or married my wife in place of me. In that sense, everything I do is delegatable and anonymous. The exercise of my capacity to draw together all the possibilities which I have, or will have, taken up and to import a significance to this totality is not, however, similarly delegatable.

To be sure, I can approach a friend or biographer and give to him the brief of providing an interpretation of my life: but this is not at all like entrusting to a doctor or a colleague judgement on the significance of my headaches or my latest book. Their verdict cannot alter the significance of headache or book, whereas my 'delegating' to a biographer an assessment of my life, as well as my response to that assessment, are themselves significant ingredients of that life. They are to be put in the melting-pot along with everything else that forms the object of the assessment I am to make. I may perhaps accept the biographer's judgement of my life as, say, a well-intentioned failure: but that I accept it is itself a contribution to my life's significance. No biographer in the future could be entitled, in coming to a verdict on the significance of my life, to ignore the significance I myself attached to it, since this is an important part of the life which he is writing. I cannot, then, irredeemably transfer to others the 'appropriation' of the elements of my life in an 'integrated and coherent way', since any such provisional transfers, and their results, are further elements for an 'appropriation' which I alone can perform. It is in this sense that my Being-as-a-whole, whose possibility is provided by the prospect of death, is uniquely my 'ownmost'.

I close this section with two remarks. In chapter 6 I suggested that, for the Existentialist, the notion of the self is dependent on hyphenated concepts like self-concern and self-estrangement, and not the other way round. This thought has received some further grounding in this section, where it has emerged that the notion of an individualized person – a self, if you wish – depends on the integrity and wholeness which only a person's self-concern can confer. He attains to individuality or selfhood only if he is concerned so to do. He fails in this if he remains 'dispersed' in the possibilities of the 'they'; remains self-estranged, that is, in the sense of evading his 'ownmost' possibility of 'appropriating' the elements of his life for his Being-as-a-whole.

Finally, we have already seen what the Existentialist could *not* mean by speaking of death as imparting meaning to a life. It is not, for example, that a heroic martyrdom can turn an otherwise worthless existence into a triumphant one. If the Existentialist is to have sympathy with Wittgenstein's thought that a beautiful death is worth a whole life, that a good death is the test of a good life, it must be along the following lines. Without at least the possibility of a final judgement as death comes close, there can be no good life – not because that judgement can transmute the bad into the good, but because, without the prospect of that judgement lying ahead, a person cannot lend to his life the integrity and direction upon which the judgement is passed. A beautiful death is worth a *whole* life – or, better, they are equivalent in value. For the possibilities of imparting wholeness to one's life and of recognizing, at the end, that this wholeness has indeed been sculpted, are not to be separated.

Absurdity

'Most people feel on occasion that life is absurd,' writes Thomas Nagel, 'and some feel it vividly and continually.'[38] The Existentialist belongs to this smaller group, and does so because the absurdity which concerns him testifies to the same truths about the human condition as *Angst* and the anticipation of death. This suggestion may sound odd. If life is absurd, why should I experience *Angst* towards the course I am to give it, rather than sink into suicidal gloom or devil-may-care apathy? Moreover, if I declare my life to be absurd, how can anticipation of death, or anything else, call me to a sense of my life as a whole having meaning? The answer to these questions is, unsurprisingly, that the Existentialist's notion of absurdity is a special one. The senses of absurdity in which it is incompatible with *Angst* or conviction of purpose are not his sense. We should not conclude, though, that he is being merely melodramatic in his choice of vocabulary. There is, I shall argue, warrant for his use of 'absurd' to speak of the phenomenon which concerns him.

Let me begin with the instructive tale of Bartlebooth, from Georges Perec's bizarre novel, *Life: A User's Manual*. This rich English émigré in Paris 'resolved one day that his whole life would be organized around a single project... with no purpose outside of its own completion... No trace would remain of an operation which would have been... [for] fifty years, the sole... activity of its author.'[39] The project was to travel abroad and to do, every fortnight, a water-colour of a sea-port, which would then be posted to Paris, there to be cut into an ingenious jigsaw puzzle. The decades of painting over, Bartlebooth returned to Paris to solve the puzzles. As each one was solved, the painting would then be completely restored, sent to the port which was its subject and there destroyed. Bartlebooth dies at his desk with the last piece of the last puzzle in his hand. Unfortunately it is shaped W, while the remaining hole is shaped X.

Most would agree that Bartlebooth's project was absurd. There is, for a start, the irony of his death, a classic instance of death's way of mocking men's best-laid plans. Then there is the peculiarly self-erasing character of a project which, if successful, leaves no trace of itself. Finally there is the gap between the triviality of the project and the amazing earnestness with which Bartlebooth devotes himself to it. As Nagel points out, 'in ordinary life a situation is absurd when it includes a consipicuous discrepancy between pretension or aspiration and reality.'[40]

I shall exploit these aspects of absurdity, suggested by Perec's tale, as we proceed. The immediate task is to set aside certain senses of absurdity to be found in existentialist writings so that the central one can be isolated.

Sartre refers to 'the absurd character of death', by which he means that, as with Bartlebooth, death is rarely 'a resolved chord at the end of a melody'.[41] More often it cuts people off in the midst of their endeavours. This is not a theme on which he harps, however, and it is certainly not a reason he gives for labelling *life* as absurd. More important is the absurdity discussed in the chestnut-root passage from *Nausea* (see p. 53f. above). Roquentin concludes that the 'key' to his nauseous experience of the sheer 'thereness' of the root lies in a sense of its absurdity. The root is experienced as utterly 'superfluous', *de trop*: and not just the root, for 'I – weak, languid, obscene . . . – I too was superfluous.' This superfluity of objects and people is due, first, to their having no allotted place in any necessary scheme of things. 'What exists appears, lets itself be encountered, but you can never *deduce* it.' Of course, people invent gods or teleologies in an attempt to lend things a place in overarching schemes but, being illusions, they do not genuinely dispel the 'perfect gratuitousness' of existence. Second, particular entities are superfluous by 'overflowing' the categories in terms of which we try to capture them. Abstract away from the root its colour, shape and function, and still there is the sheerly existing particular 'beneath all explanation'.[42]

There are two reasons not to take the absurdity of *Nausea* as the mature Sartre's central notion. First, the theme of things' 'overflowing' the categories in which we describe them all but disappears from later writings where, as we have seen, the emphasis is upon the *humanness* of the world – its inseparability from the human designs in which things have their place. Superfluity continues to dog the human condition, but it is no longer the apprehension of 'being there for nothing, or being *de trop*' which is Sartre's reason for calling that condition 'absurd'. Second, this would surely be a *bad* reason for using that label. No doubt a person hitherto convinced, on religious grounds possibly, that every object and person has a necessary place in a total scheme might respond, when this conviction suddenly evaporates, by accusing the world of absurdity. Perhaps, like Roquentin, his disillusion 'turns [his] stomach over and everything starts floating about'. But without the prior conviction that everything should have an ordained place and purpose, it is hard to see why the fact that it does not should bring down a verdict of absurdity upon reality.

Roquentin's idea of absurdity is akin to the famous one propunded by Camus in *The Myth of Sisyphus.* According to Camus, man has a fundamental 'longing for reason', especially for a world as a unitary whole within which everything has its demonstrable station and value – the sort of world Leibniz and Hegel purported to provide. Unfortunately, people have now recognized the 'irrationality' of reality and hence 'despair of true knowledge'. Yet a 'nostalgia' for reason remains, and it is the confrontation between this and reality, rather than the latter's irrationality alone, which constitutes absurdity. From the 'encounters' between a 'human need and the unreasonable silence of the world', the absurd is 'born'.[43] Here, then, there is just the kind of discrepancy between aspiration and reality of which Nagel spoke.

Popular images notwithstanding, Camus' outlook is not at all that of the Existentialist. Reality is irrational, for Camus, because it is 'chaotic' and shot through with antinomies and paradoxes. No such thought, however, is to be found in Heidegger, Sartre or Merleau-Ponty. It is true that, according to some 'religious existentialists', like Jaspers and Marcel, there are 'mysteries' which can only be resolved if the empirical world is viewed as an aspect of a larger, transcendent reality. But, for that very reason, they do not think there is something *finally* irrational about reality in Camus' sense. Here it is worth recalling why, in chapter 1, I urged that Camus not be included in a list of mainstream existentialists. Existentialism starts with an attempt to 'overcome' people's sense of alienation from the world. But it is precisely the sense of a 'divorce' between ourselves and a recalcitrant world in which Camus positively revels. In the first half of this book, the Existentialist was challenging the grounds for this divorce, while since then the estrangement which has concerned him has been *self*-estrangement. And this latter mode of estrangement is, if he is right, due to too cosy and intimate an absorption in the world about us. Self-estrangement begins only after the mollification of that 'primitive hostility of the world' which, for Camus, is ineradicable.

The final sense I want to set aside is the one indicated in one of Sartre's best-known lines, 'man is a useless passion' (*une passion inutile*).[44] This 'passion' is the human being's futile 'project to metamorphose [his] own For-itself into an In-itself-For-itself'. This is futile, since no creature can both freely determine its essence and have its existence determined by an essence. In effect, this 'useless passion' combines bad faith, wherein the person wishes on himself the status of an object, and the desire nonetheless to remain totally free. What makes it absurd is less the impossibility of success than the person's pursuit of the project despite recognizing its impossibility. Like Bartlebooth, Sartre's man presses ahead knowing that nothing will come of the project. But it cannot be this futility which prompts Sartre to regard life as such as absurd, for the simple reason that some people, the 'authentic' ones – himself included, presumably – manage to avoid it. Not everyone is for ever doomed to live in the bad faith which the 'useless passion' involves. Life as such cannot be absurd on the above count if some of us manage to resist the temptation of bad faith.

What, then, is the remaining and central notion of absurdity with which the Existentialist is left? Most of the answer is provided by Sartre through his claim that the being of the For-itself is freedom. The claim entails that 'we shall never apprehend ourselves except as a choice in the making', this 'choice' being the 'fundamental' one of a stance towards things, others and ourselves; the 'choice' which 'causes there to be a world' for the For-itself.[45] This 'choice' is not determined, since all determinations – motives and desires, for example – operate only *within* a 'chosen' world. There can be no rational basis for it, since justifications and reasons are also relative to the fundamental stance adopted.

Sartre continues: 'Such a choice made without basis of support and dictating its own causes to itself...is absurd. This is because freedom is a *choice* of its being but not the *foundation* of its being.'[46] He adds almost immediately that 'this choice is absurd...because there has never been any possibility of not choosing oneself.' But this addition makes a different, and very feeble, point. There is nothing faintly paradoxical in the idea that the freedom one enjoys is not something which is itself the outcome of free choice, Here, surely, Sartre is carried away by metaphors like his own 'Man is condemned to be free' or Ortega's 'I am free by compulsion.' If one is trying to capture the (unsurprising) thought that freedom is not itself freely chosen, one could just as well employ metaphors with a less initially paradoxical ring. Jaspers, for example, refers to freedom as a *gift*.

Let us return to the point being made in the quotation from Sartre at the beginning of the last paragraph. This becomes clearer when, a page later, he writes:

> Precisely because here we are dealing with a *choice,*... [it] indicates other choices as possibles. This possibility... is lived in the feeling of unjustifiability; and it is this which is expressed by the fact of the *absurdity* of my choice and consequently of my being.[47]

To exist at all, I must be 'engaged', for example through my having values, without which nothing could appear more worth doing than anything else – in which event, like Buridan's ass, I should remain paralysed. Yet these values, which justify my particular everyday choices, are themselves the outcome of a 'fundamental choice' for which no justification is available. It is in this tension, between the necessary seriousness with which we are engaged through our beliefs or values and their lack of a justificatory ground, that absurdity is located.

Sartre is ready with a reply to one predictable objection. Absurdity, it will be said, is a relative notion, with certain lives, like Bartlebooth's, recognizable as absurd only in contrast to others which are not. Sartre acknowledges this relative notion. Something is absurd in this sense when it is not supported by reasons we normally expect to be forthcoming. Something is *absolutely* absurd, however, when it is 'beyond all reasons' in that it is impossible that reasons should ever be forthcoming.[48] But this needs qualifying. In *Being and Nothingness,* at least, Sartre is not saying that all contingent phenomena, like the chestnut-root, are absurd, although they too are 'beyond all reason'. Absurdity is a privilege of the For-itself and is constituted not by the lack of grounds for 'fundamental choice' alone, but by the tension between this and the seriousness of engagement in the world. The following words – not Sartre's, in fact, but Nagel's – make the point with admirable clarity:

> We cannot live human lives without energy and attention, nor without making choices which show that we take some things more seriously than others. Yet we have always available a point of view outside the particular form of our lives, from which the seriousness appears gratuitous. These two inescapable viewpoints collide in us, and that is what makes life absurd. It is absurd because we ignore the doubts that we know cannot be settled, continuing to live with nearly undiminished seriousness in spite of them.[49]

There will be those who, sympathetic to such descriptions of the human condition, hesitate nevertheless to apply the label of absurdity. This hesitation is understandable given the naturalness of the inference from life's absurdity to its worthlessness, its fitness only for mockery or a speedy end. Those who, unlike Sartre, feel impelled to make such an inference are well advised to eschew the word 'absurdity' and to speak, perhaps, of life's ineradicable irony instead. But the choice of a word is of less moment than the considerations giving rise to the need for such a choice.

The relation of absurdity to the earlier topics of this chapter should now be reasonably clear. What was dimly intimated by *Angst* is one of the two aspects of existence whose confrontation makes for absurdity. The 'anxious' person, disengaged from everyday exigencies, discerns that it is up to him to 'decide the meaning of being' – a perception which fails, absurdly, to diminish the sense of exigency with which for the most part everyday life is lived. In *Angst* a person recognizes that the pavement is Virginia Woolf's 'thin strip over an abyss', yet to move around at all, he must take the stones beneath him to be built on secure foundations.

Anticipation of death is an 'individualizing' attitude which, with special poignancy, frees a person from his embroilment in the 'they'. This individuality is also an ingredient in life's absurdity. For while it is *my* 'fundamental choice' which 'causes there to be a world' for me, I act in everyday life as if a settled, determinate world dictates to me rules and values that are not subject to my 'choice'.

Angst, anticipation of death, and a sense of life's absurdity together form a triad which, for the Existentialist, indicates the radically free, individualized character of human existence. Whether the indications are genuine and, if so, how we should then respond are matters for the final chapter. In the remainder of this section I make two further points – one historical, the other critical.

All existentialist writers, I think, recognize the tension or collision which prompts Sartre to speak of life's absurdity, even though they may not follow this appellation. On one interpretation, Kierkegaard's central claim in *Either/Or* is that there can be no non-circular justification for the choice of the 'ethical' as against the 'aesthetic' way of life. Yet the person who chooses the 'ethical' must then live as if the rules which now guide his actions possess a certainty at odds with the voluntaristic nature of their adoption.[50] Nietzsche thinks that it is up to each of us to forge a 'perspective' on the world and ourselves out of many possible ones. Once it is forged, then the 'higher' man at least will live it with a seriousness for which there is no warrant beyond the individual's will.[51]

Or consider, in a little more detail, Jaspers' position. Throughout his voluminous writings, a reiterated theme is the 'tension between the apparent undecidability' of our guiding beliefs and 'the reality of resolute self-comportment'.[52] The paradox, as he sees it, is that 'we cannot be content with any standpoint that is stated as objectively valid, and yet we have to occupy a standpoint at every moment.' Without actually using the word 'absurd', Jaspers does refer to the 'inherently dubious and brittle' nature of this, the 'antinomical structure' of our existence. And there is one epithet, hardly more flattering than 'absurdity', which he likes to apply to our existence as such – 'guilt'. This is 'the true, inexculpable guilt of having spurned possibilities of *Existenz*', the thought here being Sartre's, that we must choose some possibilities at the expense of others, but without objective justification.[53]

Lastly, a final lesson to be learnt from Bartlebooth. Some existentialists give the impression that life's absurdity may be 'overcome'. De Beauvoir, for instance, thinks that we can 'escape the absurdity of [contingency] by escaping the absurdity of the pure moment'. This is done through incorporating each 'moment' of life within 'the unity of the project' of a whole life. Thereby the 'moment' ceases to be 'a stupid and opaque fact'.[54] So it seems to be the 'wholeness' discussed earlier through which life can be saved from absurdity. But this, surely, is insufficient. Few lives possess the tight structure and integrity of Bartlebooth's, with each 'moment' – each water-colour, say – taking its place in a carefully executed life-plan. Yet his life was an absurd one. More generally, the absurdity which concerns Sartre is not something which, if it is a real feature of our existence at all, could be 'overcome'. It would be an essential, ineradicable aspect of the human condition.

Religious Intimations

In the previous sections of this chapter, we have been considering the implications drawn by existentialist authors from the phenomena of *Angst,* confrontation with mortality, and the 'absurdity' or 'unfoundedness' of epistemic and moral commitments. Each of these phenomena, the authors argued, attest to or intimate the radical individuality, freedom and responsibility of human beings. And in the light of this demonstration, the authors feel entitled to what would otherwise be the loaded descriptions, encountered in chapter 7, of everyday life as something lived, for the most part, 'inauthentically', in 'bad faith' and under the dominion of the 'herd' or the 'they'.

A question raised at this point by some writers in the existentialist tradition is whether phenomena such as *Angst* attest to something more than individuality and freedom, in particular whether they are replete with *religious* significance. It has often been remarked that, of all modern philosophical tendencies, existentialism has had by far the most pronounced impact upon theology. 'Existentialist theology' is hardly a precise term, being applied to the thought of such different figures as Kierkegaard, Buber, Marcel, Paul Tillich, Rudolf Bultmann and Nikolai Berdyaev. What is characteristic of such figures, however, is precisely their conviction that phenomena of the type discussed in this chapter do carry religious significance, that in one way or another they are intimations of the divine. Thus, as Heidegger notes in *Being and Time,* 'the phenomena of anxiety and fear...have come within the purview of Christian theology,' mentioning in particular Kierkegaard's analysis of anxiety 'in the context of...the problem of original sin'.[55] He presumably had in mind such remarks of Kierkegaard's as that anxiety 'approaches sin as closely as possible'[56] – remarks enthusiastically taken up by later theologians like Bultmann, who seems actually to equate 'the real crux of [original] sin' with 'dread'.[57]

Angst is only the most prominent of existential phenomena which have offered themselves to religious interpretation. So too has the related notion of guilt. That I can still experience guilt, however rigorously I obey the dictates of morality, means for Kierkegaard that there is a higher authority than the ethical – a God in comparison with whom I am bound to feel unworthy whatever I do. In a less theistic but nevertheless religious vein, Jaspers argues that the 'inexculpable guilt of having spurned possibilities of *Existenz*' is a vivid indicator of human 'finitude', of freedom's necessity to operate within limits. Like other indicators of finitude, such as our sense of mortality, it therefore points towards 'Transcendence', to that with which finitude necessarily contrasts – to 'an origin other than that which science makes intelligible to [man] in his finite existence'.[58] Other authors, such as Marcel (see chapter 10 below) and Buber, focus upon the religious intimations of our authentic relationships with other people. In Buber's romantic example, 'He who loves a woman . . . is able to look into the *Thou* of her eyes into a beam of the eternal *Thou.*' For Buber, indeed, the whole sense that the world in which we live and act is not 'alien', but imbued with meanings – a sense, of course, defended by existential phenomenology – can only find its final 'inexpressible confirmation' through acceptance of there being a divine 'Presence' in that world.[59]

The question, then, concerns the legitimacy or persuasiveness of these and other attempts, characteristic of 'existentialist theology', to read into phenomena, whose importance the Existentialist himself emphasizes, a religious significance beyond anything that he has, as yet, assigned to them? Before addressing that question, however, we need to consider arguments which, if well taken, would stop 'existentialist theology' in its tracks. I refer to the arguments behind Sartre's claim that 'existentialist theology' is an oxymoron, that existentialism is totally incompatible with religious belief.

Early on in *Existentialism and Humanism*, Sartre divides existentialists into 'two kinds' – 'the Christians', such as Jaspers and Marcel, and 'the atheists', including himself and Heidegger. (Sartre's scholarship here is inept. Jaspers' 'philosophical faith' is far from an obviously Christian one, and Heidegger's position defies classification as theistic or atheistic.) In making this distinction, Sartre bears some responsibility for the subsequent and unfortunate tendency among commentators to suppose that the question 'religious or atheistic?' is the first and most pressing one to ask of any existentialist thinker. Be that as it may, Sartre soon makes clear his view that 'the Christians' occupy an indefensible position.

Sartre's arguments, in his lecture and in *Being and Nothingness*, are of three kinds. First, he argues that 'the idea of God is contradictory.' Various reasons are offered, couched in a Scholastic terminology which makes them sound like the 'Objections' which St Thomas Aquinas rehearsed and went on to refute. The most important one is to the effect that God, as conceived by theists, would, impossibly, have to be something both 'In-itself' and 'For-itself'. As a consciousness or For-itself, He would be 'a being who is not what he is and who is what he is not', one which is a 'lack', a 'nothingness', dependent on a reality present to His consciousness. But, as 'the foundation of the world', He would also have to be 'all positivity' or In-itself, lacking and dependent upon nothing.[60] (One is reminded of such Scholastic conundrums as how a complete and perfect God could need or want to create the world.)

A second set of arguments urges that a Creator-God is incompatible with human freedom. Sartre considers and rejects Leibniz's attempt to show that, in a sense, Adam did not *have* to take the apple, despite everything happening in accordance with divine necessity. The fact that *our* knowledge of Adam does not preclude our conceiving of Adam's possible rejection of the apple – which is Leibniz's point – cannot alter the fact that *God*'s knowledge excludes this, nor the fact that Adam did not choose to be what he was and hence was without 'responsibility for his being'. More generally, once it is conceded that a Creator-God furnished each of us with an 'essence', so that each person is 'the realization of a certain conception which dwells in the divine understanding',[61] there is no way of salvaging the central existentialist tenet that a man's 'existence comes before [his] essence,' that he *is* only what he makes of himself.

For either or both of two reasons, existentialists of a religious orientation will find these arguments of Sartre's uncompelling. First, even if they embrace a fairly traditional conception of God, of the sort Sartre has in mind, they are willing, indeed eager, to embrace the familiar 'paradoxes' which that conception seems to involve. Sartre might be right, for example, to identify a puzzle as to how men can be both free yet the creatures of an omniscient Creator: but, for Buber, this only means that I cannot and should not try to 'escape the paradox that has to be lived' in holding both that 'I am given over for disposal' and that 'It depends on myself.'[62] As for the 'paradox' that God would have to be both In-itself and For-itself, this would surely be handled by Kierkegaard, for one, in the same way he handles that of a God who is at once transcendent yet present on earth in the body of Christ. The Incarnation is an 'absolute paradox': but it is precisely a 'passion for paradox' that inspires, and is presupposed by, that 'leap of faith' which enables us to 'discover something that thought cannot think'.[63] For Kierkegaard, indeed, 'proofs' of God's *non*-existence are more conducive to authentic faith than 'proofs' of His existence. These latter 'proofs' could anyway and at best establish the existence of what Pascal called the God of 'philosophers and scientists' – one 'abhorrent to Christianity' – not the God of Abraham, Isaac and Jacob, the God of love and faith in whom we have our being.[64]

Second, it is clear that many religious existentialists do not subscribe to those traditional conceptions of God – as an exalted substance, a supreme Creator, a perfect Person or the like – against which Sartre's arguments are directed. Thus, the transcendent 'Encompassing' which is the object of Jaspers' 'philosophical faith' bears scant resemblance, to judge from the little Jaspers feels entitled to say about it, to the personal God of the Abrahamic religions. Among 'existentialist theologians' at large, above all Bultmann, the tendency has been a 'demythologizing' one which, in moving away from conceptions of God as a highly spectacular entity or person, seeks to focus our attention on the religious sense and the religious way of life. With God demythologized, it is not clear, in particular, that there remain the logical difficulties, agonized over by St Augustine and highlighted by Sartre, of reconciling human freedom with divine reality.

Sartre, however, deploys a third kind of argument, which simultaneously militates against belief in God and indicates the tension between such belief and the authentic existentialist stance to life. Crudely put, the argument is that religious belief is a symptom of bad faith. As such, it follows both that religious belief is explicable without assuming its truth, and that it cannot be part of the · authentic life. As Sartre sees it, God is an ideal projection of something that human beings, living in bad faith, impossibly aspire to be. In 'flight' from their own freedom – which, nevertheless, they cannot want entirely to forswear – they seek to enjoy the status of a being which is 'its own foundation', and hence to combine freedom with the possession of a fixed, defined nature. Because that combination is impossible, man – with his 'desire to be God' – is a 'useless passion'.[65]

Sartre's inspiration for this style of argument is surely Nietzsche. The German famously pronounced that 'God is dead,' but spent less time trying to establish this than on a 'genealogical', debunking account of why people should ever have believed He was alive. Like Sartre and many other later thinkers, Nietzsche regards religious belief as a manifestation of the incapacity of people – 'weak' ones, 'botched and bungled' ones, at least – to accept the world and human life as it is, and hence of their need to postulate a mythical 'true world', to 'imagine another, *more valuable*' world than the actual one.[66] That religious belief has such a disreputable 'genealogy' does not, of course, entail that it is false, but it does scotch any reason for supposing it is true. And certainly those with the strength to face up to the responsibility to create values and meaning – the 'Overmen' – will be without any inclination to religious belief.

Unlike his earlier ones, the Nietzschean line of argument deployed by Sartre genuinely engages with the issue raised earlier, concerning the religious intimations of phenomena such as *Angst*. For where religious existentialists detect genuine intimations of this sort, Nietzsche and Sartre look for explanations of a debunking kind for religious interpretations of the phenomena.

Consider, for instance, the phenomena of guilt and shame – that 'metaphysical' guilt or shame, as Jaspers calls it, which people can experience whatever they do, however they act, and which Heidegger had in mind when remarking '*Dasein as such is guilty.*'[67] We saw earlier how a number of authors have wanted to interpret such a phenomenon in religious terms. Akin to the Christian sense of 'original sin', 'metaphysical' guilt or shame points to a God or divine presence before whom, or in comparison with whom, it is experienced. For Nietzsche, this gets things back to front. A sense of abiding guilt is a function of belief in God, not a ground for that belief. In the story he tells, the 'weak' have a vested interest in persuading the 'strong', who might otherwise ride roughshod over them, that there exists a punitive God forever watchful of them. Guilt is then the sense of one's liability to eternal punishment at the hands of this vigilant God.[68] For Sartre too, the Christian interpretation of shame has things the wrong way round. Shame, in his view, is the disturbing sense of being a mere object before 'the Look' of other people (see pp. 105ff. above).

Now for religious believers, there is a being by whose 'Look' I am perpetually threatened and reduced to objecthood. Hence, for such believers, there is 'shame before God . . . the recognition of my being-an-object before a subject which can never become an object'.[69] 'Metaphysical' shame, then, does not 'point to' the existence of God: rather, it is the product of an antecedent belief in an ever-Lookful 'Other'. Heidegger too rejects 'any employment' of the phenomena of guilt, shame and conscience 'for proofs of God or for establishing an "immediate" consciousness of God',[70] seeing in them, rather, a sense of the final lack of justification for – the 'null basis' for – one's projects in life.

Where on this and related disputes should the Existentialist stand? With whom, if anyone, does the 'best wisdom' he seeks to extract from existentialist writings reside – with those who discern intimations of the divine in such phenomena as *Angst* and the sense of life's 'absurdity', or with those who not only deny such intimations but hold that religious conviction is incompatible with the central insights of existentialism? Should he take sides on the issue, remain studiously neutral, or perhaps seek some compromise?

The Existentialist, I suggest, is not sure. What he is sure of, however, is the need for certain clarifications and assurances from 'existentialist theologians' before he can seriously consider incorporating their perspective into his overall outlook. First, he will require more clarification than is apt to be provided by these authors on the precise sense in which phenomena like *Angst* 'intimate', 'point to' or 'manifest' matters of religious moment. Unless this is provided, the suspicion will remain that Nietzsche and Sartre have it right: while someone already committed to religious belief will interpret the phenomena in the light of that belief, the phenomena themselves provide no basis for it. What the religious existentialist needs to do, in effect, is to argue that just as phenomena like *Angst* are deeply puzzling unless seen as attesting to a dim sense of human freedom and individuality, so they remain puzzling unless they are also seen as testimony to a sense of living in the presence of God. It is far from clear to the Existentialist that any of them have produced a compelling argument of this kind.

Second, the Existentialist will seek assurance that the phenomena alleged to intimate the divine are the *same* phenomena with which he has been concerned. When discussing Iris Murdoch's remarks on *Angst* (pp. 132ff. above), we saw how easy it is to 'change the subject'. The *Angst* she describes is simply not the same phenomenon as the Existentialist had been discussing. Consider, in this connection, the theologian Reinhold Niebuhr's remark that 'Anxiety is the internal description of the state of temptation.'[71] 'Anxiety' is an elastic term, and perhaps one form of anxiety is appropriately described as an experience of temptation. But this is, rather obviously, not the form which the Existentialist had in mind under the heading of '*Angst*'. Hence, whatever religious intimations Niebuhr's 'state of temptation' might have, they are not those of the phenomenon with which the Existentialist has been engaged. Again, when theologians like Buber refer to a sense of absurdity which can only be laid to rest by recognizing that the world is imbued with divine meaning and purpose, the subject seems, once more, to have been changed. The Existentialist's sense of absurdity concerned the gap between the seriousness with which we take our epistemic or moral commitments and the perceived lack of final foundations or grounds for these. The connection between this and Buber's sense is opaque. For one thing, existentialist absurdity is, as earlier remarked (p. 144 above), not something to 'overcome', but rather to recognize and live with, whereas the sense of absurdity of which the theologians speak is something to triumph over with the realization that the world has religious purpose.

Finally, and unsurprisingly, the Existentialist will seek assurance that the religious intimations some authors find in the relevant phenomena are of a kind compatible with his general position. He need not side with Sartre in holding that a religious perspective of any sort is incompatible with that position. 'Religious perspective' is surely too generous and amorphous a category to hold that. But when, for example, Miguel de Unamuno argues that the significance for us of death displays a 'hunger for personal immortality' and a recognition, therefore, of an unbridgeable dualism between the spirit and 'the man of flesh and bone',[72] the Existentialist must of course demur. In this very important respect, at least, Unamuno has departed the existentialist fold.

Only after receiving clarification or assurances on these matters, will the Existentialist either fully understand the stance of religious existentialists or be in a position to pass some judgement upon it. In other words: whether or not there can be a 'religious existentialism' – a philosophical account in religious terms of the world, humans being and the relations between them – which is compatible with existentialism's 'best wisdom' remains a moot question.

Notes

1   *Being and Time,* 1962, p. 182H.
2   Ibid., p. 310H.
3   Stendhal, *The Red and the Black,* 1953, p. 152.
4   See, for example, Kierkegaard, *The Sickness unto Death,* 1954, pp. 80ff.
5   *Existentialism and Humanism,* 1966, p. 30. Sartre uses '*angoisse*' here, so perhaps he is not talking of *Angst,* although in *Being and Nothingness* '*angoisse*' certainly is his term for *Angst.* Incidentally, the example Sartre offers to illustrate this 'profound responsibility' – a general deciding on a costly attack – surely illustrates something quite different. It is one thing to 'decide for mankind' by risking a nuclear holocaust,

quite another to 'decide for' it in the intended sense of prescribing a universal principle or maxim.

6 *Being and Time,* pp. 186, 187H.
7 *Being and Nothingness: An Essay on Phenomenological Ontology,* 1957, p. 29.
8 Ibid., p. 31.
9 Ibid., pp. 35, 39.
10 Soren Kierkegaard, *The Concept of Anxiety,* 1980, p. 61: Karl Jaspers, *Philosophy,* vol. 2, 1970, p. 232.
11 *Diaries,* 1985, entry for Oct. 1920.
12 Sartre, *Being and Nothingness,* pp. 36–7.
13 Ibid., p. 556.
14 Heidegger, *Being and Time,* p. 182H.
15 Ibid., pp. 187–8H.
16 Ibid., p. 187H.
17 Ibid., p. 190H.
18 Iris Murdoch, *The Sovereignty of the Good,* 1985, pp. 38–9.
19 *Being and Time,* p. 266H.
20 *Philosophy,* vol. 2, p. 198.
21 *Being and Time,* p. 245H.
22 De Beauvoir, *The Ethics of Ambiguity,* 1948, p. 7; Jaspers, *Philosophy,* vol. 2, p. 200.
23 Quoted in H. C. Robbins-London, *1791: Mozart's Last Year,* 1988, p. 58.
24 'Wittgenstein's meaning of life', 1989, p. 18.
25 *Cahiers pour une morale,* 1983, pp. 338–9.
26 *The Prime of Life,* 1965, p. 606.
27 *Cahiers pour une morale,* pp. 53–4.
28 *The Prime of Life,* p. 601.
29 *Being and Time,* p. 266H.
30 Kierkegaard, *Either/Or,* 1974, vol. 2, p. 240.
31 Ibid., p. 164.
32 *Being and Time,* pp. 264, 249H. Jaspers puts it by saying that death is 'the test that proves *Existenz* and relativizes mere existence'. *Philosophy,* vol. 2, p. 196.
33 Ibid., p. 258H.
34 Ibid., p. 240H.
35 Ibid., p. 274H. The critics referred to include Sartre, *Being and Nothingness,* pp. 533ff., and Paul Edwards, *Heidegger on Death,* 1979. Sartre, always impatient to press on towards his own theses, is rarely at his best when analysing the writings of others. For Edwards' scoffing little book, there is less excuse.
36 Ibid., pp. 242ff., 264H.
37 *Heidegger and the Problem of Knowledge,* 1983, p. 135.
38 'The absurd', in his *Mortal Questions,* 1979, p. 11.
39 Georges Perec, *Life: A User's Manual,* 1988, pp. 117–19.
40 'The absurd', p. 13.
41 *Being and Nothingness,* p. 533.
42 Sartre, *Nausea,* 1986, pp. 184ff.
43 Albert Camus, *The Myth of Sisyphus,* 1986, p. 22ff.

44 *Being and Nothingness*, p. 615.
45 Ibid., p. 479.
46 Ibid.
47 Ibid., p. 480.
48 Ibid., p. 479. See also *Nausea*, p. 185.
49 'The absurd', p. 14.
50 See Alasdair MacIntyre, *After Virtue*, 1981, pp. 38ff. Elsewhere Kierkegaard has a good deal to say about absurdity, but he has in mind the religious paradoxes which a 'knight of faith', like Abraham, is able to take on board. See the final section of this chapter.
51 Alexander Nehamas, *Nietzsche: Life as Literature*, 1985, is good on this aspect of Nietzsche's philosophy.
52 *Einführung in die Philosophie*, 1985, p. 74.
53 Jaspers, *Philosophy*, vol. 2, pp. 109, 218. Heidegger, too, speaks of this kind of 'guilt' in an especially opaque section of *Being and Time*, pp. 280Hff.
54 *The Ethics of Ambiguity*, pp. 26–7.
55 *Being and Time*, p. 492, n. iv.
56 *The Concept of Anxiety*, p. 92.
57 Quoted in David Brown, *Continental Philosophy and Modern Theology*, p. 91.
58 *The Perennial Scope of Philosophy*, pp. 64ff.
59 *I and Thou*, pp. 106, 110.
60 *Being and Nothingness*, pp. 615, 90.
61 Ibid., p. 468; *Existentialism and Humanism*, p. 27.
62 *I and Thou*, p. 96.
63 *Philosophical Fragments*, pp. 37ff.
64 *Pensées*, No. 449.
65 *Being and Nothingness*, pp. 566, 615.
66 *The Will to Power*, Section 579.
67 *Being and Time*, p. 285H.
68 See especially Essay I of *The Genealogy of Morals*.
69 *Being and Nothingness*, p. 290.
70 *Being and Time*, p. 269H.
71 *The Nature and Destiny of Man*, vol. I, p. 182.
72 *Tragic Sense of Life*, pp. 36, 115.

9

Existential Freedom

In my original plan, the middle chapter was to have been on freedom, thereby attesting to the importance of this concept for existentialists rather as the position of the *Crucifixus* in some Masses symbolizes the centrality, for Christians, of the event depicted. But this would have been a mistake, for existential freedom is more the culmination of a movement of thought described in my earlier chapters, and is only intelligible in terms of that. Too many commentators rush into discussion of this concept without due attention to the larger philosophy in which it is set. By postponing discussion to this late stage I do not relegate the concept, but do justice to its culminative position.

Existential freedom is a fusion of earlier considerations – the 'human world', ex-istence, individualization and wholeness, etc. – brought into the orbit of practical philosophy, into connection, that is, with matters of responsibility and commitment. When Sartre writes of his doctrines of the For-itself and the precedence of existence over essence that 'all this is to say one and the same thing...that man is free,'[1] he makes clear that, in a sense, he adds nothing new by proclaiming human freedom. Rather, he switches the focus on to the practical. A man, being free, 'carries the weight of the whole world on his shoulders...[He] is the one by whom it happens that *there is* a world;...he is also the one who makes himself...It is therefore senseless to think of complaining since nothing foreign has decided what we are.'[2] Here, the existential phenomenologist's insistence on the 'humanness' of the world is yoked with the later insistence on the 'individualization' which makes you or me, not man in general, 'the maker of a world'. The practical purpose of this fusion is to bring out the radical responsibility each of us bears. Judgement on the concept of existential freedom would depend, therefore, on assessments of existential phenomenology, the accounts of *Angst* and 'individualization', and the success of combining these with a thesis of each person's total responsibility for his life.

Freedom and Constraint

These preliminaries already help to dispel some misconceptions about existential freedom. First, it needs to be distinguished sharply from political or social liberty. Since we are all 'condemned to be free', our freedom cannot depend on the liberal or Draconian complexion of our society. Jupiter thinks he is being clever in pointing out that, on Orestes' account, even a prisoner in his cell would be free. 'And why not?' retorts Orestes, for the freedom of which he speaks is indeed that which belongs to man as such.[3] It is important to stress this point, since there are passages in *Existentialism and Humanism* where Sartre might be taken as construing freedom in a political sense. For example, 'I am obliged to will the liberty of others at the same time as mine.'[4] Since he immediately adds that 'freedom as the definition of man cannot depend upon others', he cannot, however, be offering a political construal. (I suggest what his meaning might be on pp. 182ff. below.)

A related misconception is that existentialist freedom is a 'passion and ideal', a 'supreme value' to be 'preserved and increased'.[5] But this freedom is something which, for the Existentialist, each person necessarily possesses, and it cannot be increased or decreased. And a person's attitude towards this freedom is no more likely to be one of celebration than one like the 'horror' with which Mathieu 'shrivels' on appreciating its scope.[6] Were it something to celebrate, people would not try to suppress this appreciation through the devices of bad faith. If the Existentialist does have an 'ideal', it is not freedom itself, but an authentic 'facing up' to it.

Finally, one should be rid of the common misconception that existential freedom is supremely manifested in the commission of unmotivated *actes gratuits*. Here, as elsewhere, it is unfortunate that Meursault – Camus' 'outsider' – has been regarded as the model existentialist 'hero'. Most of our writers, in fact, issue explicit rebuttals of this conception. 'Freedom is not the caprice . . . of inclining in this or that direction,' writes Heidegger, for example.[7] Indeed, their accounts of human behaviour are designed, as we shall see, with an eye to avoiding the conclusion that only *actes gratuits* can be free. If a person decides to live capriciously, it is the decision, not the subsequent capriciousness, which exhibits his freedom.

Freedom, for the Existentialist, is to be contrasted with two kinds of constraint, which I label 'causal' and 'rational'. A person may be causally constrained, through brain-washing perhaps, to accept a certain conclusion even though it is not rationally determined by the available evidence. Conversely, a conclusion may be rationally required even though no causal process guarantees that a person will in fact draw it. Previous discussion shows that the Existentialist upholds a freedom from both kinds of constraint. *Angst* and the sense of absurdity indicate that there is no final, rational determination of the large decisions in life, of our 'fundamental projects'. And in chapter 4 it was argued that the course of a human existence is not amenable to sufficient explanation of a causal kind.

Is the Existentialist therefore using 'freedom' ambiguously? No, for he is, rather, attending to two dimensions of a single, albeit rough, intuitive idea of freedom. This is an idea intimately related to that of responsibility. The sense of being a fully responsible agent may be threatened from two directions. By the thought, first, of being in the grip of inexorable causal processes. And by the thought, second, that one's decisions – to marry, join the Resistance or whatever – are all subject to rational decision-procedures with determinate outcomes (to a Benthamite utilitarian calculus, for instance). If they were so subject, then problems of choice could only arise as a result of irrationality or ignorance. This offends against the conviction that even a fully informed and rational person occupies a space within which large decisions are for him to settle. He would experience neither *Angst* nor a sense of independence if the right decisions could always be determined by a sufficiently well programmed calculating machine.

Of the two kinds of constraint with which existential freedom is contrasted, it will be with the causal variety that this chapter is mainly concerned. The Existentialist's denial of the other kind will receive more attention in chapter 10.

It is useful to think of the Existentialist as engaged in criticism of what may be called the Humean approach to freedom. For Hume, our actions are causally explicable, so that freedom cannot be a 'liberty of indifference' towards causal processes. It can only consist in a 'liberty of spontaneity' – the capacity to act on desires stemming from one's character.[8] My act is unfree when caused by an 'external' factor, like the threats of a torturer. *Pace* Orestes, the prisoner in his cell is a paradigm of *un*freedom.

One of the Existentialist's criticisms of Hume is that he construes explanation by character as causal in nature. Consider Sartre's hiker who gives way to his fatigue while his companions soldier on. Is this because he is a 'sissy'? Perhaps, but 'to be a "sissy" cannot be a factual given, and is only a name given to the way in which [he] suffers [his] fatigue.'[9] Sissiness or machismo does not explain action in the way bronchitis explains coughing. They are patterns which my actions tend to fit, not forces or states which cause them (though it is a common ploy of bad faith so to regard them).

More pertinent is a criticism often levelled against Hume to the effect that acting on characteristic desires is insufficient for freedom. The agent must, additionally, possess the capacity to reflect upon and manage the desires.[10] The

Existentialist pushes this point to the limit. I am the 'incontestable author' of my actions only if I am responsible for what they stem from – my desires, temperament, situation. I must, says Ortega, be *causa sui* by 'determining which self' I become.[11] Sartre refers to a person's responsibility as 'overwhelming', since he not only makes things happen, but 'makes himself be'. Freedom is everything or nothing. It is not enough that we are 'self-creators' through 'shaping our characters in the light of our attitudes and values'.[12] We must, as well, be responsible for those attitudes and values.

Clearly there are going to be problems here. Can I, as Ortega's remark implies, create myself *ex nihilo*? 'Hume's fork', as it is sometimes called, will also be brandished. If actions are not causally explicable, Hume argued, then they are fortuitous. But how can a person be held responsible for what is chance and random? I return to these problems in the next section, 'Choice and Refusal'. A different problem is raised, if only to be set aside, over the next few paragraphs.

Most recent writers on the subject regard as the main issue about freedom its compatibility or otherwise with neurophysiological explanation of behaviour. Existentialist writers, however, have given much less attention to this issue than might be expected. Perhaps, as David Wiggins surmises in the case of Sartre, they are confident that neurophysiology can never deliver the goods, in the shape of deterministic explanations. (Though this surmise is based on a passage where Sartre is only challenging the idea that social conditioning could determine behaviour.)[13] More likely, the existentialists' near-silence is owed to the belief that neurophysiology, whether it delivers the goods or not, is tangential to issues of freedom and responsibility.

An argument popular among followers of Wittgenstein might be at work here.[14] Neurophysiology can at best explain bodily movement, with which action is not to be confused. Such would be the consequence, perhaps, of the claim in chapter 4 that actions, unlike mere movements, cannot be specified without reference to the future. The agent is always 'ahead of himself'. In the jargon of chapter 5, neurophysiology pertains to the career of the 'objective' body, but not the 'lived' body or 'embodied point of view'. These bodies are, of course, no more separate from one another than a painting and the molecules which compose it. Equally, however, the categories of neurophysiology are no more germane to the explanation of the 'lived' body's actions than are those of chemistry to that of a painting's aesthetic qualities.

A further argument may be that it is not the possibility of neurophysiological determinism which induces worries about the reality of freedom. What does is the thought that some familiar kinds of explanation, which are certainly incompatible with freedom, may be *much more* generally applicable than we usually suppose; explanations, for example, in terms of social conditioning, irresistible drives, or *idées fixes*. That all our actions may be explicable, at some level, in terms of (normal) brain functions does not prompt a corresponding worry, and is therefore marginal to the issue of freedom.[15]

Readers familiar with the massive literature on free will know that arguments like these get challenged, then defended against the challenges and so on. We are only at the early stages of a seemingly interminable dialectic. If I do not pursue the matter further, this is partly because of excusable cowardice and shortage of space, but mainly because the writers who concern us have, wisely or not, had so little to say on it themselves.

Choice and Refusal

The Existentialist's sanguine attitude towards the threat of physical determinism does not extend to the other worries just sketched. If responsibility for my actions entails responsibility for the desires, etc. from which they stem, and responsibility for the desires, etc. entails responsibility for their source, we seem to be embarked on a regress which could only be halted by the unlikely sounding event of my having created myself *ex nihilo*. A second worry – allied to the thought that, his denials notwithstanding, the Existentialist turns free actions into *actes gratuits* – was that, unless actions are causally explicable, they are fortuitous events for which no responsibility can be attributed.

To appreciate how existentialists seek to allay these worries, we need to distinguish a simple account of freedom urged by Sartre and Ortega from a modified one argued by Merleau-Ponty and Heidegger. Since the modification turns out to be welcome, it is this second account with which I shall identify the Existentialist, that embodiment of existentialism's best wisdom.

I begin, though, with the familiar Sartrean version. The key notion, already encountered, is that of an 'initial choice' (or project). Sartre deploys it in order to reconcile the explicability of our actions with our complete responsibility for them. The tired hiker *could* have soldiered on but, remarks Sartre, 'at what price?' It is because there would have been a price that his actual behaviour was not gratuitous. The price would have been collision with the man's 'initial choice'. An action is explained when we connect it up, 'through going further and further back', with 'the original relation which the For-itself chooses with...the world'.[16] Ortega puts the same point by saying that actions are typically explained through their 'accordance with the general programme' a person set himself.[17] Although vital to the intelligibility of all of a person's subsequent behaviour, the 'initial choice' or 'programme' is not rigid. It can be 'renewed' or 'modified', and in times of *Angst* we are conscious that 'we can abruptly invert the choice and "reverse steam"'.[18]

The 'initial choice' is vital since, without it, there would not be the motives and situations in terms of which we ordinarily account for behaviour. The hiker's fatigue is a reason to give up only because, unlike his companions, his relation to the world is not to something he feels the need to overcome in the face of adversity. He has opted for a stance towards the world in which such physical accomplishments count for little.

Situations too are not brute, factual givens. Rather, they are 'intentionally' constituted through the projects and values whereby we lend significance to things. Two prisoners in a cell are in different situations if their 'fundamental projects' differ. The one who relates to the world as something to savour in all its variety is not in the situation of the one who regards the world as itself being a prison from which to retreat into his inner self. A situation is defined by the 'coefficient of adversity' it presents: hence it is a function, not a cause, of the projects a person has adopted. Like a motive, a situation is exigent only in relation to how a person has decided to 'sculpt his figure' in the world. We are not, then, confronting external forces which press in on us, but factors that emerge only on the ground of our 'initial choices' and their modifications.

Explanation of behaviour, says Sartre, is 'hermeneutical', not causal: for it 'attempt[s] to disengage the *meanings* of an act' which is not 'the simple effect of prior psychic states', not part of a 'linear determinism', but is 'integrated in . . . the totality which I am'.[19] With a nod to Freud, Sartre calls this hermeneutical task 'existential psychoanalysis'. The best analogy, though, is with understanding words in relation to the larger linguistic contexts to whose significance they in turn contribute. Ortega's metaphor of man as the 'novelist' of his life is not banal: for it indicates that the episodes in life, as in fiction, are made intelligible not as causal products of earlier happenings, but as items within a whole narrative structure.[20]

Reverting to a point from the first section, 'Freedom and Constraint', it should now be clearer why existentialist freedom is not the privilege of the rebel, the outsider or any other popular existentialist 'hero'. The hen-pecked husband, the obedient soldier, the bourgeois *salaud* and others from some existentialists' demonologies have also made 'initial choices' which inform the actions for which, therefore, they are responsible. *All* of us are 'novelists' even if, as Ortega complains, most of us are 'plagiarists'. It may be that the rebel is more likely than the *salaud* to be 'facing up' to his freedom, and less likely to be borrowing the plot for his life from those around him. But in good existentialist fiction we meet rebels and outsiders no less guilty of bad faith and 'plagiarism' than the *salauds* – Daniel in *The Roads to Freedom* trilogy, Hugo in *Les Mains sales*, and others.

How successfully, returning to the main theme, does Sartre's account cope with the worries about freedom mentioned on p. 156? I have read, foisted on Sartre, the claim that for any choice to be free it must be preceded by a further free choice of the reasons or motives behind the first one.[21] This would mean that freedom could never begin, for there could never be a first free choice.

Obviously, however, this is not Sartre's (or anyone's) view. There is a choice, the 'initial' one, which presupposes no other. 'Is this [initial] project... *selbständig* [dependent only on itself]? Certainly' − and for the reason Euclid's Postulate is: all explanation in the relevant domain derives from it.[22] But, if my 'initial choice' has no background to it, am I not creating myself *ex nihilo*? That, however, does not sound coherent, for who would the I be prior to this making of myself? Let us take this objection alongside another one.

Sartre tries to escape 'Hume's fork' by holding that actions, while not the products of causal processes, are nevertheless explicable through their relation, finally, to an 'initial choice'. But what of this choice itself? As Sprigge writes, '[There is] little difference between saying that it just happens, as Sartre would not say, and saying that it is something one does freely, as he insists.'[23] De Beauvoir, in fact, *does* say that the 'initial choice' is a 'pure contingency', a 'stupid upsurge':[24] and if Sartre would be unhappy to say 'it just happens,' the reason is a rather deep one. Such a phrase suggests that a person is something indentifiable quite independently from an 'initial choice', something *to* which the latter happens. But this idea of a person divorced from the projects in which he is engaged is one rejected by Sartre and other existentialists (see p. 96ff. above). Ortega, for instance, refers to a person as 'but a project of life... nothing but this devised programme'.[25] The 'initial choice' is not, therefore, an accident which befalls me: and I am responsible for it not through being its author, but in virtue of being *it* and its subsequent modifications. At any rate, I cannot slough off responsibility for the choice on to an agency outside of myself which has lumbered me with it: for, taken apart from the choice, there is no I for anything to happen to or be foisted upon.

It is in these terms that Sartre could respond to the postponed objection about self-creation *ex nihilo*. While an 'initial choice' cannot be based upon or derive from anything, nor is it the act of an I which both preceded it yet somehow manages to create itself through it. As we might expect from the discussion in chapter 6, self-creation is not to be construed as creation by a self. The I is not to be separated from the 'initial choice' and its modifications which individuate a life as mine. Self-creation through that choice is not an act performed by anyone but, in de Beauvoir's words, the 'upsurge' of someone into existence.

Whether or not Sartre's defence against the objections just discussed succeeds, his account is open to other criticisms levelled by fellow existentialists, such as Merleau-Ponty. The last chapter of *Phenomenology of Perception* is, in fact, the most considered statement of existential freedom. It should not be read as a 'moderation' of Sartre's 'excessive' idea of total freedom and responsibility, for Merleau-Ponty is equally insistent that nothing 'can act from outside upon a consciousness', or 'cancel out freedom'.[26] He attempts, rather, to defend a freedom more in harmony with those tenets of existential phenomenology subscribed to by Sartre himself, among others.

We might begin with his criticisms of the ability to 'reverse steam' and 'abruptly invert' choices, which forms part of Sartrean freedom. First, 'it is necessary that what [freedom] does should not be immediately undone by a new freedom.'[27] A responsible choice bears with it the sense that it is not liable to inversion the next moment. If I suspect that tomorrow I might, 'just like that', convert to Marxism or Daoism, I must doubt my status as an autonomous, rational being. Anxiety at this prospect would not be existential *Angst*, but Iris Murdoch's sense of being in the grip of unpredictable forces.

Second, it is not true that my freedom has 'the power to transform me instantaneously' or to 'annul' my stance towards the world.[28] This is not a mere psychological limitation, for it is not even *conceivable* that, 'just like that', I decide to be a Daoist. I might don the right clothes and recite the right verses, but this is not to understand the world in the Daoist way. That understanding cannot spring from nowhere, but must be acquired, like a foreign language, on the basis of what is already familiar to a person. The great anthropologist Evans-Pritchard, it seems, could 'see the world' through Zande eyes: but to do so he had to leave his Oxford study and become immersed in a new form of life. This is not because he was lacking in a 'will to believe', but because without acquiring understanding there can be no belief, wilful or not.

Merleau-Ponty's point has fatal implications for 'initial choice'. If 'choice' of a framework of interpretation and belief presupposes the acquisition of understanding, then there can be no 'initial choice' – since this is supposed to give rise to all understanding, to bring it about that *there is* a world for a person. In *all* choice, however, 'there is presupposed a previous acquisition which [it] sets out to modify', and it can operate only within a received 'field' of interpretation.[29] Even the most independent child must be the fairly passive recipient of most of what he is told: and although nothing need remain immune to his inquisitiveness and scepticism, the 'modifications' he makes cannot occur at one fell swoop.

Merleau-Ponty's criticisms derive from Heidegger's insistence on the 'thrown' character of existence, and from Jaspers' on the 'boundary' imposed by our 'historical definiteness'. *Dasein*, writes Heidegger, 'has been thrown... [and] is not itself the basis of its own Being'.[30] 'Thrownness' is immersion at the outset in a world already interpreted by one's fellows, a world a person must first be 'in' before he can make an 'issue' of it and of himself. I noted earlier that where Sartre speaks of *losing* authenticity through bad faith, Heidegger speaks of *winning* it from 'thrown' existence in the 'they'. Merleau-Ponty's criticisms suggest we should speak with Heidegger.

A further criticism is that Sartre's account is infected with concepts of which, ironically, his own critique of Husserl helped cure us. For example, his 'chooser' is 'acosmic', lacking in that 'specific weight' by which real people are kept attached to an already interpreted world. And he sounds like a 'pure intellect', classifying and evaluating everything as he decides, and not a 'natural self' immersed through physical activity in a world already replete with significance for him. Such a 'chooser' is the pure, spectatorial ego against which Sartre has elsewhere railed so effectively.

For Merleau-Ponty, the demise of 'initial choice' does not at all mean the end of existential freedom: and he accuses Sartre of an elementary confusion in tying choice and freedom together: 'We must not say that I continually choose myself, on the excuse that I *might* continually refuse what I am. Not to refuse is not the same thing as to choose.'[31] I need not choose something in order to be responsible for it, since I may be guilty of negligence or culpable ignorance, for example. In the case of fundamental projects, it is illegitimate to assume that a person has chosen them, since he may simply not have exercised his capacity to review and modify them. That assumption, indeed, is bad phenomenology, since it implies that people are permanently in the process of considering and selecting competing interpretations and values. In reality, we 'natural selves' are normally embroiled in the business of *living* in a world whose contours are not experienced as products of will.

None of this, however, reduces our existential freedom. While 'I can no longer pretend... to choose myself continually from... nothing at all,' I do possess the power of 'general refusal' and the power to 'begin something else'.[32] It is these powers which constitute existential freedom, for it is they, exercised or not, which make a person responsible for his stance towards the world and for the actions which arise from it. This claim will be elaborated shortly.

Before that, we should ask why Sartre confuses choice and non-refusal. Or is it, perhaps, rhetoric rather than confusion: a desire to ram home our responsibility by calling everything for which we are responsible a 'choice'? Merleau-Ponty certainly thinks that Sartre's language does not reflect his real position since, for most of the time, he emphasizes that freedom is 'incorporated in [a] world' which is not experienced as 'the theatre of our free will'.[33] But Sartre's own later verdict is harsher: 'The other day I reread [my preface] to a collection of [wartime] plays... and was truly scandalized. I had written: "Whatever the circumstances... a man is always free to choose to be a traitor or not"... It's incredible, I actually believed that.'[34] These are not the words of someone ruing rhetorical excess. Under the influence of his Marxist friends, moreover, Sartre came to view the condition of his earlier, unattached 'chooser' not as *man's* lot, but as the hopeless aspiration of floating bourgeois intellectuals such as he himself had been.

A clue to the earlier confusion is the reference to the traitor in the lines just quoted. The issue of resistance versus collaboration informs much of the fiction written by Sartre and Simone de Beauvoir during the 1940s. The German occupation presented a context in which, arguably, the dictum 'If you're not for us, you're against us' applied. Not actively to resist the Germans was, in effect, to accept them. A person could hardly plead ignorance, or a busy diary, by way of excusing himself from having to decide. The situation was, in effect, one where the distinction between choosing and not refusing or resisting was easily elided. Mathieu performs this elision when he declares that by remaining indecisive he has actually chosen the defeat of France.[35] In the normal course of life, however, we are not in the position of opting *for* whatever we are not actually refusing. The source of Sartre's confusion, then, may be his generalizing from the special issue with which he was preoccupied when developing his account of freedom. He concedes this, perhaps, when years later he writes that 'during the Resistance there appeared to be a possibility of free decision,' but now he has 'found that the world was more complicated'.[36]

Despite the simple, dramatic appeal, it was never Sartre's 'initial choice', but something more akin to Merleau-Ponty's 'power to refuse', which dominated in existentialist accounts of freedom. Marcel condemns Sartre's 'fatal error' of making freedom equivalent to choice, while Buber understands freedom as an 'open confrontation' with sedimented ways that have become 'adverse' to the emergence of new meanings.[37] It is this kind of reactive freedom too, which Heidegger ascribes to *Dasein*: a freedom 'released from the illusions of the "they"', yet 'within the limitations of its throwness'.[38] Moreover, it is this strain of existential freedom which persists among recent philosophers sympathetic to the existentialist tradition. Charles Taylor, for example, defends the responsibility for oneself which is 'not that of radical choice, but [of] radical evaluation . . . essential to our notion of a person'.[39]

The rejection of Sartrean 'initial choice', and the substitution in many contexts of 'non-refusal' for 'choice', do not then mitigate existential freedom. Rather, they secure that freedom by locating it, with greater consistency, within the account of human life provided by existential phenomenology. It is important to recognize this location if the distinctive character of existential freedom is to be appreciated.

The central proposition of existential phenomenology is that we exist in a 'human world' whose contents are articulated in terms of the significance they have through the intentional projects in which we engage. Our relation to this world is not that of substances causally interacting with others, but what Heidegger calls 'care'. This is a relation to things in so far as they matter to us for the 'issue' that each of us is to himself. This central proposition serves as a premise for freedom in two related ways. Because the 'human world' is constituted by situations, 'signs', *négatités* and other intentional items, it cannot be an outside agency causally dictating our attitudes and actions. I am not free, as the Stoic would have it, because I am an inner citadel protected against outside incursion by impregnable walls. Rather, as Merleau-Ponty puts it, 'nothing determines me from the outside... because I am from the start outside myself and open to the world.'[40] This is the doctrine of intentionality, as revised by the Existentialist. The 'human world' is not 'outside' us – nor, of course, 'inside us', if by that is meant that the 'external world' is really a projection of the imagination. The mode in which I am 'there', outside in the world, is intentional and not natural, as with a bird in its habitat. My situation is not an environment with which I interact. It is, in Ortega's metaphor, something I carry like the vagabond his bundle.[41] The vagabond cannot survive or begin his journey without a bundle: but how he carries it, and where to, are his responsibility.

The second implication for freedom of the 'human world' is that if human beings 'make' it, they can also 'unmake' it. People can alter their projects and thereby 'refuse' the interpretations and values which projects carry. They are not spectators of a show, destined, unless mad or handicapped, to register and share a particular impression of what passes before them. These powers to 'refuse' and 'begin something else', moreover, go deep which is why the *Angst* in which they are intimated may exhilarate or disturb, but not leave us indifferent. To take the kind of example to which Sartre and Merleau-Ponty are partial, it is not only the habits, opinions and tastes of the 'typical member of the working class' from which a person has the power to step back and demur. He may so act as to reorientate his stance towards his society, coming to view its history as, say, a story of exploitation that can be brought to an end, instead of an inevitable chapter in the natural evolution of the species. Or, to go deeper still: we may reject Sartre's reference to his hiker having 'chosen' what amounts to a philosophy of the body and the significance of physical endeavour, but agree that just such a philosophy is manifested in the ways the hiker comports himself towards the world – ways which he can 'refuse', thereby restructuring the manner in which he resolves the 'issue' that his relation to the world poses.

As these examples indicate, existential freedom should not be 'over-intellectualized'. Its powers are not exercised, typically, by deciding in the quiet of one's study to submit this or that aspect of one's attitude to the world to critical analysis. Once this deliberation occurs, then, as Sartre argues, the chips have already been put down: 'les jeux sont faits.' The person is already on the way, as part of the business of living, to 'refusing' aspects of how he has so far been. He will be on his way not through contemplation, but through embarking on a new career, say, or through the value he finds himself placing on a new personal relationship, or through his response to a colleague's chiding him about his habits.

The priority of practice over intellect has a further consequence. If the behaviour of 'refusal' is to be intelligible to the agent, it must have real continuity with the previous behaviour which has embodied his interpretations and evaluations of things. While there are no limits on the scope of freedom's powers, there are nevertheless limits on the manner and velocity of their exercise. In Neurath's famous analogy, the ship's planks may well get replaced, but not all at once, for the carpenter must have some to stand upon while he removes others. *Pace* Sartre's talk of the ability to 'reverse steam', a person's exercise of freedom's powers cannot be a nihilist assassination of his former self, its convictions and comportments. To continue the nautical figures, the order has to be 'Slow ahead!'

We can now see, finally, why existential freedom is not an 'ideal' or 'passion'. Its powers are those a person is 'condemned' to possess in virtue, simply, of enjoying a human existence. A creature for whom the world and his place in it are an 'issue', which he is constantly in the business of resolving through the projects in which he engages, is a free one. This freedom is not, like a sun-roof on a car, an 'optional extra' with which a human life may or may not come equipped. To be free *is* to have that kind of life, viewed from the perspective of the responsibility which such a life has for itself.

Individuals and Tribes

How much credence is to be given to the Existentialist's account of freedom? Are we in fact capable of the authentic existence which clear-sighted, self-conscious exercise of the powers of freedom would constitute? Or is such an existence, as Heidegger wonders, merely a 'fantastical exaction'?[42] Before I address these questions, I want to say a few more words on another question we have already seen asked of the Existentialist. Even if we are sympathetic to his account, is he justified in using the pejorative vocabulary of 'inauthenticity', 'self-estrangement' and 'bad faith' to describe the way in which, for the most part, we live? In the light of the notion of existential freedom just articulated, my inclination is to allow him this vocabulary. Let us take the three pejorative terms in order.

In virtue of his powers of disengagement, refusal and recommencement, a person is responsible for his stance and comportment towards the world and others. If he will not recognize these powers, or having recognized them, ignores them, then he is sloughing off responsibility on to shoulders other than his own – society's, God's, Nature's, the 'they's or whatever. Given the root meaning of the term (see p. 109 above), 'inauthenticity' would not be a bad label for these failures to own to one's responsibility and to see as one's 'ownmost' that for which this responsibility is borne – namely, one's life and its possibilities.

Nor is talk of self-estrangement inappropriate. Taylor was right to emphasize the role played by the capacity for 'radical evaluation' of one's desires and values in our concept of what it is to be a person. Here is a capacity as plausible as most for marking off the distinctively human from the generally intelligent orders of existence. If the capacity is as large as The Existentialist supposes, the failure to exercise it will be a major abdication from something distinctively human. The capacity, after all, is not an 'optional extra'. Moreover, the way a person is must be due to how he has exercised, or failed to exercise, this capacity. It would not then be excessive to describe someone who cannot identify himself in terms of this capacity – one which partly constitutes our notion of what it is to have a self – as being estranged or alienated from himself.

We might expect, finally, that powers so integral to our being the creatures we are would be the objects of familiar, pre-philosophical awareness. *Angst*, of course, is supposed to be just such an awareness. People who then act and speak as if they did not possess such powers would be denying something of which, perhaps only spasmodically and inchoately, they are aware. This is equivalent to saying that they would be in bad faith.

This defence of the Existentialist's vocabulary will be of small interest unless one is sympathetic to his account of freedom. That account, I suggested, results from a fusion of the tenets of existential phenomenology with a thesis of individual responsibility. One way to attack the account, then, is to take issue with existential phenomenology. If the world is not a 'human' one but an objective one spectatorially mirrored by a certain scheme, then there will be no freedom from what I called 'rational constraint' to 'refuse' that scheme. And if the exigency of situations and motives is not conferred on them through the projects in which we engage, and through the significance these projects impart to things, then the Existentialist's reasons for rejecting a causal model for the explanation of behaviour will vanish. I shall not, however, discuss these objections to existential phenomenology. The sympathy with which I described that position in earlier chapters must serve for its defence.

I want, however, to discuss a different line of criticism of existential free-dom, one already prefigured in chapter 7. Sprigge writes: 'The nearest to a definite outside factor [that Sartre] acknowledges is the world produced by... a group of... others, which there is a special difficulty for me in not taking over as my world too.'[43] The problem indicated here – and it is not one for Sartre alone – is with the thesis of 'individualization'. Someone will argue that responsibility for the 'human world' is inevitably plural – ours or theirs, not mine. In Heidegger's jargon, the permanent answer to 'Who is *Dasein?*' would be 'The "they"'. On this view, the 'construction' of a world is always the enterprise of a collective, and the individual is to be understood as a unit within such a collective.

As I have interpreted the Existentialist's idea of freedom, he displays none of Sartre's spasmodic hostility towards recognizing the individual's 'thrownness' in an already interpreted, public world. He may not need to object, therefore, to a passage like the following, even though existentialism is an intended target: 'the human power to evaluate experiences and adopt goals...depends on...the individual's...accepting as binding on him the norms, ends and disciplines presupposed in [public] practices.'[44] Heidegger, indeed, seems to outbid this claim when he refers to our 'fateful destiny in and with [our] "generation"' and to our 'fates [having] already been guided in advance, in our Being with one another in the same world'.[45]

Certainly, though, accentuation of collectivity can reach a degree that is incompatible with existential freedom. When this occurs, I shall refer to 'tribalism',[46] of which we have already encountered several varieties. One of these was represented by Debray's pronouncement – a slogan, virtually, for today's fashions for 'roots' and 'cultural identity' – that a man is not a 'personal possession, but a patrimonial construct'. Then there was the idea that, even in the most private recesses of his life, a person is only a place-holder for the roles which his society makes available. One might mention, too, the 'linguistic relativism' associated with Benjamin Lee Whorf, for whom the shape of a person's view of the world is dictated by his society's language. The price of 'refusal' would then be silence. Recently, a sophisticated version of 'tribalism' has emerged by way of opposition to modern social contract theories, like that of John Rawls. These are taken to task for the pretence that there could be creatures 'unencumbered' by social traditions, as parties to a contract setting up society would have to be. Such a creature would be 'at sea', without bearings on where or who it is.[47] It is not simply that a person cannot begin from nowhere, nor disengage and 'refuse' in one lightning stroke. A radical disengagement from a form of social life will either destroy or transmute a person's identity. It will destroy it if there is no compensating immersion in an alternative form, and it will transmute it if there is.

Some commentators, I have complained, wrongly attribute solipsistic proclivities to existentialism. The self, for the Existentialist, far from being a hermetically sealed 'pure ego', is an embodied engagement in a world where, necessarily, it is alongside others. But to the varieties of 'tribalism' just sketched the Existentialist cannot, of course, subscribe. Central to the notion of authenticity is the idea that a person can, without loss of either intelligibility or self-identity, disengage himself from the public schemes, the ways of the 'they', in which he has been embroiled. Far from 'losing' himself through this operation, the person appropriates his 'ownmost Being'.

The ramifications of the issue which divides the Existentialist from the 'tribalists' are immense, for it is nothing less than the issue of the proper account to be given, at the most fundamental level, of a person's relation to the community of his fellows. Before I elaborate the Existentialist's stand on this issue, I need to say a few words about Heidegger's apparently 'tribalist' remarks quoted on p. 166. They occur in the context of the question of 'whence *Dasein* can draw' the possibilities which the authentic person makes his own. Heidegger's point is that these cannot be plucked out of thin air and must instead be sought in the traditions of a people, its 'heritage'. Far from making the 'tribalist' claim that self-identity requires immersion in the prevailing ways of a society, Heidegger is arguing that recovery of self from the 'they' necessitates a search for alternatives to '*their*' ways within a larger historical tradition. Authenticity requires 'authentic historicality', an 'authentic repetition of a possibility of existence that has been'. This may take the form of 'choosing' a past 'hero' as an inspiration.[48] This 'repetition' should not, of course, be the hopeless attempt to re-create a past form of life. The past is always 'outstripped', and it is absurd to 'bind the "Present" back' to it.[49] (Heidegger is not, then, talking of the authenticity to which performers on valveless trumpets or keyless flutes nowadays pretend.) In sum, Heidegger is joining with Kierkegaard and Nietzsche in urging us to look to the past as a means of ascending from that 'levelling down' of possibilities for existence on which, at any given time, the 'they' is busy.

I do not have the space to do justice to the large issue between the Existentialist and the 'tribalists'. Admitting my partiality, I shall therefore restrict myself to giving room only to the Existentialist to raise some points against his opponents.

First, he will recall the violence that 'tribalism' does to the perception a person has, from the 'inside', of his beliefs and values. Here, he does not have in mind the sporadic glimpses of the power to disengage from these beliefs and values which *Angst* is supposed to afford. He is thinking, rather, of the status which the 'directives' that guide his life have for a person (see p. 114 above). The 'tribalist' treats these from a third-person perspective: as expressions of cultural membership, perhaps, or as ideological concomitants of the roles one plays in society. Unless the person is viewing himself from the 'outside', as one specimen among the rest, this is not his perspective. If it were, he could not have any 'directives': for they can 'direct' only if he accepts them – takes them, that is, to be true or warranted. Now he cannot do this while simultaneously regarding them as mere expressions or ideological symptoms. Taking a given 'directive' to be true requires the person to suppose that, in principle at least, he might occupy a position from which the 'directive' could be examined and endorsed. This position, moreover, must be one 'above' the particular society or tradition which has furnished him with the 'directive', if he is to have any confidence that the examination is not *parti pris*. (It does not follow that the position must be a kind of Kantian kingdom inhabited not by flesh-and-blood people, but by purely rational souls. The choice is not, I think, between regarding the truth of a belief as relative to a given culture and regarding it as obtaining independently of actual human practices of verification, criticism and appraisal.[50] Regarding it as thus independent would, in fact, be incompatible with the tenets of existential phenomenology and with the anti-foundationalism discussed in chapter 8 under 'Absurdity'.)

The second point is that 'tribalists' exaggerate or misunderstand the kind of constraints which the public practices into which the individual is 'thrown' exert. Properly viewed, attempts at radical disengagement from them need not end up in loss of intelligibility or self-identity.

Consider, here, that repository *par excellence* of a society's interpretations of the world – its *language*. As we might predict, the Existentialist rejects the image of language as a straitjacket on the thinking that goes on inside it. My language, as Merleau-Ponty puts it, is not the 'clothing' of my thought, but its 'body'. 'Thought is no "internal" thing, and does not exist independently of the world and of words.'[51] This is not, of course, something the 'tribalist' need deny. In Whorf's view, it is precisely the inextricability of thought from language that makes the language of a society the determinant of its view of the world. Only if thought took place inside an 'inner' retreat, he implies, could people seek refuge from their society's schemes of interpretation.

The Existentialist's reply to this is that, while there can be no retreat *from* language, a person can retreat *with* and *through* it. Important here is the idea that a language is not only, or even primarily, a system for the communication of information. Language is also *expression*. This is not the expression of cultural affiliation of which the 'tribalist' spoke but, in Merleau-Ponty's words, the individual's 'project[ing] himself towards "a world" . . . [his] taking up a position in the world of his meanings'.[52] If anyone doubts this dimension of language, he should ask himself how language ever got going. For, in order for a 'sedimented' system of communication to have become established, people must once have expressed themselves more idiosyncratically – in a manner akin, Merleau-Ponty suggests, to that of the singer or dancer.

With the 'sedimentation' of language, expression does not disappear, but now it utilizes words belonging to a relatively stable system. The grand testimony to this is the rhetorical and figurative power of language – its potential for metaphor, metonymy, irony and the rest. In the exercise of this potential, words with more or less fixed meanings are put to novel work: the expression of individual visions, the inspiring of images, the prompting of unsuspected analogies and new classifications, and so on. Here, perhaps, is the most important aspect of that 'open and indefinite power to giving significance' of which Merleau-Ponty speaks.[53] And it is one reason why Sartre can write that, while the language I speak does not 'emanate' from me, it 'cannot constitute an external limit of [my] freedom'.[54]

I do not know if it is reasonable to hold, with Whorf and other 'tribalists', that a language may somehow incorporate a whole metaphysics. It is worth noting, though, that this is a view shared by Nietzsche. 'I am afraid we are not free of God' – nor of souls, substances and much else – 'because we still believe in grammar.'[55] But as Nietzsche's own writings demonstrate, the metaphysics is one that can be challenged using just the language which purportedly incorporates it. It is wrong, then, to imagine that intelligibility is necessarily sacrificed when a language is put to uses well beyond its ordinary communicative functions, including that of 'refusing' the interpretations which the language may be thought to incorporate. Nor, therefore, is a person's identity as a member of the linguistic community necessarily lost when he turns poet or revisionary metaphysician.

Consider next the moral code and practices into which, as a member of a society, a person is 'thrown'. Just as the speaker of metaphor must draw on the resources of 'sedimented' language, so the moral innovator or iconoclast must, if he is to be intelligible to anyone, himself included, start from the moral conceptions that have currency in his society. But just as the power to speak in novel ways is 'open and indefinite', so too there is no clear limit to moral revision and originality. The cord which connects the innovator to his society can, it seems, be stretched indefinitely. The example of Nietzsche is again instructive. Radical as his new 'table of values' was – in praise of hardness, inequality, even suffering – it is one which someone starting out with the raw materials of Christian morality might, using a suitably unusual angle of projection, intelligibly come to construct. The person who practises what Nietzsche preached will be an 'outsider' in the sense of a moral pariah. But as is amply illustrated by the many 'Nietzschean' figures who populate twentieth-century fiction – Mann's Leverkühn, London's 'sea-wolf', Gide's 'immoralist', even Conrad's Kurtz – he need not be 'outside' in the sense of being unfathomably alien and the purveyor of moral gibberish.

Finally, the Existentialist will of course concede that there are societies, including those described by anthropologists as 'tribal', where the conditions for exercising the powers to 'refuse' and 'begin something else' are hardly favourable. But this is not to concede that, in such societies, these distinctively human capacities simply do not exist. After all, some of the 'tribal' societies of yore are the 'open' ones of the present. Some people in those societies must manage, therefore, to 'refuse' and 'begin something else'. In so doing they manifest a more authentic human dignity, if the Existentialist is right, than would be permitted us by contemporary preachers of 'roots' and 'cultural identity'.

Notes

1   *Being and Nothingness: An Essay on Phenomenological Ontology*, 1957, p. 439.
2   Ibid., pp. 553–4.
3   Sartre, *Les Mouches*, 1947, p. 110.
4   *Existentialism and Humanism*, 1966, p. 52.
5   Mary Midgley, *Beast and Man: The Roots of Human Nature*, 1979, p. 287; John Macquarrie, *Existentialism: An Introduction, Guide and Assessment*, 1973, p. 180.
6   Sartre, *The Reprieve*, 1986, p. 199.
7   'On the essence of truth', in *Martin Heidegger: Basic Writings*, ed. D. F. Krell, 1978, p. 128. See also Sartre, *Being and Nothingness*, p. 453, and *Cahiers pour une morale*, 1983, pp. 52–3.
8   *A Treatise of Human Nature*, 1960, Book 2, Part 3.
9   *Being and Nothingness*, p. 455.
10 See the articles by Harry Frankfurt, Gary Watson and Charles Taylor in *Free Will*, ed. Gary Watson, 1982.
11 'History as a system', in his *History as a System and Other Essays towards a Philosophy of History*, 1962, p. 204.
12 Jonathan Glover, *I: The Philosophy and Psychology of Personal Identity*, 1988, p. 132.
13 David Wiggins, *Needs, Values, Truth*, 1987, p. 294.
14 See, for example, G. E. M. Anscombe, *Intention*, 1957, and Norman Malcolm, 'The conceivability of mechanism', in *Free Will*, ed. G. Watson.
15 This is a main theme in P. F. Strawson's 'Freedom and resentment', in his *Freedom and Resentment and Other Essays*, 1974.
16 Sartre, *Being and Nothingness*, p. 457.
17 'History as a system', in his *History as a System and Other Essays*, p. 205.
18 *Being and Nothingness*, p. 465.
19 Ibid., p. 459.
20 'History as a system', in his *History as a System and Other Essays*, p. 205.
21 Galen Strawson, *Freedom and Belief*, 1986, ch. 2. For a brief and effective retort, see Ted Honderich, *A Theory of Determinism*, 1988, pp. 179–80. Strawson's book, I should add, is generally a very illuminating one.
22 Sartre, *Being and Nothingness*, p. 457.
23 T. L. S. Sprigge, *Theories of Existence*, 1984, p. 148.
24 *The Ethics of Ambiguity*, 1948, p. 25.
25 'Man the technician', in his *History as a System and Other Essays* pp. 111–12.
26 *Phenomenology of Perception*, 1962, pp. 443, 454.
27 Ibid., p. 437.
28 Ibid., p. 447.
29 Ibid., p. 439.
30 *Being and Time*, 1962, pp. 284–5H.
31 *Phenomenology of Perception*, p. 452.
32 Ibid.
33 Merleau-Ponty, 'Partout et nulle part', 1960, p. 196.

34   *New York Review of Books*, 26 March 1970, p. 22.

35   Sartre, *Iron in the Soul*, 1974, p. 78.

36   *New York Review of Books*, 26 March 1970, p. 22.

37   Gabriel Marcel, 'Existence and human freedom', in his *The Philosophy of Existence*, 1948, p. 58; Martin Buber, *I and Thou*, 1937, pp. 53–4.

38   *Being and Time*, pp. 226, 366H.

39   'Responsibility for self', 1982, p. 126.

40   *Phenomenology of Perception*, p. 456.

41   'History as a system', in his *History as a System and Other Essays*, p. 216. Ortega himself applies the metaphor to a person's past.

42   *Being and Time*, p. 266H.

43   *Theories of Existence*, p. 150.

44   Anthony O'Hear, *The Element of Fire: Science, Art and the Human World*, 1988, p. 77. Sartre is a specific target here, but O'Hear's aim is spoiled by foisting on Sartre an *acte gratuit* view of free action.

45   *Being and Time*, p. 384H.

46   I borrow the term in roughly this sense from Jonathan Glover, *I...*pp. 196ff., though his use is wider than mine.

47   See, for example, Michael Sandel, *Liberalism and the Limits of Justice*, 1982, and Leszek Kolakowski, *Metaphysical Horror*, 1989.

48   Heidegger, *Being and Time*, p. 385H. Charles Guignon, *Heidegger and the Problem of Knowledge*, 1983, is good on this neglected area of Heidegger's thinking.

49   Ibid.

50   The issue here is large and complex, and central to contemporary discussions of realism versus anti-realism. There is a helpful discussion by David Wiggins in 'What is a substantial theory of truth?', 1980.

51   *Phenomenology of Perception*, pp. 182–3.

52   Ibid., pp. 191–2, 193. On the topic of expression and information, see Charles Taylor, 'Language and human nature', in his *Human Agency and Language*, 1985, and my 'Assertion, phenomenology and essence', 1987.

53   Ibid., p. 194.

54   *Being and Nothingness*, p. 519. In his section on language, Sartre does more justice to our 'thrownness' into social practices than his talk of 'initial choice' would indicate, as we shall see in the appendix.

55   *Götzen-Dämmerung, Werke*, vol. 2, 1979, p. 960.

10

Existentialism and Ethics

Existentialism versus Ethics?

Existentialism has been described as 'a philosophy for living', and I have suggested there is a truth to this. Not only does it address people's real concerns but, through delineating their Being-in-the-world and their freedom, it aims to release them from illusions or deceptions which estrange them from the world, each other, and themselves. Existentialism not only talks about, but calls people to, the authentic attitude.

Does this exhaust existentialism's contribution as practical philosophy? Mary Warnock thinks so, for she writes that existentialism cannot make 'any contribution to moral philosophy at all', since it can at best tell us what we ought to 'think and feel', not 'that there is anything that we ought to do'.[1] Might we not hope for something more – guidance as to how we should live and treat one another, guidance as to the conduct of an authentic existence? This is sometimes put as the question, 'Can there be an existentialist ethic?' This rephrasing of the question is not without its dangers. Kierkegaard described his hero of authenticity, the 'knight of faith', as 'suspending the ethical', while Nietzsche described his, the 'Overman', as being 'beyond good and evil'. Generally, terms like 'ethical' and 'moral' are not ones to which existentialists are partial. Certainly, if questions are not to be begged, we need to use 'ethics' in a broad sense which does not tie it down to notions of moral rights and duties. With this and a similar proviso about the word 'ought', I shall take the questions, 'Can there be an existentialist ethic?' and 'Can the Existentialist tell us how we ought to live and treat one another?' as interchangeable.

An initial reason for doubting that there can be *an* existentialist ethic is that various of our writers have furnished very different and incompatible prescriptions for conduct. At the political level, for example, these range from Nietzsche's *a*political, solitary aristocratism, through Ortega's elitist liberalism, to the left-wing activism of Sartre. Do all or any of these have any sort of grounding in a general existentialist outlook? But this kind of consideration is hardly decisive – no more than disputes between Thomist and 'liberation' theologians are for the non-existence of a basic Christian ethic. Perhaps we are looking for an existentialist ethic at too particular and concrete a level.

More serious are arguments for ruling out the very possibility of an existentialist ethic. An individual man or woman who happens to be an existentialist philosopher will doubtless have views on how people ought to behave: but these, it gets argued, will be ones that he or she holds 'privately' or 'unofficially', and not *qua* existentialist. One such argument is visible in Iris Murdoch's complaint that 'moral philosophy of an existentialist type is still Cartesian and egocentric...our picture of ourselves has become too grand...We have lost the vision of a reality separate from ourselves.'[2] This, she continues, is incompatible with the 'unselfing' which is a precondition of a genuinely moral outlook. 'In the moral life the enemy is the fat relentless ego.'[3]

But while the Existentialist does in a sense deny 'a reality separate from ourselves', he is no friend of the Cartesian ego. Indeed the two go together, for a 'separate reality' requires a separate ego, and vice versa. 'The fat relentless ego', in fact, reminds one of Sartre's description of the Cartesian self as 'a bloodthirsty idol which devours all one's projects' (see p. 17 above). The Existentialist is as much an 'unselfer' as Murdoch. Self-concern, it is true, is a dimension of authenticity, but this is not to be a self-engrossed 'grubbing about in one's soul' of the 'Californian' variety (see p. 96 above). Self-concern is towards one's Being-in-the-world, hence towards the world and towards those who are 'in' it. There is no warrant for assuming that this self-concern will be 'egocentric' in a pejorative sense. A constant theme in Marcel's writings, for instance, is the way rigid 'self-occupation' alienates a person from others and from himself.[4] Like Murdoch, he pins the blame on a Cartesian conception which, with fellow existentialists, he rejects. True self-concern will, he thinks, be 'selfless'.

A very different reason for thinking there could be no existentialist ethic is the common belief that existentialism treats evaluative judgements as merely 'emotive' or expressive of 'subjective' preferences. If this were so, the Existentialist could not have any business, in his capacity as philosopher, passing such judgements.

One thing wrong with this interpretation is, as we have seen (p. 90ff. above), that it foists on the Existentialist a number of dualisms – fact versus value, description versus evaluation – which he is in fact keen to dissolve. We do not, as Heidegger put it, 'stick' values on to a world first described in its naked state. A description of the world is of things and situations 'disclosed' through projects that manifest what we value. If values do not belong to an objective, 'separate reality', neither do facts.

The inspiration for this misinterpretation, I suggested earlier, is some remarks from *Existentialism and Humanism*, and I want now to look more closely at the famous example of the student who has to decide between looking after his mother and joining the Free French. Sartre's only 'advice' was 'You are free, therefore choose – that is to say, invent,' for it is impossible to 'find any sort of guidance whatever' as to the right choice.[5] Critics have rightly pointed out that the example is badly designed to support a general subjectivist thesis. For it only illustrates a serious dilemma, unlike that of selecting a liqueur chocolate, because there are good reasons, independent of subjective preference, for each course of action. But Sartre, here, is at one with his would-be critics. The dilemma is indeed due to there being good reasons for each action. The problem is that the reasons are culled from two different 'kinds of morality': so different that they cannot be compared on a single scale.

On the one hand is 'the morality of sympathy, of personal devotion'; on the other, a more universalistic kind concerned with the good of, say, 'a national collectivity', or even humanity as a whole.[6] There can indeed be no rule for making decisions when these two kinds of moral concern collide, since every rule is rooted within one or the other. Compare, for example, 'Honour thy father and mother' with 'Act so as to maximize the greatest happiness of the greatest number.'

It would be incompatible with this diagnosis of moral dilemma to hold that, in general, moral decision can find no guidance beyond personal preference. Sartre would not, I am sure, have told his student, 'You are free, therefore choose and invent' if the 'dilemma' were between joining the Free French and peddling heroin to children in Marseilles. For that second option cannot be supported by reasons from either of the two kinds of morality. Because reasons of the two kinds are incommensurable, yet in frequent conflict, there is a recurrent need to 'invent' resolutions to dilemmas. It is unclear to me why people take this talk of 'invention' to indicate an attitude of moral *laissez-faire*. Inventors have to work with appropriate materials and their inventions are not immune to appraisal. If we can adjudicate between those of Leonardo and Heath Robinson, why not between different resolutions 'invented' by Sartre's student? Sartre does indeed say, 'You are unable to judge others' when those others decide 'in all clearness and authenticity'.[7] But without yet knowing the conditions for 'clear and authentic' decision, there is no reason to take this as a counsel of relaxed tolerance.

Sartre, in fact, clearly does believe that there is an absolute condition which authentic moral decision must meet. 'Freedom,' he writes, is 'the foundation of all values,' and while we may have no way of calculating the solution to the student's dilemma, 'the one thing that counts is to know whether the invention is made in the name of freedom.'[8] To be sure, it is unclear what Sartre means here. He cannot, as I have already shown, be referring to a political ideal of freedom (p. 154 above). I will return to what he might mean in the last section, 'Reciprocal Freedom'; but by way of a brief preview, it goes something like this. It is always a criticism of a person's 'invention' that it fails to register appreciation of his and others' existential freedom. The one imperative, not at all 'negotiable', which should govern the exercise of both the morality of 'personal devotion' and its more 'universalistic' rival, is respect of existential freedom.

Even this much makes it clear that Sartre is not preaching the 'do your own thing' freedom from convention – the licence and inconoclasm – which 'café existentialists' seem to have picked up from his remarks about values not belonging to the objective order. If those remarks really were intended to preserve any behaviour from moral criticism, they would also preclude moral congratulation. If *carte blanche* were given to black-sweatered youths to make love in jazz clubs, it would also be given to bowler-hatted businessmen to make profits in their offices. If *anything* goes, this includes the conventional behaviour despised by the 'café existentialist' as much as his own. (There may, anyway, be little to distinguish, in terms of conformism, between the bowler-hatted brigade and regiments of black-clad or spiky-haired youths all being shocking in unison.)

Because they are often both in conflict and incommensurable, moral rules or principles are, for Sartre, of limited use for guidance. This point might be taken further and then used as a third reason for denying the possibility of an existentialist ethic. 'What would you have done in my place?' asks Henri in Simone de Beauvoir's The Mandarins. 'I can't tell you,' replies Dubreuilh, 'because I wasn't in your place. You'd have to tell me everything in detail.'[9] Taken literally, Dubreuilh's point would render moral rules entirely nugatory: for whereas these are supposed to have general application, he is saying that each person's situation is too unique to fall under any general rubric. If an ethic comprises such rules, and if Dubreuilh represents existentialist thinking, there could be no existentialist ethic. But despite some of their wilder remarks, Sartre's and de Beauvoir's point is not Dubreuilh's. It is, rather, to warn against 'principles that are *too* abstract', and against the mechanical application of principles to situations that are only superficially similar.[10] (It is worth bearing in mind here, and elsewhere, that when Sartre and de Beauvoir make remarks of the 'No general rule can give you guidance' variety, they are thinking of real, serious, moral dilemmas, and not of the simple, everyday decisions where general principles often speak unambiguously.)

It is important, in connection with the second part of this warning, to recall that a situation is not a wholly external circumstance. Remember the very different situations of the two prisoners in their cell (p. 158). Care must indeed be taken, then, before judging that people are in situations of the same general kind. Still, there is nothing inaccessibly 'private' about a person's interpretation of his circumstances, nor therefore about his situation. Situations are publicly identifiable, and they are sometimes sufficiently alike in morally salient features for the same principle to be applicable. Influenced perhaps by Kierkegaard, commentators have, in my view, wildly exaggerated the importance of existentialist references to the 'concrete', 'particular' or 'unique' aspects of our decisions and actions.

Some of the popular reasons, then, for denying the possibility of an existentialist ethic are unconvincing. But a problem remains. It was central to the Existentialist's accounts of absurdity and freedom that the 'directives' by which people guide the large decisions in life cannot be given a final, foundational justification. Life was judged to be absurd because of the discrepancy between this lack of foundations and the confidence with which people embrace and enact their 'directives'. Existential freedom was understood in terms of a capacity to distance oneself from, and perhaps 'refuse', any of the beliefs and values which shape one's 'directives'.

The problem is whether it would be consistent with these anti-foundational claims for the Existentialist, in his capacity as such, to promulgate his own 'directives'. How can he urge us to behave in a certain way when, in the previous breath, he has insisted that there are intelligible stories to be told in which this would be not at all the way to behave? How, for example, could he exhort us to devote ourselves to the pursuit of a certain ideal of justice whilst reminding us that this, like any other ideal, can be 'refused' by sane men? More generally, if conceptions are not mirrors of an objective moral reality, but the achievements of men who might have exercised themselves differently, what business does he have promoting any particular conceptions?

Now it is true, certainly, that there are countless 'directives' which the Existentialist cannot promote or censure *ex cathedra*, with his philosophical hat on, so to speak. These include the kinds which Sartre refused to urge on his student. But it does not follow that the Existentialist is reduced to silence, unable to offer anything describable as an ethic. For there is, one might say, a 'super-directive' which he can consistently promulgate: to live authentically, to live, that is, in full appreciation of absurdity, the significance of *Angst*, freedom, and the other truths which he believes he has communicated. It is open to the Existentialist, therefore, to try to articulate the conditions which a life must meet if it is to manifest appreciation of these truths. The hope would be for a characterization in general, but not vacuous, terms of an authentic stance towards life – one which might provide some genuine guidance on how to behave. It should be pretty obvious, for example, that the *acte gratuit*, iconoclastic programme of the 'café existentialist' would not meet the conditions of authentic life. Exercise of the powers to 'refuse' and 'begin something else' is, of necessity, hard and gradual work, and not the accomplishment of an evening in the jazz club. The perpetual-motion iconoclast, if such there can be, would be a paradigm of bad faith and irresponsibility.

There must be the further hope, moreover, that the articulation of the conditions for authentic existence would show that some 'directives' of a relatively specific kind concerning our dealings with one another are more consistent with those conditions than are others. There is an analogy here, perhaps, with the position of the political liberal, who does not begin with any particular conception of 'the good life', but only with the imperative that people should, as far as possible, be able to pursue their own conceptions. But this does not preclude him from then arguing that some conceptions of 'the good life' are more compatible than others with this imperative.[11] Those in pursuit of sybaritic luxury, for instance, are more likely to thwart the aspirations of others than those who favour frugality and fraternity as prime constituents of 'the good life'.

In the next section, 'Commitment and Availability', I look at two attempts in existentialist writings to specify a general condition of authentic existence. These turn out to be less antithetical than they appear at first. In the last section, 'Reciprocal Freedom', I consider the prospects, encouraged by the convergence of these attempts, for an existentialist ethic.

Commitment and Availability

It would be hopeless in the space available to attempt a general survey of the ingredients which different existentialist writers have deemed essential to an authentic life. Most of the proposals, though, fall into two rough, and seemingly opposed, categories. On the one hand, there are those – Sartre, de Beauvoir, Kierkegaard – who emphasize the place of *commitment* in an authentic life. On the other, there are those – Marcel, Jaspers, Heidegger – for whom the authentic stance is one of *openness* and a refusal, it would seem, to be tied down by even a self-imposed commitment to attitude and action. I shall look, in turn, at an exemplar of each of these categories: Sartre's well-known, if ill digested, theory of *engagement*, and Marcel's theory of *availability*. It is possible, I shall suggest, to develop these accounts so that they are complementary rather than antagonistic.

The idea of a committed life might appeal to the Existentialist on a number of counts. For one thing, it sounds consonant with his insistence on the primacy of action as the medium through which things, situations and values are disclosed. The authentic life, it seems, is not that of the detached spectator, but of the actor in the thick of the action. Second, since inauthentic existence is supposed to consist, in large part, of docile concurrence in the ways of the 'they', the antidote might be a resolute commitment to action which embodies a person's own order of values and meanings. In the unfinished final volume of *The Roads to Freedom* novels, Mathieu was intended to 'commit himself freely, which would give the world a meaning for him'.[12] Finally, commitment might confer on a person's life precisely that wholeness and integrity which, according to the Existentialist, secure the person against self-dispersal in the pursuit of passing fancies. By committing myself, writes Sartre, I transform myself from a contingency into a passion.[13] To switch metaphors, commitment could serve as the anchor for those who would otherwise suffer the sense of 'weightlessness', Milan Kundera's 'unbearable lightness of being', which the experience of freedom induces. In *Les Mouches*, Orestes gives 'weight' to himself by his commitment to killing his mother and her consort.

Sartre, at one point, defines commitment as the 'complete consciousness of being embarked'.[14] However, he means something more than this recognition that one is always engaged in projects for which one is responsible. Commitment is, rather, a way of resolving how one should live in response to that recognition. It is the free, self-conscious, clear-headed dedication of oneself to a great project. As in the case of Mathieu, it is through commitment that a person discharges the 'burden' of being 'free to no purpose'. It is nothing short of fastening upon 'something for which [one] is prepared to die'.[15] A problem with this kind of talk is raised by Martin Buber. Recalling Sartre's claims that values are not there like things 'sown in my path' to be 'discovered', and that a person must 'invent' resolutions of moral issues, Buber writes: 'one can believe in and accept a meaning or value, one can set it as a guiding light over one's life, if one has *discovered* it, not if one has *invented* it.'[16] He then compares Sartre's call to total commitment with the syndicalist, Georges Sorel's, call for a workers' revolution in the name of a 'social myth'. Such calls can only be heard and obeyed by those who do not understand the basis, or rather the lack of a basis, for what they are being called to.

Sartre might reply, I suppose, that some choices, by their very nature, imply a thorough commitment and must, therefore, act as 'guiding lights' for future conduct and attitudes. The student could hardly have chosen to join the Free French, but with the proviso that he could visit his mother whenever he felt like it. But this hardly dissolves the problem, for Buber could now ask why Sartre, given his apparent denial of moral objectivity, does not urge us to avoid choices which carry this kind of commitment, the kind one is 'prepared to die for'.

On the few occasions where Sartre does address the problem, he misunderstands it, imagining that the difficulty is the merely psychological one of whipping up commitment for something whose moral validity is open to question. His solution to *that* difficulty is mouthed by several of his fictional characters. Doubt disappears through the decision to act in a committed manner. 'My dear chap, one doesn't believe, straightaway, what one wants to: it needs practice.'[17] 'Do you imagine that I was convinced when I joined the Communist Party? A conviction has to be created.'[18]

Buber's problem, however, is not the psychological one of how a person manages to acquire total conviction, but the logical one of whether managing to do this is consistent with good faith – with the appreciation that there is no final foundation for one's beliefs and that one is free to 'refuse' and 'begin something else'. And the 'solution' mouthed by Sartre's characters does indeed smack of bad faith. Can it really be a choice in good faith which I make when 'in choosing myself. . . I choose to subordinate myself to the Communist Party and its victory'?[19] If Sartre himself had not finally decided against joining the Party, for fear of 'losing [himself] in [its] comforting paternal embrace',[20] one would be tempted to regard that kind of talk about choice as a disingenuous apologia.

Sartre is able, however, to offer a better answer to Buber; one that depends on an aspect of his account of engagement which has scarcely surfaced so far. Before it is brought into the open, though, I want to look at Marcel's remarks on availability (*disponibilité*), a notion seemingly at odds with Sartrean commitment. Indeed, while Marcel's ideas were developed before Sartre's career had begun, later on he is keen to stress the difference between the two of them. Like Buber, he wonders how Sartre can advocate total commitment to, say, the Resistance, while harping on the 'invented' character of a person's values.[21] Earlier he had described total commitment to a principle or cause as 'idolatrous', since there is nothing I should not hold open to revision. I betray a 'sacred duty' if I set myself to stick to a principle come what may. Commitment may induce complete conviction, as with those characters from Sartre, but this would be a 'sclerosis of habit' incompatible with freedom.[22]

This does not mean that I should, even if I could, remain 'aloof and indifferent'. In fact, I am always and necessarily 'embarked' as an embodied activity in a world from which I cannot retreat. 'Aloofness' would be possible only for Cartesian *cogitos* 'spectating' an independent world. But I am not, as Marcel puts it, 'watching a show': I am an actor in it. It is essential, however, that the actor does not fall victim to a hubris which makes him 'unavailable', unable to listen and learn from his fellow actors.

Unavailability, in one of its forms, is a 'sclerosis' or 'crispation': a 'hardening of the categories in accordance with which we conceive and evaluate the world'.[23] In another metaphor, the unavailable person draws concentric circles around himself, allowing only those experiences which fall within the nearest zones to influence his concepts and values. Those which fall further out are ignored, or filtered through so as only to confirm a pre-established conception – rather as a dogmatic scientist will twist recalcitrant data to the advantage of his hypothesis. The available person will break up 'the lines of this...ego-centric topography' and be ready to accept, for example, that 'from a stranger, casually met, may come a call too strong to be resisted: suddenly all our perspectives are turned inside-out...Such experiences...force us to become sharply aware of the accidental character of...our mental space, and of the rigidities on which [it] rests.'[24]

Availability of this kind may, at first, seem like a pretty uncontroversial condition of authentic existence. In fact, it runs into a similar difficulty to Sartrean commitment. While he rejects talk of 'invention', Marcel concurs in the general existentialist claim that there is nothing 'about which we can be certain that its spell could hold out against the attack of a fearless critical reflection'. We must renounce the 'naïvely rationalist idea' which implies otherwise.[25] What, one now asks, are we holding ourselves available to and for? The analogy with the virtuous open-mindedness of a scientist breaks down. The dogmatic scientist debars himself from progress to the best-con-firmed hypothesis, but at the level of fundamental categories which concerns Marcel, the notion of correct or probable hypotheses is, by his own insistence, ruled out. In this situation, it may well be improper to advocate total commit-ment to principles, but does it not become equally pointless to advocate 'maintaining oneself in a permeable state'? Whatever we are holding ourselves available for, it cannot be the dawning of a secure certainty.

It is important, no doubt, to bear in mind that, for Marcel, availability is ultimately a spiritual condition, informed by a sense of the existence of a divine being. Indeed, 'spiritual life' is defined as 'the sum of activities by which we try to reduce...unavailability'.[26] But this does not help with the present problem, for in Marcel's elusive theology God is not a being whose nature, will and even existence could be matters of rational certainty. He would endorse Jaspers' pronouncement that 'whatever we think we *know* about the deity is super-stition.'[27] Openness to the divine cannot, therefore, be argued for in the way the openness of a scientist to the evidence can. On what grounds, one asks, could Marcel object to the Kierkegaardian religious figure who commits himself totally and without reason to certain beliefs about God and His purpose? That figure, indeed, may seem to enjoy the advantage of gaining 'weight', a constancy of direction which protects him against dissipation into the ways of the 'they'.

I have, though, been overlooking an aspect of Marcel's account, just as I did in the case of Sartre's. When these aspects are brought in, not only do the two accounts become much less distant from one another, but the problem which arose for both accounts is eased. Moreover, it is in the region where the accounts converge that one might look for the Existentialist's attempt to state the ethical conditions for authentic existence. In the remainder of this section, I confine myself to sketching in the missing aspects.

'In the end,' writes Marcel, 'there must be an absolute commitment', and what 'matters most' is the 'fidelity' demanded by this commitment.[28] This squares with his earlier rejection of commitment to principles as 'idolatrous', since the commitment now in view is to *persons* – to other people and to God. (Like Buber, Marcel thinks that fidelity to people is intelligible only through a similar relation to God. I do not follow him here, and I discuss his account of human relations in isolation from their divine counterpart.)

Corresponding to this commitment to others is a further form of availability. Earlier, unavailability was understood intellectually, as a 'hardening' of a person's descriptive and evaluative categories. What matters more to Marcel is unavailability to other people. This is 'rooted in alienation' from them, an inability to allow them a 'presence' or 'influx' in one's life. They are mere 'cases' or 'objects'. 'When I am with an unavailable person, I am conscious of being with someone for whom I do not exist.'[29] The last volumes of Proust's novel depict, in Marcel's opinion, a coterie of people chronically unavailable to each other, obsessively enclosed in their private worlds as Proust himself was in his cork-lined room.

The remedy for such unavailability is commitment: for it is only through this that others come to 'have a hold' on me. And it is through this 'hold', and the reciprocal one which I have on them, that our lives interpenetrate and we become truly 'present' to one another. But what are the constituents of this reciprocal commitment? In part, the mutual exercise of the Christian virtues of faith, hope and charity. In charity or 'generosity', for instance, I must be permanently 'on call' for the other person, in case he is in need. More interesting is the point made, in very Buberian terms, in this passage: 'if I treat the Thou as a He, I reduce the other to . . . nature: an animated object . . . If I treat the other as Thou, I treat him and apprehend him *qua* freedom . . . what is more, I help him . . . to be freed, I collaborate with his freedom.'[30]

Availability, then, is a reciprocal relation through which each party is committed not only to treating the other as a free person, but to enabling and 'collaborating with' his freedom. This has an important implication. A person can only realize himself '*qua* freedom' as a participant in such reciprocal relations. For, outside of them, he is without 'collaborators' to 'help him . . . to be freed'. This is what Marcel emphasizes when he writes that in contrast to the 'captive soul', the one which is available to others 'knows that . . . its freedom . . . does not belong to itself'.[31]

With remarks like these, it is clear that Marcel is in the territory not only of Buber, but of Sartre who, we know, also states that a person's freedom 'depends entirely upon the freedom of others'. Taken literally, this statement is inconsistent with our being 'condemned', willy-nilly, to be free. Let us, for the time being, overlook that and recognize how this thesis of reciprocal freedom provides the aspect so far missing from our account of Sartrean commitment.

Marcel and Sartre seemed at odds because the total commitment urged by the one appeared to exclude the openness demanded by the other. But Marcel, it turns out, does after all urge commitment as a precondition of availability; while Sartre, it will now emerge, holds that it is something like the reciprocal freedom of availability which is the one end of true commitment.

His main discussion of commitment is found in *What is Literature?*, a series of essays in which Sartre justifies his chosen profession. 'The writer,' he tells us, 'should commit himself completely in his works.'[32] This is so, at least, with the 'serious' writer as distinct from the mere entertainer and from the 'poet'. The latter, as Sartre defines him, is not using words to *say* things, but 'to produce puns' and other 'word-things', as part of a concern with form rather than the communicative content of what he writes. The 'serious' writer's commitment, however, is not to particular views and causes that he may embrace. Writing has 'only one subject – freedom', and its single 'end is to appeal to the freedom of men so that they may realize and maintain the reign of human freedom'.[33]

Such remarks can, however, give a misleading impression of a primarily political concern. For although Sartre clearly does want writers to engage in criticism of political oppression – there can be no good novel in praise of anti-Semitism, he says – it is not to political freedom that writing, in its very essence, appeals. Freedom is the one 'end' and 'subject' of writing because the relation between author and reader is a paradigm of that true relation between people where 'the more we experience our freedom, the more we recognize that of the other.' By the very act of writing, by placing words before an audience with the intention that they employ their intelligence to interpret, consider and respond to those words, 'the writer appeals to the reader's freedom.'[34] Titillation, propaganda, invective and affectation are not only literary sins, they are moral ones: for they occlude the way to transparent communication and mutual understanding which must be kept to by people engaging with one another as free individuals.

Crucial, here, is the implication that the freedom of the writer, or indeed anyone, is itself diminished by the failure to 'appeal' to the freedom of others. To paraphrase an earlier line: the less we recognize the freedom of the other, the less we experience our own. This is the thesis already encountered in *Existentialism and Humanism*, and it runs through the *Cahiers*, where Sartre writes, for instance, that 'in oppression, the oppressor oppresses himself.'[35] From 1945 onwards, Sartre committed himself to a number of causes – the victory of post-war socialism in France, the end of colonialism in Indo-China and Algeria, student power in 1968 and so on. In his own view, at least, these commitments were implied by the one underlying commitment to the freedom of others that one's own presupposes. In the preface he wrote to Fanon's *Wretched of the Earth*, for example, the end of colonialism will mean liberation for the oppressors, their 'ideology of lies' now exposed, as well as for the oppressed.[36]

The positions of Marcel and Sartre have now converged into a thesis about the reciprocity of freedom. There is much which still calls for elucidation. How is the thesis to be squared with our being 'condemned' to freedom, and with Sartre's agonistic account of human relations in *Being and Nothingness*? What, anyway, is the argument for the thesis that my freedom requires that of others? What, in reasonably concrete terms, might be entailed by a commitment to reciprocal freedom?

These problems I leave to the final section, but there is one which can now be left behind. Buber complained that if 'directives' have no final, rational foundation, it is bizarre to encourage total commitment to any of them. What, moreover, would be the point in remaining available and open to new 'directives' if rational security were never to be had? Marcel and Sartre can now combine voices in reply to this problem.

First, the availability which 'matters most' is not an intellectual one, but an interpersonal one. Being available, which is never a solo feat, is participation in relations characterized by mutual 'collaboration' with the freedom of each party. Second, it is just this reciprocal freedom which is the real object of commitment. This commitment is not subject to anti-foundational worries, whatever the case may be with people's other 'directives'. Sartre writes:

> when I recognize, as entirely authentic, that man is a being whose existence precedes his essence, and that he is a free being who cannot . . . - but will his freedom, at the same time I realize that I cannot not will the freedom of others.[37]

This is less than clear, and not only because of the convoluted grammar. But it means at least this: willing one's own freedom is not an optional 'directive' adopted by some people, but a condition of authentic existence. Since it is impossible to will one's own freedom without willing that of others, then this latter is also a condition of authenticity. In the requirement of reciprocal freedom, then, there is nothing 'unfounded', 'invented', 'negotiable' or 'subjective'. It is the 'plane' upon which we can form judgements on the 'cowards' and 'scum' who 'seek to hide from themselves' their freedom and that of others.[38]

Reciprocal Freedom

The Existentialist's treatment of the question of why a person ought to be ethical bears comparison with Aristotle's. For one thing, each of them treats it as a serious and difficult question, and not as one which answers itself in virtue of an alleged meaning of the word 'ought'. A person who asks it expects, and deserves, to be shown what is 'in it' for him to concern himself with others. Neither Aristotle nor the Existentialist is, however, an 'egoist', for what is 'in it' for a person is not the satisfaction of desires and avoidance of danger that Hobbesian men look for from morality. For Aristotle, the pursuit of the ethical virtues is a dimension of one's 'flourishing' as a human being, of one's realization of the human 'essence' or 'function' (*ergon*). For the Existentialist, likewise, proper relations with others are necessary for a person's existence to be authentically human.

Aristotle offers a clear, if not convincing, case for his belief that justice, friendship and the other ethical virtues are components of human 'flourishing'. The distinctive human *ergon* is *reason* and the virtues, by falling 'in the mean' between 'excess' and 'deficiency', are manifestations of reason. The Existentialist, however, has yet to explain how ethical behaviour – that is, 'collaboration' in the freedom of others – should be a condition of the individual's free and authentic existence.

The best way to understand his position is by considering the difficulties, mentioned earlier, into which his ethic of reciprocal freedom seems to run. The first of these arose from his claim that we are 'condemned' to be free: for if that is true, then my freedom cannot depend on anything, the freedom of others included. When Sartre writes of 'my freedom implying mutual recognition' of freedom, he cannot be taken literally.[39] And for the most part, indeed, he writes more circumspectly. While I cannot lose my freedom, I can 'lose sight' of it and fail to 'seize hold' of it. When I do so, mine is an 'alienated freedom'.[40] Existential freedom, it was argued, resides in capacities to 'refuse' and to 'begin something else'. What depends on 'collaboration' in the freedom of others cannot be these capacities themselves, but recognition and clear-sighted exercise of them. It must be the authentic 'seizing hold' of one's freedom which, for the Existentialist, requires 'collaboration' with others.

It is not, parenthetically, arbitrary of the Existentialist to understand by 'freedom' the possession, rather than the actual exercise, of certain capacities. For the main point of introducing the word was to emphasize people's responsibility for their situations: a responsibility not diminished by the failure to reflect and 'refuse'. My illness, writes Sartre, does not restrict my freedom, since I am 'without excuses' for what I make, or fail to make, of it. I can do nothing about the virus I catch, but this is not true of the 'horizon' and 'perspective' I then construct out of my condition. It is because the formula 'condemned to be free' expresses this responsibility 'without excuses' that it states, according to Sartre, 'the basis of [his] morality'.[41]

The second difficulty concerned the apparent tension between the ethic of reciprocal freedom and the agonistic accounts of human relations, notably in the sexual domain, offered by some existentialists. Sartre, after all, wrote that 'conflict is the original meaning of Being-for-others.' If there is reciprocity, it is because 'while I seek to enslave the Other, the Other seeks to enslave me.' Within this Hobbesian scenario, 'respect for the Other's freedom is an empty word.'[42]

Sartre's remarks here should be set against his discussion of 'the Look', the experience of which is one of the dimensions of a person's original encounter with others (see p. 105 above). 'The Look' is felt as a threat to one's freedom, and the varieties of interpersonal attitudes described in Part 3 of *Being and Nothingness* are the devices people employ in their attempts to ward off that threat. The dark message seems to be that all these attitudes, including love and desire, are the continuation by other means of the perverse strategies of sadism and masochism. In desire, for example, I attempt to 'possess' or 'appropriate' the Other as a body: which is only at one remove from the sadist's reduction of the Other to a helpless, fleshly instrument. In love, somewhat as in masochism, I try to 'glue down' the Other's freedom: to 'captivate' it by making of myself a 'seductive' fleshly object. More generally, treatment of others continually oscillates between assaulting their freedom and, as a kind of pre-emptive strike, annulling one's own so as to immunize oneself against assault by others.

Certain passages and footnotes make it clear that Sartre is here describing the relations and attitudes obtaining among people in bad faith. The possibility is allowed of a 'radical conversion' from bad faith, enabling the 'possibility of an ethics of deliverance and salvation' from the regime of conflict.[43] This is the ethics of reciprocal freedom which Sartre proclaims in his writings over the next few years. Three points about the connection between the agonistic account in *Being and Nothingness* and the subsequent ethical position should be made. First, it is quite wrong to suppose that, in the former, a rival view of how an individual realizes his freedom is being offered. For Sartre insists that the strategies there described are all *failures*. Each involves 'the impossible ideal of the simultaneous apprehension of [the Other's] freedom and of his objectivity'.[44] The sadist, for example, requires his victim to be a mere instrument, no longer a source of 'the Look': but if he succeeds in this, he no longer has a human being before him, nor therefore a human freedom in his possession. Second, if there is a tension between the earlier and later positions, it is one between pessimism and optimism. In *Being and Nothingness*, bad faith is 'the normal aspect of life' and the 'radical conversion' from it only a 'possibility'. In the *Cahiers* and elsewhere, authentic attitudes of reciprocal freedom, though hard to accomplish, are spoken of as ones which most of us can, with effort and clear heads, realistically develop. (Sartre's optimism was fairly short-lived, for in the later, Marxist period he argues that reciprocal freedom is impossible without a radical transformation of social conditions and the abolition of economic scarcity.)

The third and most important point is that the agonistic account, far from contradicting the subsequent ethical position, provides an essential clue to its interpretation and underlying argument. The thesis of *Being and Nothingness* is that conflict is the way of Being-for-others of people who are in bad faith. The implication is that people who 'convert' from bad faith will, and must, relate to one another in a different way, that of 'intersubjective solidarity'. This implied thesis is, I suggest, equivalent to that of reciprocal freedom. That is, the claim that my freedom depends on my 'collaborating' in the freedom of others is a restatement of the claim that I exist in good faith only through adopting the perspective of 'intersubjective solidarity', and abandoning the 'oppressive' attitudes which obtain in the regime of conflict.

The reasoning is as follows. Bad faith, we know, is first and foremost the view of oneself as object-like, as something In-itself or present-to-hand. This view is a false one: in particular it is a failure to recognize one's capacities of existential freedom. Now we also know that the primary mode of bad faith is 'the predominance of the Other': the tendency to view oneself through the eyes of others, as just one more series of events in the universe. However, and crucially, it is only because I regard others in this objectifying manner that, looking at myself through their eyes, I regard myself in this manner too. If others are objects for me, I am an object for them – and hence, via the prism they provide for self-understanding, an object for myself as well. Having broken with 'intersubjective solidarity', I receive back from others the objectifying conception I form of them, an 'image of myself as the Other'.[45] Through treating others as alien, I become alienated from myself, and my freedom becomes an 'oppressed freedom' through my effective denial of others' freedom. This is what Sartre meant by saying that 'in oppression, the oppressor oppresses himself.'

The abstract form of the Existentialist's argument for an ethic of reciprocal freedom, then, is this: since my view of myself is indelibly coloured by how I take myself to stand in the eyes of others, then an authentic understanding of myself as freedom – one released from 'connivance' in bad faith – requires me to view others as possessed of this same kind of existence. Unless I so view them, I cannot expect them to view me in that manner. Only if I regard and treat others – or better, regard them *through* treating them – as loci of existential freedom will I receive back an image of myself as just such a locus.

If this argument is well taken, there is no conflict between the Existentialist's 'individualism' and his insistence on a person's entwinement in the lives of others. On the contrary, it is because a person is, in Saint-Exupéry's words, so much a 'network of relationships' with others that Merleau-Ponty can write that my 'freedom cannot be willed without leaving behind its *singular* relevance.'[46] As Sartre puts it, reversing the 'loner' image of the existentialist 'hero', 'one cannot achieve the conversion [from bad faith] *alone*.'[47]

The position now reached is one to which most of our writers would subscribe. To earlier quotes one could add Jaspers' remark that 'man becomes free only in so far as the other one becomes free' and Heidegger's reference to people being 'authentically bound together' only when each 'frees the Other in his freedom for himself'.[48] The Existentialist would concede, however, that this ethic of reciprocal freedom so far remains depressingly abstract. It is impossible to judge it without knowing what it might indicate by way of concrete relations with others. To secure conviction, the Existentialist must provide illustrations, from various provinces of life, to clarify how my 'seizure' of my freedom requires 'collaboration' in a like 'seizure' by others. We want illustrations, that is, of how my exercise of the capacities for self-reflection, 'refusal' and 'beginning something else' imply my 'solidarity' with others in their exercise of these capacities. Clearly there is a lot of work for the Existentialist to do here, for the exercise of the capacities of freedom can, as we know, be broken down into various components – distancing oneself from the 'they', obtaining a clear-sighted appreciation of one's situation, gaining a relatively cohesive conception of one's life as a whole and so on. Each of these components would have to be tested at a reasonably concrete level for their reciprocal character. The most the Existentialist can do in the space remaining is to offer a few samples of his ethic in action, so to speak.

One sample was met with earlier, in connection with Sartre's discussion of committed literature. The relationship between the 'serious' author and his readers was Sartre's paradigm of authentic human intercourse. Not only does this writer 'appeal to the reader's freedom' but, through doing so, his experience and exercise of his own are enhanced. More generally, my 'seizure' of freedom requires me to engage in a certain kind of open communication with others. The point, in part, is of the sort made by J. S. Mill: unless I speak openly and honestly to my audience, I shall not receive back from them informed critical responses that are of any value for purposes of self-criticism. The refusal to communicate openly, says Jaspers, is 'the most seductive form of inauthentic self-assertion'.[49] But there is a deeper point as well.

A criticism often levelled by 'continental' writers – structuralists, post-structuralists, critical theorists – is that Sartrean authenticity is rendered nugatory by the impossibility, in our kind of society at least, of transparent communication. All communication, we hear, is 'systematically distorted', or replete with hidden rhetorical devices which work on hearers even despite the speaker's intention: or a 'code' intervenes, so that the speaker is never able to get across his message 'neat'. These critics are, of course, agreeing with Sartre on the essential point that authenticity does require transparent communication. If my speech is infected in the ways supposed, I do not 'appeal to the hearer's freedom', for to a degree I manipulate him, keep him in the dark, and mean more (or less) than I appear to. But if this is how I view the hearer's situation, then this must be my situation when I am the hearer. I must regard myself as the unknowing target of rhetorical devices, the victim of a distorting 'code' through which words are filtered, and unable to receive just what the speaker intended to emit. Jaspers wrote that 'what is not realized in communication does not yet exist', and Merleau-Ponty that 'speech does not translate ready-made thought, but accomplishes it.'[50] The person who regards himself as engaged in distorted communication can have no confidence as to what speakers, including himself, are 'realizing' and 'accomplishing'. In particular, he can have no confidence in the sense and mutual intelligibility of the exercises of self-reflection and 'refusal' which are conducted, paramountly, in and through dialogue with writers and other speakers. The ethical implication for a person who so conceives the character of communication is that he should work towards the construction of what Habermas calls 'ideal speech situations': conditions under which men can speak with one another without distortion, intervention and hidden agendas; conditions, that is, under which a person can view the language he speaks and hears as one through which he can really exercise the capacities of existential freedom. It is just this towards which Sartre envisages the 'serious' author to be working.

A second sample is suggested by Heidegger's distinction between two kinds of 'solicitude': 'that which leaps in and dominates, and that which leaps forth and liberates'. The former, inauthentic kind 'take[s] away "care" from the Other', 'disburdens' him of his problems and so makes him dependent on someone else's dealing with matters. The second, authentic kind does not 'disburden' the Other, but calls him to face up to his concerns, and so 'helps the Other to become transparent to himself *in* his care and to become *free for* it'.[51]

Heidegger then claims that the kind of 'solicitude' one displays towards others is not independent of one's comportment towards oneself. 'Solicitude proves to be a state of *Dasein*'s Being...bound up with its...authentic Being towards itself.'[52] To the degree that I treat others as creatures to be relieved of their 'care', I regard them and myself as ready-to-hand or present-at-hand.

His point can be elucidated by comparing it to one made by Stefan Zweig in his neglected novel *Ungeduld des Herzens (The Heart's Impatience)*. A young soldier, drunk at a party, crassly insists on dancing with a girl who turns out to be badly crippled. His remorse develops into a 'weak-willed and sentimental' pity. His attempts to distract the girl from her condition, and to cheer her up with false hopes of a cure, are contrasted with the 'unsentimental, but creative' sympathy of a doctor who encourages her to face up and accommodate to her situation, without illusions or despairing obsession. (Zweig must surely have read Nietzsche's distinction between the 'moraline', 'Christian' pity, which 'belittles' people by applying to 'the creature in man', and a 'noble' pity for the person who 'lags behind what could have come of him'.)[53]

Zweig describes the cloying pity of the soldier as an attempt to 'escape from the painful emotion felt at another's misfortune'. By distracting the girl, by never mentioning her legs except when encouraging hopes of a cure, he is in effect 'disburdening' *himself*. And this, I think, illustrates Heidegger's point. The problems, misfortunes and concerns of those I am close to fall within my own sphere of 'care'. By 'taking away "care" from the Other', I do not so much shoulder his concerns as 'disburden' *myself* of the issue which their 'care' constitutes for me – lover, son, colleague, or whatever I may be. At its crudest, I evade the suffering which his suffering would cause me by blinding him as to his situation. Conversely, an acceptance of my responsibility to integrate into my life those concerns which arise from the concerns of someone close to me requires that I do not distract him from his concerns, but help him 'become transparent to himself' in those concerns. Put differently: a true appreciation of my situation – a precondition for the exercise of existential freedom – requires that I 'collaborate' in others' appreciation of theirs, warts and all.

The final sample is suggested by a passage not from an existentialist writer, but from someone who, despite her criticisms of Sartre and others, admits and appreciates their influence on her – Iris Murdoch. A character in her novel *The Philosopher's Pupil* remarks:

> We have simply 'cut free', and what we have done is not really so mysterious (or grand) after all. There are many aspects to our freedom. One is certainly an absence of vanity ... a complete indifference to 'what people say'. We are outside the power of censure, as ... *very few* people are.

When we achieve this, and also eliminate 'apathy and a desire to be liked',

> have we not reached a place which some deny exists? Not by a dramatic leap, or by the development of some narrow specialized super-virtue, but by a simple movement of escape, like an eel slipping out of a trap.[54]

There are two points to make about this passage. First, it captures much of what the Existentialist intends by existential freedom. When that notion is understood, not as an 'original choice' or Kierkegaardian 'leap', but in terms of powers for withdrawal, 'refusal' and 'beginning something else', then it indeed incorporates a 'movement of escape'. The exercise of these powers will certainly require an 'indifference to "what people say"' when 'people' here are the 'they'.

The second point is to underline the 'we' in the passage. The 'movement of escape' described is not one a person can make alone: not, at any rate, if he is to have confidence that the escape route is realistic. Misconceptions notwithstanding, the Existentialist does not think that each of us is an island. A person will find the courage and discipline to resist 'apathy and the desire to be liked' by 'people', the 'they', only in the company of others, 'very few' perhaps, who are also trying to find them. At its simplest, this person will need others to *talk* to. (Even Zarathustra, in his mountain eyrie, needed his talking animals for his attempt to go 'beyond' the valuations of the 'herd'.) But these others, the 'very few', must themselves be embarked on a similar movement, so that they turn to this person as much as he does to them for 'collaboration' in their 'escape'. The person who cajoles and browbeats those close to him, who in these and other ways stymies their efforts at self- reflection and 'refusal', cannot find in them the sounding-boards, the companions, he requires. It is itself a mode of bad faith to abandon entirely a concern for how others regard one, and a perverted mode of heroism to dispense completely with the succour and encouragement that others can afford. Unless I keep company with, and listen to, those whose own efforts I respect, I cannot be sure that mine are more than exercises in the kind of eccentricity which the 'they' is happy to encourage and pass off as the essence of freedom and individuality. Unless I 'collaborate' with others, then who can I trust to tell me that the picture I form of my life is not, to quote Murdoch again, a mere 'concoction', designed as a 'consolation' or 'cure', rather than a serious reflection of my situation with all its 'rough contingent rubble'?[55]

The samples lend some substance and credence to an ethic of reciprocal freedom. Each suggests in its different way that a person's exercise of freedom requires 'collaboration' in similar exercises by others, and so provides sense and support for the claim that to will one's own freedom is to will that of others too.

There is one difference among the samples which deserves special attention. In the first of them, the others whose freedom is to be 'appealed to' by the 'serious' writer are intended, by Sartre, to be everyone. In the remaining samples, however, the others are people who are more or less close to me: a friend in trouble, say, or a fellow student, or a girlfriend, whose life impinges upon mine. This suggests there may be a tension among existentialist writers as to where the emphasis should be placed: upon a universal reciprocity of freedom, or upon a limited, intimate reciprocity which could obtain only among people whose lives are intertwined. And we do find a rough division between those like Sartre and Merleau-Ponty, whose main concern is with the former, and those like Marcel, Jaspers and Buber, who concentrate on the latter. It would be wrong to exaggerate this division. While Merleau-Ponty's focus may be on a global 'slavery' and that freedom which 'cannot be willed ... without willing freedom for all', he also writes of 'the task of a true communication' with those who are bodily, perhaps sexually, present to me.[56] Jaspers, on the other hand, may emphasize, somewhat glutinously, the mutual freedom to be won through 'loving struggle' with a 'beloved wife', but he is also the champion of a new 'world-order' through which 'everyone can be united, because it maximizes the chances of freedom for all.'[57]

The tension is nevertheless there. That it is should not occasion any great surprise, for it is a reflection within existentialist ranks of the division between two 'kinds of morality' noted by Sartre: that, roughly, of 'sympathy and personal devotion', and that of 'wider scope' (see p. 175 above). This is a division which, in its various manifestations, runs through the history of moral thought. No one should expect the Existentialist, therefore, to produce a short, sharp argument which clinches the case for one or other of the two kinds.

Nevertheless, he does have reasons for thinking that the reciprocity which it is the more plausible to regard as a requirement of an individual's exercise of freedom will be the more limited, intimate kind. For one thing, it is hard to take seriously the idea that my exercise of freedom depends on a like exercise by *everyone*. Even the best-selling 'serious' writer, whose 'experience of freedom' is alleged to depend on 'appealing' to others' freedom, will be selling to only a very limited number of educated readers. One cannot see how the condition of everyone else is supposed to impinge on his 'experience of freedom'. The rhetoric of Sartre and Merleau-Ponty, to the effect that the freedom of us oppressors in the West demands the emancipation of the world's oppressed, is either just that, rhetoric, or it invokes a quite different concept of freedom from that of existential freedom.

Second, the Existentialist has a reason for denying the requirement of a more global reciprocity which is similar to Richard Rorty's reason for denying that his 'ironist' has any immediate concern for a general 'human solidarity'. This 'ironist' is strikingly similar, in several respects, to the Existentialist's authentic individual. He is someone who renounces the possibility of a 'final vocabulary' as a yardstick for beliefs and values, and so subscribes to the Existentialist's anti-foundationalist thesis of 'absurdity'. 'Ironists', moreover, are engaged in the task of 'mak[ing] the best selves for ourselves that we can' through challenging the vocabularies which have been inherited.[58] This transcendence of prevailing vocabularies through 'constant redescription' is a large part of the Existentialist's withdrawal from, and 'refusal' of, the ways of the 'they'. Rorty then writes that 'in the ideal liberal society, the intellectuals would still be ironists, although the non-intellectuals would not.' It is neither possible nor desirable that most people in a society should be 'continually dubious about their own process of socialization'. It is not, at least, desirable for the 'ironist', since she 'cannot get along without the contrast between the final vocabulary she inherited and the one she is trying to create for herself'. Irony is 'intrinsically...reactive'.[59] The way Rorty puts this is by saying that 'irony' is 'inherently a private matter', but by 'private' he does not mean solitary, for his 'ironists' are very much engaged in conversing with and reading one another.

Rorty's, and the Existentialist's, point is that it is impossible for people to exercise powers of 'redescription', withdrawal and 'refusal' – impossible, therefore, to pursue authenticity or 'private perfection' – except against a background of relative stability in the thought and vocabulary of their society. The person intent on an authentic existence or 'private perfection' cannot, therefore, think it desirable, even if it were possible, for too many of his fellows to be bent in a similar direction. The point is, in effect, a milder version of Nietzsche's aggressive insistence on a 'pathos of distance' between 'free spirits' and the 'herd' whose 'opposition' they need and which they 'live off'.[60]

Those who charge existentialism with yielding an 'elitist' ethic, whether or not they do so for the right reasons, are not without justification. The exercise of existential freedom looks to be one conducted by the few in the company of the few. To be sure, this exercise is not, as Iris Murdoch would say, a 'grand' one in all of its aspects. There are many 'little' ways in which each of us, with the help of those around us, can 'appeal' to the freedom of others and 'collaborate' in an indifference to 'what people say'. It remains, however, that there is a 'grand' aspect to the exercise. It is called 'philosophy'; for what else shall we call reflection on the schemes and vocabularies which we have inherited? Philosophy so understood will be tangentially related to what is pursued by a handful of people in university philosophy departments, yet it could hardly be a demotic pursuit. Few people will have the leisure, inclination or education seriously to engage in it, so that under any foreseeable conditions it will remain a minority privilege.

We end this section where we began it: with a comparison with Aristotle. He argued that above what he named the 'ethical virtues' there lay the 'intellectual virtues', for it is in the latter that the distinctive human *ergon*, reason, is most fully manifested. Philosophy in particular is the theatre for the display of these virtues. The Existentialist does not share Aristotle's view of reason as the human *ergon*, nor does he follow the division into ethical and intellectual virtues. Philosophy, for him, is inextricably woven into the wider collaborative endeavour of self-reflection, withdrawal, 'refusal' and 'beginning something else': the endeavour to be free from the 'they' and the 'predominance of the Other'. But, like Aristotle, he is not shy to proclaim that human beings realize their authentic existence in a transcendence of the commonplace, in philosophizing. It is no objection to either of them that, according to the egalitarian sentiment of our age, this is snobbery. If they are wrong, it is because they have misidentified the character of human existence or the conditions for its authentic manifestation.

On a radio programme about Camus, Pierre Boulez reminisced about the excitement generated by existentialism in the Paris of his youth. His somewhat 'franglais' conclusion, however, was that 'when the *actualités* have gone, it is a lot of noise about not very much!' I hope this book will have overturned verdicts like Boulez'. For all the sensation, existentialism was never just 'news' or a 'current event'. The journey made by the Existentialist has taken him from an initial sense of people's alienation from the world, each other and themselves, to a tentative conclusion on how human dignity is to be secured. This journey has been too long and complicated for a neat synopsis, but it is clearly one of perennial interest which now crosses, now coincides with, other journeys traced by the great philosophical traditions. No doubt it is a journey which could only have been made in just the way it was during our own century. But that does not reduce it to a trip around the Latin Quarter, ending up at the Tabou or the Pergola somewhere around 1950.

Notes

1   *Existentialism*, 1970, pp. 125–6.
2   *The Sovereignty of the Good*, 1985, p. 47.
3   Ibid., p. 52.
4   See, for example, Gabriel Marcel, *Being and Having*, 1949, pp. 69ff.
5   *Existentialism and Humanism*, 1966, pp. 38, 49.
6   Ibid., pp. 35–6. Anthony Manser, *Sartre: A Philosophic Study*, 1966, is one of the few commentators to appreciate the importance of this point about two kinds of morality for Sartre.
7   *Existentialism and Humanism*, p. 50. Actually he uses the word 'sincerity', but he is clearly talking about authenticity rather than the sincerity discussed in *Being and Nothingness*.
8   Ibid., pp. 51, 53.
9   De Beauvoir, *The Mandarins*, 1982, p. 646.
10 Sartre, *Existentialism and Humanism*, p. 52.
11 See, for example, Ronald Dworkin, 'Liberalism', 1978.
12 Quoted in Ronald Hayman, *Writing Against: A Biography of Sartre*, 1986, p. 250.
13 *Cahiers pour une morale*, 1983, p. 498.
14 *What is Literature?*, 1967, p. 59.
15 Sartre, *The Age of Reason*, 1961, p. 122.
16 *The Eclipse of God*, 1979, p. 70.
17 Sartre, 'L'enfance d'un chef', in his *Le Mur*, 1939, p. 226.
18 Sartre, *The Age of Reason*, p. 121. Jaspers also misses the point, when he refers to how 'difficult psychologically' it is to 'carry out [one's] own beliefs' while admitting they have no greater 'objective validity' than competing ones. Quoted by Charles F. Wallraff, *Karl Jaspers: An Introduction to his Philosophy*, 1970, p. 17.
19 *Cahiers pour une morale*, p. 435.

20 David Caute, Introduction to Sartre's *The Reprieve*, 1986, p. vii.
21 Gabriel Marcel, 'Existence and human freedom', in his *The Philosophy of Existence*, 1948, p. 64.
22 Gabriel Marcel, 'On the ontological mystery', in ibid., p. 22. On Marcel, see my articles on him and existentialist ethics in the Routledge *Encyclopedia of Philosophy*.
23 Ibid., p. 27.
24 Marcel, *Being and Having*, p. 71.
25 Ibid., pp. 119–20.
26 Ibid., p. 69.
27 Jaspers, *Philosophy*, vol. 3, 1971, p. 207. Marcel's acknowledgement of a 'real debt to this noble and profound thinker', Jaspers, indicates the close affinity between them: Marcel, *The Philosophy of Existence*, p. vii.
28 *Being and Having*, pp. 45, 120.
29 Ibid., p. 72.
30 Ibid., pp. 106–7.
31 'On the ontological mystery', in his *The Philosophy of Existence*, p. 28.
32 *What is Literature?*, p. 22.
33 Ibid., pp. 32, 119.
34 Ibid., pp. 36, 32.
35 *Cahiers pour une morale*, p. 443.
36 Preface to Frantz Fanon, *The Wretched of the Earth*, 1963, pp. 24–5.
37 *Existentialism and Humanism*, p. 52.
38 Ibid.
39 *Cahiers pour une morale*, p. 487.
40 Ibid., pp. 463, 490, 485.
41 Ibid., pp. 447–9.
42 Sartre, *Being and Nothingness: An Essay on Phenomenological Ontology*, 1957 pp. 364, 409.
43 Ibid., p. 412n.
44 Ibid., p. 408.
45 Sartre, *Cahiers pour une Morale*, p. 443. My account of the relation between *Being and Nothingness* and the later writings owes a good deal to Thomas Baldwin, 'Sartre, *Existentialism and Humanism*', 1986.
46 *Phenomenology of Perception*, 1962, p. 456.
47 *Cahiers pour une morale*, p. 16.
48 Jaspers, 'Philosophical autobiography', 1957, p. 85; Heidegger, *Being and Time*, p. 122H.
49 *Einführung in die Philosophie*, 1985, p. 95.
50 Ibid.; Merleau-Ponty, *Phenomenology of Perception*, p. 178.
51 Heidegger, *Being and Time*, p. 122H.
52 Ibid.
53 Nietzsche, *Beyond Good and Evil*, section 225; Nietzsche, *The Will to Power*, 1968, Section 373.
54 Iris Murdoch, *The Philosopher's Pupil*, 1983, p. 406.
55 Ibid., p. 81.

196 Existentialism and Ethics

56 *Phenomenology of Perception*, p. 456; 'The primacy of perception and its philosophical consequences', 1974, p. 203.
57 'Philosophical autobiography', p. 85; *Einführung in die Philosophie*, p. 83.
58 Richard Rorty, *Contingency, Irony, and Solidarity*, 1989, pp. 96, 80.
59 Ibid., pp. 87–8.
60 *The Will to Power*, Section 866.

Appendix
Heidegger and Sartre:
an 'erroneous conflation'?

This book has been organized, not around individual philosophers, but around themes and directions of thought that the Existentialist has culled from various figures in the existentialist tradition. Some names, however – above all those of Heidegger and Sartre – have occurred with great frequency. More significantly, it was by reference to these two thinkers that I made my preliminary identification of the existentialist tradition. If Heidegger and Sartre are not existentialists, I said in chapter 1, no one is. I duly noted a possible problem with this strategy: maybe it over-assimilates the philosophies of these two men. Thus I cited one commentator's wild remark that these 'two philosophers... are radically opposed in every respect.' Having offered a few reasons, in staccato style, for rejecting such remarks, I left it to subsequent chapters to show up the affinities between the two thinkers, instead of devoting an explicit discussion to those affinities.

For two reasons, I now take advantage of the opportunity which a revised edition provides to add such a discussion. First, there have continued to appear, over the last decade, books and articles by authors – let's call them 'separatists' – which challenge the older assumption that Heidegger and Sartre belong, as it were, in the same camp. One reads, for example, of the 'erroneous, but highly influential conflation between [Sartre's] existentialism and Heidegger's thought'.[1] 'Separatist' claims are worth examining in their own right. But a second reason for examining these claims is that, if they were correct, then my approach in this book would be misguided. Heidegger would not be an existentialist at all, so that any wisdom culled from his writings could not be assimilated by anyone appropriately dubbed 'the Existentialist'. This appendix defends the book's starting-point and approach against 'separatist' critics.

Before examining the 'separatist' case, three preliminary remarks are in order. First, all the 'separatists' I know of are enthusiasts for Heidegger's philosophy which, they think, was misunderstood and bowdlerized by Sartre and people like myself who 'conflate' the two thinkers. Unsurprisingly, therefore, they rely heavily on Heidegger's own hostile comments on Sartre in the 1947 essay, 'Letter on Humanism', in which he disowns the label of 'existentialist' and suggests that his philosophy was never significantly similar to the Frenchman's. The questions this essay raises concerning the relation between Heidegger's earlier and later thinking, and the accuracy of his retrospective account of his earlier views, are too complex to discuss here.[2] Suffice it to remark, however, that many commentators are sceptical, and reasonably so, about the reliability of that retrospective account.[3]

Second, I nowhere disguised that there are interesting differences, at several points, between Heidegger and Sartre – ones, for example, over the essential aspects of our Being-for-others and over the political implications of authenticity. I could have mentioned others, had they been relevant to the direction of thought taken by the Existentialist. It is clear, however, that such differences are neither sufficient to warrant talk of a totally 'erroneous conflation' of the two thinkers, nor in fact those which 'separatists' tend to harp on.

Third, even if the differences were more momentous than I allow, it would still be quixotic to publish a book called *Existentialism* without drawing on the writings of Heidegger as well as Sartre, and I know of no general book on existentialism which does not devote considerable space to Heidegger. For one thing, the word 'existentialist' has become something of a proper name: it labels certain figures – Sartre, de Beauvoir, Jaspers, and others, *including* Heidegger. Existentialism, as commonly perceived, *is* what one finds in such authors. A book with my title that omitted Heidegger would resemble one called *The British Empiricists* which left out John Locke. In both cases, readers would feel short-changed. That Locke may have differed substantially from later empiricists, like Hume, would not excuse the omission. 'The British Empiricists' *means* Locke, Berkeley, Hume and co. For another thing, it cannot seriously be denied that both Sartre and Heidegger were exponents of existential pheneomenology, and that both were concerned to address those issues of human existence, such as *Angst* and authenticity, bequeathed by Kierkegaard and Nietzsche. And existentialism, I suggested, is reasonably understood as a fusion of existential phenomenology and concern for those issues. That said, my reasons for giving Heidegger a prominent place were not solely fear of disappointing readers' expectations and his fusion of phenomenology with 'problems of life'. If the 'separatists' are right, I concede that my starting-point was a misleading one. So I need to examine their case.

Consider the following remarks by the author, Tom Rockmore, whose accusation of 'erroneous conflation' I cited above. In Sartre, he writes, 'everything happens as if the subject were understood on a "Cartesian" model.' Indeed, 'the prominence of "Cartesian" subjectivity . . . is a major factor in existentialism of all kinds.' Central to Sartre's thought is 'the theme of freedom' which he explains by 'developing a view of human consciousness as independent of its surroundings'.[4] Such remarks are typical of 'separatism', and in them we find deployed the three terms which loom largest in 'separatist' criticism: 'Cartesian', 'subjectivity' and 'consciousness'. The terms, of course, form a triad, for Descartes was the philosopher *par excellence* to have given a central place to the subject considered as a conscious 'thinking thing'.

The 'separatist' claim, then, is this: Sartre was a Cartesian thinker, wedded to the pivotal idea of the conscious subject, whereas Heidegger was a robust anti-Cartesian who rejected the very idea of the subject and in whose account of human existence the notion of consciousness plays virtually no role. My concern is not to challenge this characterization of Heidegger's outlook, though it will require qualifications. The characterization of Sartre, on the other hand, seems to me entirely mistaken.

Let's begin with the charge of 'Cartesianism'. In current parlance, this term does not apply to Descartes' philosophy alone, but to philosophical approaches, especially in the philosophy of mind, which, in essential respects, follow the Frenchman's. Which respects are 'essential' can, to be sure, be contested, but it is not necessarily objectionable, and may be illuminating, to describe as 'Cartesian' views which, in certain respects, contradict Descartes' own. For example, a materialist who identifies the mind with the brain may be 'Cartesian', for while he disagrees with Descartes over the 'stuff' which composes the mind, he shares with him the more basic view that the mind is a 'substance', a 'thing which thinks', logically independent of the (rest of the) body and material world.

Still, there are clearly limits on how far the philosophy of a 'Cartesian' can differ from Descartes' own. Surely he must subscribe to a significant number of the following propositions advanced by Descartes:

a   The existence of the external world, including the body, can sensibly be doubted.

b   The mind/self/*cogito*, whose existence cannot be doubted, is entirely distinct from the external world and the body.

c   The mind is an intellectual substance, whose connections with the world are contingent and causal.

d   The mind is indirectly related to the external world through 'ideas' or 'representations' which are immediately present to it and transparent to introspection.

e   The external world is a 'machine', its nature and operations entirely explicable in terms of mathematical physics: hence, it makes no sense to suppose that external things as such have meaning and value. (This would need qualification, not germane to the present discussion, in the light of Descartes' theology.)

f   Intellect and will are independent faculties: hence, understanding how things are and what things there are has nothing to do with considerations of desire, purpose and will.

Sartre, like Heidegger, rejects *every one* of these propositions (a)–(f). Hence it is absurd to describe him as a 'Cartesian'. Those who so describe him are either failing to obey proper constraints on the use of the label, or they have not read Sartre with care. One wonders, for example, what on earth one author can have in mind by the label when he describes as 'Cartesian' Merleau-Ponty's view, largely shared by Sartre, of a person as 'the lived body' – a view expressly opposed to Descartes' conception of a person as a mind *plus* a body. As for reading Sartre rightly, I hope that the previous chapters have amply documented his rejection of *all* the Cartesian tenets. We have, for instance, encountered his references to 'Descartes' substantialist illusion', to the *cogito* as an 'idol', to Descartes' and Husserl's error in placing the world behind a veil of 'ideas' or 'representations' ('*representation* . . . is a pure invention of philosophers'),[5] to the world as a 'human world' which is the 'product' of our purposive activities, to the absurdity of isolating consciousness from the world that is present to us, to the impossibility of regarding a person as 'the union of soul and body' ('the very nature of the For-itself demands that it be body')[6] – and so on.

Nor are any of these claims of Sartre's occasional ones which he sometimes abandons. In the 1948 essay *Truth and Existence*, for example, we find him reaffirming, *inter alia*, his hostility to the idea that there are pre-interpretative 'givens' transparent to the mind, to any attempt to describe the world in isolation from human purposes and projects, and to the thought that the For-itself exists 'in a state of indifferent exteriority' to the world. 'The world appears to a being in the midst of the world...[a being] *of* the world.'[7]

I can think of only two objections that a 'separatist' might raise at this stage. The first is that, however radically Sartre rejected Cartesian doctrines like (a)–(f), he was, like the Master, a 'dualist': he divided reality into Being-for-itself and Being-in-itself. So he did, but this calls for a couple of remarks. First, this is not a division between different kinds of entities or beings (immaterial substances *versus* material substances, souls *versus* bodies, etc.), but between the kinds of being or existence enjoyed by people and by 'mere' material objects respectively. Being a conscious, intelligent creature endowed with mentality or 'mindedness' is very different from being a thing not so endowed. If this is 'dualism' then, of course, Heidegger was equally a 'dualist', insisting on the gulf between the kind of being we have (*Dasein*) and the kinds possessed by mere things ('presence-at-hand', 'readiness-to- hand'). Second, Sartre is himself keen to ward off misleading metaphysical implications suggested by the 'dualist' tenor of his distinction. Having made it, he quickly warns that 'we have chosen an unfortunate approach', treating as separate what are really abstractions, terms 'not capable of existing in isolation'. Both consciousness and what appears to consciousness are abstractions from that basic and 'concrete...union of man with the world which Heidegger...calls "being-in-the-world"'.[8]

The only other 'separatist' objection I can envisage is that we have it from the horse's mouth that Sartre was a 'Cartesian'. Does he not write that 'our point of departure is...the subjectivity of the individual' and the 'absolute truth of consciousness' expressed by Descartes' 'I think therefore I am'?[9] He does, but since a page later he disassociates himself from Descartes' own construal of the 'I think' as referring to a self that might exist in splendid isolation, it is to Sartre's understanding of 'subjectivity' and 'consciousness' that we should attend – terms which, I noted, invariably loom large in 'separatist' accusations.

I take it as obvious that the mere fact that one philosopher does, while a second does not, speak of 'starting out' from subjectivity and consciousness is no reason for suppos-ing that their positions are importantly different and that the first is a 'Cartesian' while the second is not. It all depends what they have in mind by the two terms. Sartre, I hold, understands subjectivity and consciousness very differently from Descartes and Husserl. Heidegger, on the other hand, generally understands the terms as they figure in those thinkers' acounts and *for that reason* refuses to allot to subjectivity and consciousness any central role in his own philosophy. The importance of subjectivity and consciousness on Sartre's understanding of the concepts is not something, as Sartre himself saw, that Heidegger should have denied.

Let's start with consciousness. Heidegger rarely employs this word and when he does it usually comes with scare-quotes. This is not, of course, because he denied that human beings are conscious beings. 'Formally, it is unassailable to speak of the ego as consciousness-*of*-something.'[10] He is, however, chary of using the term, given the grip that the wayward philosophies of Descartes, Natorp, Husserl and others have got on people's conceptions of consciousness. For one thing, these philosophers are guilty of an erroneous 'reification of consciousness', treating consciousness as some kind of stuff, container or gossamer-like secretion of the soul, like 'act-rays issuing from an ego-center'. Second, as the expression 'act-rays' suggests, these philosophers treat consciousness as, essentially, consisting in the performance of conscious acts – explicit, reflective judgements. Combined with their equation of consciousness with intentionality, this results in a 'perverted' view of intentionality as fundamentally the performance of discrete mental acts (see chapter 3 above). Each of these erroneous accounts contributes, for Heidegger, to the disastrous conclusion – which Husserl, for one, enthusiastically embraces – that conscious existence is something that might exist in isolation from the world which we are 'in'.

Sartre is not simply in total agreement with Heidegger on these points, but makes them pivotal to his account of consciousness. The whole thrust, for example, of describing consciousness as a 'nothing', and of parenthesizing the word 'of' when referring, say, to 'consciousness (of) a table', is to reject the 'reificatory' idea of consciousness as some thing or container distinct from the world in the midst of which we are conscious. (How, in the light of this, anyone can attribute to Sartre 'a view of human consciousness as independent of its surroundings' is beyond my comprehension.) Sartre even follows Heidegger in ridiculing the image of consciousness as 'light rays' emitted from some source. Such ridicule, as with Heidegger, signals an attack on the view that intentional life is, fundamentally, the performance of so many explicit conscious acts. Truly fundamental is an 'operative intentionality', where consciousness is 'pre-reflective', as when I am absorbed in counting my cigarettes but without directing any reflective attention to what I am doing.[11]

As Gregory McCulloch persuasively argues, the 'separatist' complaint that Sartre invokes a Cartesian view of consciousness in opposition to Heidegger's anti-Cartesian stance may, in a sense, be 'back to front'. For while

> Heidegger rightly offers skills and coping as the bedrock of our experience of the world, [he] sometimes seems to leave a 'strict' form of consciousness to the Cartesians. Sartre, on the other hand, sees more clearly that skills and coping are *forms* of the only non-reflective consciousness we are capable of.[12]

In other words, Heidegger surrenders the *concept* of consciousness to the Cartesians and hence tries to provide an account of intelligent, intentional activity without invoking that concept. Sartre, more plausibly perhaps, regards the notion of consciousness as indispensable, and so tries to offer an account of such activity in terms of a concept of consciousness purged of all Cartesian trappings.

There remains the notion of 'subjectivity'. Do we find a substantial difference, registering a Cartesian *versus* anti-Cartesian approach, between Sartre and Heidegger over this?

As we saw in chapters 1 and 5, the word 'subject' and its cognates are highly ambiguous, and the targets of the many authors – Foucault, Lévi-Strauss, Derrida and so on – who have denounced 'subjectivity' in recent years have varied wildly. Hence one should be cautious in assuming that the 'subjectivity' which is Sartre's 'point of departure' is the same animal that Heidegger, in *Being and Time* and related writings, is hunting down. In fact, neither of them employs the term in a single sense, but for the most part they have quite different notions in mind. With one qualification to come, I suggest that Heidegger is as much a 'subjectivist' in Sartre's preferred sense as Sartre is an 'anti-subjectivist' in Heidegger's.

Despite the impression given by some 'separatist' commentators, Heidegger did not deny the existence of 'subjects' and 'subjectivity' *tout court*. There are many references in *Being and Time* to *Dasein* as a 'factical' or 'actual' subject, and as a 'subject-entity'.[13] Heidegger's animosity to talk of subjects and subjectivity is always directed against the bad theories in which such talk has, since Descartes, become entangled. In particular, he objects to 'the idea of a subject which has intentional experiences merely inside its own sphere' and to the view that 'self and the world' are 'two beings, like subject and object', which happen to come into contact.[14] In short, his hostility to 'subjectivity' is to substantialist accounts of minds and their objects. *Dasein* is not a 'subject' if that term is understood as it is on those accounts.

And nor, of course, is Sartre's human being or For-itself a 'subject' in that sense. As we have seen in previous chapters and this appendix, Sartre's rejection of substantialist treatments is no less robust than Heidegger's. So in what senses, if any, is Sartre a friend of subjectivity? We have already encountered other senses of the term in which he is certainly no subjectivist. He is not, for example, a 'subjective idealist' like Bishop Berkeley; nor does he hold that truth and value are 'subjective' in the sense of being matters of mere personal opinion (see pp. 16ff. and 174ff. above).

What Sartre means by 'subjectivity' and 'subjectivism' is made tolerably clear in *Existentialism and Humanism*. 'Subjectivism,' he writes, 'means . . . the freedom of the individual subject and . . . that man cannot pass beyond human subjectivity,' where 'subjectivity' in turn means that 'man is nothing else but that which he makes of himself . . . something which propels itself towards a future.'[15] So what Sartre has in mind is entirely different from the notion of subjectivity which Heidegger criticizes in the texts which concern us. Indeed, Heidegger himself is clearly a subjectivist in Sartre's sense, for he too insists on the freedom of the individual *Dasein* to 'choose itself' and on *Dasein*'s being a 'project' that is always 'ahead-of-itself'. For neither philosopher is there *first* a self or subject which then 'projects' itself: rather, to be a self or subject *is* to be a 'projection'.

Some paragraphs back I flagged a qualification to the claim that Sartre is no more a subjectivist than is Heidegger. One thing that recent critics of subjectivity sometimes have in mind is a thesis of individualism – hyper-individualism, one might call it – which wrongly, as they see it, minimizes the reliance of an individual person's under-standing and capacities for action on his or her intercourse with others. Now at more than one place in this book, I noted a tension between Heidegger and Sartre in this connection. Thus, on pp. 159ff. I remarked that Merleau-Ponty's criticisms of Sartre's 'initial choice' – that 'choice' which 'depends only on itself' and in whose light all later choices are made – derive from Heidegger's insistence on the 'thrown' character of human existence. For Merleau-Ponty, as for Heidegger, before someone can 'choose' and 'refuse', he must already be immersed in a world as understood and interpreted by his fellows. And whereas, for Heidegger, authentic existence is something *won*, only after a struggle, from inauthentic life led under the dominion of the public 'they', Sartrean authenticity sounds like something we begin with but then, with the onset of bad faith, abandon.

I do not want to minimize the significance of this qualification, of the tension, that is, between Sartre and Heidegger over the issue of the reliance of individual choice on conditions 'outside of itself'. But nor should its significance be overdone, in the 'separatist' manner, to the point of denying that Heidegger belongs in the existentialist tradition at all. My qualification itself stands in need of several qualifications.

To begin with, it is not Heidegger but Sartre himself who is the odd man out in this debate. The Existentialist, indeed, made no bones about preferring the accounts of freedom offered by Merleau-Ponty, Jaspers, Marcel, Buber and others who, like Heidegger, reject the implausibly asocial view of freedom encapsulated in the doctrine of 'initial choice'. In fact, if rejection of that doctrine means abandonment of the existentialist cause, then existentialism is being stipulatively identified with Sartre's, and no one else's, thinking.

Second, the hyper-individualism of the doctrine of 'initial choice' is something Sartre himself quickly abandoned, and an interview of 1975 in which he recalls that abandonment makes it clear that this came well before those works, like *Critique of Dialectical Reason*, whose existentialist credentials may indeed be doubted.[16] The doctrine has, in fact, disappeared from such writings, otherwise largely continuous with *Being and Nothingness*, as *Truth and Existence* (1948).

Third, and more important, the hyper-individualistic thesis was never essential to Sartre's overall position, as in effect I (or the Existentialist) argued on pp. 161ff. At the heart of the existentialist conception of freedom are the twin claims that our choices and actions are not explicable in the causal terms employed for 'mere' things, and that our capacity for reflective assessment and 'refusal' of the beliefs and values into which we have been 'thrown' is a radical one. Neither of those claims requires the doctrine of 'initial choice', with its corollary that we begin as asocial isolates. And neither claim is one that Heidegger would take issue with. For him, as much as for Sartre or Merleau-Ponty, authenticity entails a capacity for an 'individualizing' escape from immersion in the ways of the 'they'. (One might, to be sure, argue that Heideggerian authenticity is incompatible with Heidegger's emphasis on the degree of our 'thrownness' in the 'they', but that is another matter.)[17]

Finally, and relatedly, Sartre's hyper-individualism was always badly at odds with aspects of his own existential phenomenology, as Merleau-Ponty perceptively noted (see p. 160 above). Consider especially Sartre's constant stress on the 'situated' character of our freedom. We always choose and act in situations. Now a situation, in his terminology, is never a set of 'objective' circumstances, but circumstances interpreted, experienced and encountered in a certain way. Crucially, a person's interpretation or mode of encountering these circumstances is not, in the first instance, some solo feat performed without any reliance on how others interpret and encounter them. Thus, in a passage which virtually reiterates Heidegger's view of the matter, Sartre writes:

> the For-itself arises in a world which is a world for other For-itselfs. Such is the *given*. And thereby...the meaning of the world is *alien* to the For-itself. This means simply that each man finds himself in the presence of *meanings* which do not come into the world through him. He arises in a world which is given to him as *already looked-at*, furrowed, explored, worked over in all its meanings, and whose very contexture is already defined by these investigations.[18]

Here we have, not the doctrine of solipsistic 'initial choice', but of Heideggerean 'thrownness' into an already interpreted world from which only subsequently can the authentic individual stand apart.

Or consider the following passage from *Truth and Existence*: 'judgement is an inter-individual phenomenon. *I* do not need to judge: I *see*. I judge only for the other. Judgement is an indicative gesture to the other.'[19] Sartre's point here, as he goes on to elaborate it, sounds themes salient in several other philosophers, including Wittgenstein and Habermas. No sense is to be made of notions like statement and judgement – nor, therefore, of the understanding and beliefs which these manifest – as the 'private' products or possessions of isolated individuals. To state, judge and understand is possible only for creatures that participate in ongoing social practices – of interpretation, verification and criticism – in terms of which such achievements have sense and purpose. Here too, then, we find that Sartre's considered position belies the individua-listic rhetoric of 'initial choice' and lonely abandonment.

With these qualification to my qualification in place, the immediate conclusion is that Sartre's hyper-individualistic 'subjectivism' is either not what it seems or something that he himself elsewhere mitigates. A further conclusion is that, given Sartre's unquestion-able rejection of 'subjectivity' in the other senses of that term identified earlier, he is no more to be diametrically pitted against Heidegger over this issue than he was over that of consciousness. Hence, Sartre is no more a Cartesian philosopher of subjectivity and consciousness than is Heidegger, and the 'separatist' claim fails.

Someone might, I suppose, still insist that it is 'more accurate' to describe Heidegger as an 'existential philosopher' than as an 'existentialist'.[20] But given the overwhelming tendency to include Heidegger among 'the existentialists', this would be a Canute-like gesture. It could only be warranted by a powerful argument demonstrating that the differences between Heidegger and Sartre are so significant that this tendency, even if unstoppable, is one to deplore. I have tried to show that no such argument can be made out.

Notes

1   Tom Rockmore, *Heidegger and French Philosophy*, p. 81.
2   I am more fulsome about these questions in my *Heidegger*, ch. 5 and 6.

3   See, for example, Frederick A. Olafson, *Heidegger and the Ground of Ethics*, 1998, introduction.

4   *Heidegger and French Philosophy*, 1995, pp. 56, 78ff. Rockmore, incidentally, does not quite make the 'separatist' claim as I go on to describe it, since he thinks that even *Being and Time* contains 'Cartesian' elements which Heidegger fully expunged only in later works.

5   *Being and Nothingness*, p. 217.

6   Ibid., p. 309.

7   *Truth and Existence*, p. 8.

8   *Being and Nothingness*, p. 3.

9   *Existentialism and Humanism*, p. 44.

10 *The Basic Problems of Phenomenology*, p. 158.

11 *Being and Nothingness*, pp. liii ff.

12 *The Mind and its World*, p. 148.

13 *e.g., Being and Time*, p. 229H.

14 *The Basic Problems of Phenomenology*, pp. 64, 297.

15 pp. 28ff.

16 Quoted in the editor's introduction to *Truth and Existence*, p. xl.

17 Hubert L. Dreyfus argues this in his *Being-in-the-World*.

18 *Being and Nothingness*, p. 520.

19 p. 7.

20 See Richard Schacht, 'Existentialism', p. 150.

Bibliography

Adorno, Theodor, *The Jargon of Authenticity*, trans. K. Tarnowski and F. Will, Northwestern University Press, 1973.

Anscombe, G. E. M., *Intention*, Blackwell, 1957.

Aristotle, *The Ethics of Aristotle*, trans. J. A. K. Thomson, Penguin, 1976.

Baldwin, Thomas, 'Sartre, *Existentialism and Humanism*', in *Philosophers Past and Present*, ed. G. Vesey, Cambridge University Press, 1986.

—— 'Phenomenology, solipsism and egocentric thought', *Proceedings of the Aristotelian Society*, suppl. vol. LXII, 1988.

Barrett, William, *Irrational Man: A Study in Existential Philosophy*, Heinemann, 1960.

Beauvoir, Simone de, *The Ethics of Ambiguity*, trans. B. Frechtman, Citadel, 1948.

—— *The Second Sex*, trans. H. M. Parshley, New English Library, 1962.

—— *The Prime of Life*, trans. Peter Green, Penguin, 1965.

—— *The Mandarins*, trans. L. M. Friedman, Fontana, 1982.

—— *The Blood of Others*, trans. R. Moyse and R. Senhouse, Penguin, 1984.

—— *Force of Circumstance*, trans. Richard Howard, Penguin, 1987.

Bell, David, 'Phenomenology, solipsism and egocentric thought', *Proceedings of the Aristotelian Society*, suppl. vol. LXII, 1988.

Berkeley, George, *Philosophical Writings*, Nelson, 1952.

Brown, David. *Continental Philosophy and Modern Theology*, Blackwell, 1987.

Buber, Martin, *I and Thou*, trans. R. Gregor Smith, T. & T. Clark, 1937.

—— *The Eclipse of God*, Humanities Press, 1979.

Camus, Albert, *The Outsider*, trans. J. Laredo, Penguin, 1960.

—— *The Myth of Sisyphus*, trans. Justin O' Brien, Penguin, 1986.

Caws, Peter, *Sartre*, Routledge & Kegan Paul, 1979.

Chuang-Tzu, *Chuang-Tzu*, in *Wisdom of the Daoist Masters*, trans. and ed. D. Bryce, Llanerch, 1984.

Cooper, David E., *Philosophy and the Nature of Language*, Longman, 1973.

—— *Authenticity and Learning: Nietzsche's Educational Philosophy*, Routledge & Kegan Paul, 1983.

Cooper, David E., 'Assertion, phenomenology and essence', *Proceedings of the Aristotelian Society*, suppl. vol. LXI, 1987.

—— 'Life and narrative', *International Journal of Moral and Social Studies*, 3, 1988.

—— *World Philosophies: An Historical Introduction*, Blackwell, 1995.

—— *Heidegger*, Claridge, 1996.

—— 'Existentialist ethics' and 'Gabriel Marcel', in *Routledge Encyclopedia of Philosophy*, ed. E. Craig, Routledge, 1998.

Danto, Arthur C., *Sartre*, Fontana, 1975.

Descartes, René, *Philosophical Letters*, trans. and ed. A. Kenny, Oxford University Press, 1970.

Dreyfus, Hubert L., Introduction to *Husserl, Intentionality and Cognitive Science*, ed. H. L. Dreyfus, MIT Press, 1982.

—— 'Husserl, Heidegger and modern existentialism', in *The Great Philosophers*, ed. B. Magee, Oxford University Press, 1987.

—— *Being-in-the-World: A Commentary on Heidegger's* Being and Time *Division I*, MIT Press, 1991.

Dreyfus, Hubert L. and Haugeland, John, 'Husserl and Heidegger: philosophy's last stand', in *Heidegger and Modern Philosophy*, ed. M. Murray.

Dworkin, Ronald, 'Liberalism', in *Public and Private Morality*, ed. S. Hampshire, Cambridge University Press, 1978.

Earle, William, 'Anthropology in the philosophy of Karl Jaspers', in *The Philosophy of Karl Jaspers*, ed. P. A. Schilpp.

Edwards, Paul, *Heidegger on Death*, Hegeler Institute, 1979.

Fell, Joseph J., *Heidegger and Sartre: An Essay on Being and Place*, Columbia University Press, 1979.

Finkielkraut, Alain, *The Undoing of Thought*, trans. Dennis O'Keeffe, Claridge, 1988.

Føllesdal, Dagfinn, 'Husserl's notion of noema', in *Husserl, Intentionality and Cognitive Science*, ed. H. L. Dreyfus.

Foot, Philippa, 'Moral beliefs', in *Theories of Ethics*, ed. P. Foot, Oxford University Press, 1967.

Frege, Gottlob, 'On sense and reference', in his *Philosophical Writings*, trans. Max Black and Peter Geech, Blackwell, 1966.

Gardiner, Patrick, *Kierkegaard*, Oxford University Press, 1988.

Gide, André, *Les Caves du Vatican*, Pléiade, 1958.

—— *Journals 1889–1949*, trans. Justin O'Brien, Penguin, 1978.

Gillespie, M. A., *Hegel, Heidegger, and the Ground of History*, University of Chicago Press, 1984.

Glover, Jonathan, *I: The Philosophy and Psychology of Personal Identity*, Penguin, 1988.

Guignon, Charles B., *Heidegger and the Problem of Knowledge*, Hackett, 1983.

Guignon, Charles and Pereboom, Derk (eds), *Existentialism: Basic Writings*, Hackett, 1995.

Haar, Michel, 'Sartre and Heidegger', in *Jean-Paul Sartre: Contemporary Approaches to his Philosophy*, ed. H. Silverman and F. Elliston.

Habermas, Jürgen, *The Philosophical Discourse of Modernity*, trans. Frederick Lawrence, Polity Press, 1988.

Hampshire, Stuart, *Thought and Action*, Chatto & Windus, 1959.

Hayman, Ronald, *Writing Against: A Biography of Sartre*, Weidenfeld & Nicolson, 1986.

Hegel, G. W. F., *The Philosophy of History*, trans. J. Sibree, Dover, 1956.

—— *The Philosophy of Right*, trans. T. M. Knox, Oxford University Press, 1962.

—— *The Philosophy of Mind*, trans. W. Wallace and A. V. Miller, Oxford University Press, 1969.

—— *Phenomenology of Spirit*, trans. A. V. Miller, Oxford University Press, 1977.

—— *Introduction to the Lectures on the History of Philosophy*, trans. T. M. Knox and A. V. Miller, Oxford University Press, 1985.

Heidegger, Martin, *An Introduction to Metaphysics*, trans. R. Manheim, Yale University Press, 1959.

—— *Being and Time*, trans. J. McQuarrie and J. Robinson, Blackwell, 1962.

—— Letter to Husserl (22 Oct. 1927), *Husserliana*, vol. I, 1962.

—— *Poetry, Language, Thought*, trans. Albert Hofstadter, Harper & Row, 1971.

—— *Martin Heidegger: Basic Writings*, trans. and ed. D. F. Krell, Routledge & Kegan Paul, 1978. (Includes 'Letter on humanism' and 'On the essence of truth'.)

—— *Prolegomena zur Geschichte des Zeitbegriffs*, Klostermann, 1979. (Trans. Theodore Kisiel as *History of the Concept of Time*, Indiana University Press, 1985.)

—— *The Basic Problems of Phenomenology*, trans. Albert Hofstadter, Indiana University Press, 1982.

Hoffman, Kurt, 'The basic concepts of Jaspers' philosophy', in *The Philosophy of Karl Jaspers*, ed. P. A. Schilpp.

Honderich, Ted, *A Theory of Determinism*, Oxford University Press, 1988.

Hume, David, *A Treatise of Human Nature*, Oxford University Press, 1960.

Husserl, Edmund, *Cartesian Meditations*, trans. D. Cairns, Nijhoff, 1960.

—— *Ideas: General Introduction to Pure Phenomenology*, trans. W. R. Boyce Gibson, Collier Macmillan, 1962.

—— *Phenomenology and the Crisis of Philosophy*, trans. and ed. Q. Lauer, Harper & Row, 1965. (Contains 'Philosophy as a rigorous science' and 'Philosophy and the crisis of European man'.)

—— *The Crisis of European Sciences and Transcendental Phenomenology*, trans. D. Carr, Northwestern University Press, 1970.

—— *The Paris Lectures*, trans. Peter Koestenbaum, Nijhoff, 1975.

Jaspers, Karl. *The Perennial Scope of Philosophy*, trans. R. Manheim, Yale University Press, 1950.

—— 'Philosophical autobiography', in *The Philosophy of Karl Jaspers*, ed. P. A. Schilpp.

—— *Philosophy*, 3 vols, trans. E. B. Ashton, University of Chicago Press, 1969–71.

—— *Reason and Existence*, in *Existentialism from Dostoievsky to Sartre*, trans. and ed. W. Kaufmann, New American Library, 1975.

—— *Einführung in die Philosophie*, Piper, 1985. (Trans. as *The Way to Wisdom*.)

Kenny, Anthony, 'Wittgenstein's meaning of life', *Times Higher Education Supplement*, 19 May 1989.

Kierkegaard, Søren, *The Sickness unto Death*, trans. Walter Lowrie, Doubleday, 1954.

—— *The Present Age*, trans. Alexander Dru, Harper & Row, 1962.

—— *Either/Or*, 2 vols, trans. Walter Lowrie, Princeton University Press, 1974.

Kierkegaard, Søren, *Concluding Unscientific Postscript*, trans. H. V. and E. H. Hong, Princeton University Press, 1974.

—— *The Concept of Anxiety*, trans. H. V. and E. H. Hong, Princeton University Press, 1980.

—— *Fear and Trembling*, trans. A. Hannay, Penguin, 1985.

—— *Philosophical Fragments*, trans. H. V. and E. H. Hong, Princeton University Press, 1985.

Kockelmans, Joseph J. (ed.), *Phenomenology: The Philosophy of Edmund Husserl and its Interpretations*, Doubleday, 1967.

Kolakowski, Leszek, *Main Currents of Marxism*, vol. 1, trans. P. S. Falla, Oxford University Press, 1981.

—— *Metaphysical Horror*, Blackwell, 1989.

Kundera, Milan, *The Unbearable Lightness of Being*, trans. Michael Heim, Faber & Faber, 1985.

Leach, Edmund, *Culture and Communication*, Cambridge University Press, 1976.

Lowe, E. J., 'Substance', in *An Encyclopaedia of Philosophy*, ed. G. Parkinson, Routledge & Kegan Paul, 1988.

McCown, Joe, *Availability: Gabriel Marcel and the Phenomenology of Human Openness*, Montana Press, 1978.

McCulloch, Gregory. *Using Sartre: An Analytical Introduction to Early Sartrean Themes*, Routledge, 1994.

—— *The Mind and its World*, Routledge, 1995.

McDowell, John, 'Singular thought and the extent of inner space', in *Subject Thought and Context*, ed. P. Pettitt and J. McDowell, Oxford University Press 1986.

MacIntyre, Alasdair, *After Virtue*, Duckworth, 1981.

Macquarrie, John, *Existentialism: An Introduction, Guide and Assessment*, Penguin, 1973.

Malcolm, Norman, 'The conceivability of mechanism', in *Free Will*, ed. G. Watson.

Manser, A. R., *Sartre: A Philosophic Study*, Athlone Press, 1966.

Marcel, Gabriel, *The Philosophy of Existence*, trans. M. Harari, Harvill, 1948. (Contains 'On the ontological mystery' and 'Existence and human freedom'.)

—— *Being and Having*, trans. Katherine Farrer, Dacre, 1949.

—— 'I and Thou', trans. Forrest Williams, in *The Philosophy of Martin Buber*, ed. P. A. Schilpp and M. Friedmann.

Marx, Karl, *The Portable Karl Marx*, trans. and ed. E. Kamenka, Penguin, 1983. (Includes 'On the Jewish question', 'Contribution to the critique of Hegel's *Philosophy of Right'*, *A Contribution to the Critique of Political Economy, Economico- Philosophical Manuscripts of 1844*, and *The German Ideology* (selections).)

Mauriac, François, *A Woman of the Pharisees*, trans. Gerard Hopkins, Penguin, 1988.

Merleau-Ponty, Maurice, 'Partout et nulle part', in his *Signes*, Gallimard, 1960.

—— *Phenomenology of Perception*, trans. Colin Smith, Routledge & Kegan Paul, 1962.

—— *The Structure of Behaviour*, trans. A. L. Fisher, Methuen, 1963.

—— 'The philosopher and his shadow', in his *Signs*, trans. R. C. McCleary, Northwestern University Press, 1964.

—— 'The primacy of perception and its philosophical consequences' in *Phenomenology, Language and Sociology: Selected Essays of Maurice Merleau-Ponty*, trans. and ed. J. O'Neill, Heinemann, 1974.

Midgley, Mary, *Beast and Man: The Roots of Human Nature*, Methuen, 1979.

Morris, Phyllis, S., 'Self-deception: Sartre's resolution of the paradox', in *Jean-Paul Sartre: Contemporary Approaches to his Philosophy*, ed. H. Silverman and F. Elliston.

Murdoch, Iris, *The Philosopher's Pupil*, Penguin, 1983.

—— *The Sovereignty of the Good*, Routledge & Kegan Paul, 1985.

Murray, M. (ed.), *Heidegger and Modern Philosophy*, Yale University Press, 1978.

Nagel, Thomas, *Mortal Questions*, Cambridge University Press, 1979. (Includes 'The absurd', 'Death' and 'Subjective and objective'.)

Nehamas, Alexander, *Nietzsche: Life as Literature*, Harvard University Press, 1985.

Niebuhr, Reinhold. *The Nature and Destiny of Man*, Scribners, 1964.

Nietzsche, Friedrich, *Twilight of the Idols*, in *The Portable Nietzsche*, trans. and ed. W. Kaufmann, Vintage, 1954.

—— *The Genealogy of Morals*, in *Basic Writings of Nietzsche*, trans. and ed. W. Kaufmann.

—— *The Will to Power*, trans. W. Kaufman, Random House, 1968.

—— *The Gay Science*, trans. W. Kaufman, Random House, 1974.

—— *Werke*, in 5 vols, ed. K. Schlechta, Ullstein, 1979.

—— 'Schopenhauer as educator', in *Untimely Meditations*, trans. and ed. R. Hollingdale, Cambridge University Press, 1983.

O'Hear, Anthony, *The Element of Fire: Science, Art and the Human World*, Routledge & Kegan Paul, 1988.

Olafson, Frederick A., *Principles and Persons: An Ethical Interpretation of Existentialism*, Johns Hopkins University Press, 1967.

—— *Heidegger and the Philosophy of Mind*, Yale University Press, 1987.

—— *Heidegger and the Ground of Ethics: A Study of Mitsein*, Cambridge University Press, 1998.

Ortega y Gasset, José, *The Modern Theme*, trans. J. Cleugh, C. W. Daniel, 1931.

—— *History as a System and Other Essays towards a Philosophy of History*, trans. H. Weyl, E. Clark and W. Atkinson, Norton, 1962. (Includes 'History as a system' and 'Man the technician'.)

—— *The Revolt of the Masses*, Allen & Unwin, 1972.

Parfit, Derek, *Reasons and Persons*, Oxford University Press, 1984.

Pascal, Blaise, *Pensées*, trans. A. J. Krailsheimer, Penguin, 1980.

Passmore, John, *Man's Responsibility for Nature*, Duckworth, 1980.

Perec, Georges, *Life a User's Manual*, trans. David Bellos, Collins Harvill, 1988.

Plato, *The Republic*, trans. Desmond Lee, Penguin, 1986.

Platts, Mark, *Ways of Meaning*, Routledge & Kegan Paul, 1979.

Popper, Karl, *The Open Society and its Enemies*, vol. 2, Routledge & Kegan Paul, 1963.

Putnam, Hilary, 'The meaning of "meaning"', in his *Mind, Language and Reality*, Cambridge University Press, 1979.

Rilke, Rainer Maria, *Ewald Tragy*, Insel, 1980.

Robbins-Landon, H. C., *1791; Mozart's Last Year*, Thames & Hudson, 1988.

Roberts, J. M., *Europe 1880–1945*, Longman, 1977.

Rockmore, Tom. *Heidegger and French Philosophy*, Routledge, 1995.

Rorty, Richard, *Contingency, Irony and Solidarity*, Cambridge University Press, 1989.

Roubiczek, Paul, *Existentialism – For and Against*, Cambridge University Press, 1964.

Ryle, Gilbert, Review of Heidegger, *Sein und Zeit*, in *Heidegger and Modern Philosophy*, ed. M. Murray.

Sandel, Michael, *Liberalism and the Limits of Justice*, Cambridge University Press, 1982.

Sartre, Jean-Paul, 'L'enfance d'un chef', in his *Le Mur*, Gallimard, 1939.

—— *Huis clos* and *Les Mouches*, in *Théâtre* I, Gallimard, 1947.

—— 'Une idée fondamentale de la phénoménologie de Husserl: l'intentionnalité', in *Situations* I, Gallimard, 1947.

—— *Being and Nothingness: An Essay on Phenomenological Ontology*, trans. Hazel Barnes, Methuen, 1957.

—— *The Transcendence of the Ego: An Existentialist Theory of Consciousness*, trans. Forrest Williams and Robert Kirkpatrick, Noonday, 1957.

—— *The Age of Reason*, trans. Eric Sutton, Penguin, 1961.

—— *Sketch for a Theory of the Emotions*, trans. P. Mairet, Methuen, 1962.

—— Preface to Frantz Fanon, *The Wretched of the Earth*, trans. Constance Farrington, Grove Press, 1963.

—— *The Problem of Method*, trans. Hazel Barnes, Methuen, 1963.

—— *Existentialism and Humanism*, trans. P. Mairet, Methuen, 1966.

—— *What is Literature?*, trans. Bernard Frechtman, Methuen, 1967.

—— *Saint Genet: Actor and Martyr*, trans. Bernard Frechtman, as partially reprinted in *The Philosophy of Jean-Paul Sartre*, ed. R. D. Cumming, Methuen, 1968.

—— *Iron in the Soul*, trans. Gerard Hopkins, Penguin, 1974.

—— *Cahiers pour une morale*, Gallimard, 1983. (Trans. D. Pellaver, as *Notebooks for an Ethics*, University of Chicago Press, 1992.)

—— *Nausea*, trans. Robert Baldick, Penguin, 1986.

—— *The Reprieve*, trans. Eric Sutton, Penguin, 1986.

—— *Truth and Existence*, trans. A. Van Den Hoven, University of Chicago Press, 1992.

Satta, Salvatore, *The Day of Judgement*, trans. Patrick Creagh, Collins Harvill, 1988.

Schacht, Richard. 'Existentialism', in *A Companion to Metaphysics*, ed. J. Kim and E. Sosa, Blackwell, 1995.

Schapiro, Meyer, *Van Gogh*, Thames & Hudson (n.d.)

Schilpp, P. A. (ed.), *The Philosophy of Karl Jaspers*, Tudor, 1957.

Schilpp, P. A. and Friedmann, M. (eds), *The Philosophy of Martin Buber*, Open Court, 1967.

Scruton, Roger, *Sexual Desire*, Weidenfeld & Nicolson, 1986.

Searle, John R., 'Literal meaning', in his *Expression and Meaning*, Cambridge University Press, 1979.

Silverman, H. and Elliston, F. (eds), *Jean-Paul Sartre: Contemporary Approaches to his Philosophy*, Duquesne University Press, 1980.

Solomon, Robert C., *Continental Philosophy since 1750*, Oxford University Press, 1988.

Sprigge, T. L. S., *Theories of Existence*, Penguin, 1984.

Stendhal, *The Red and the Black*, trans. R. Adams, Random House, 1953.

Strawson, Galen, *Freedom and Belief*, Oxford University Press, 1986.

Strawson, P. F., *Freedom and Resentment and Other Essays*, Methuen, 1974.

Taylor, Charles, *The Explanation of Behaviour*, Routledge & Kegan Paul, 1964.

—— 'Responsibility for self', in *Free Will*, ed. G. Watson.

—— Human Agency and Language, Cambridge University Press, 1985. (Includes 'Self-interpreting animals' and 'Language and human nature'.)

Unamuno, Miguel de, Tragic Sense of Life, trans. J. E. Crawford-Flitch, Dover, 1954.

Wahl, Jean, Philosophies of Existence, trans. F. M. Lory, Routledge & Kegan Paul, 1969.

Wallraff, Charles F., Karl Jaspers: An Introduction to his Philosophy, Princeton University Press, 1970.

Warnock, Mary, The Philosophy of Sartre, Hutchinson, 1965.

—— Existentialism, Oxford University Press, 1970.

Watson, Gary (ed.), Free Will, Oxford University Press, 1982.

Whorf, Benjamin Lee, Language, Thought and Reality, MIT, 1969.

Wiggins, David, 'What is a substantial theory of truth?', in Philosophical Subjects: Essays for P. F. Strawson, ed. Z. van Straaten, Oxford University Press, 1980.

—— Needs, Values, Truth, Blackwell, 1987.

Wittgenstein, Ludwig, Philosophical Investigations, trans. G. E. M. Anscombe, Blackwell, 1969.

—— Culture and Value, trans. Peter Winch, Blackwell, 1980.

Woolf, Virginia, Diaries, Penguin, 1985.

Zweig, Stefan, Ungeduld des Herzens, Fischer, 1976.

Index